Learning Cascading

Build reliable, robust, and high-performance big data applications using the Cascading application development efficiently

Michael Covert

Victoria Loewengart

BIRMINGHAM - MUMBAI

Learning Cascading

Copyright © 2015 Packt Publishing

First published: May 2015

Production reference: 1250515

Published by Packt Publishing Ltd.
Livery Place
35 Livery Street
Birmingham B3 2PB, UK.

ISBN 978-1-78528-891-3

www.packtpub.com

Credits

Authors
Michael Covert

Victoria Loewengart

Reviewers
Allen Driskill

Bernie French

Supreet Oberoi

Commissioning Editor
Veena Pagare

Acquisition Editor
Vivek Anantharaman

Content Development Editor
Prachi Bisht

Technical Editors
Ruchi Desai

Ankita Thakur

Copy Editors
Sonia Michelle Cheema

Ameesha Green

Project Coordinator
Shipra Chawhan

Proofreaders
Stephen Copestake

Safis Editing

Indexer
Monica Ajmera Mehta

Graphics
Disha Haria

Production Coordinator
Nilesh R. Mohite

Cover Work
Nilesh R. Mohite

Foreword

The Cascading project was started in 2007 to complete the promise that Apache Hadoop was indirectly making to people like me — that we can dramatically simplify data-oriented application development and deployment. This can be done not only from a tools perspective, but more importantly, from an organizational perspective. Take a thousand machines and make them look like one: one storage layer and a computing layer. This promise means I would never have to ask our IT group for another storage array, more disk space, or another overpriced box to manage. My team and I could just throw our data and applications at the cluster and move on. The problem with this story is that we would have to develop our code against the MapReduce model, forcing us to think in MapReduce. I've only ever written one MapReduce application and it was a terrible experience. I did everything wrong.

Cascading was originally designed to help you, the developer, use your existing skills and do the right thing initially, or more importantly, understand whether assumptions about your data were right and wrong so that you can quickly compensate.

In the past couple of years, we have seen the emergence of new models improving on what MapReduce started. These models are driven by new expectations around latency and scale. Thinking in MapReduce is very difficult, but at least you can reason in it. Some of the newer models do not provide enough mental scaffolding to even help you reason out your problem.

Cascading has been evolving to help insulate you from the need to intimately know these new models while allowing businesses to leverage them as they become stable and available. This work started with Cascading 2.0 a few years ago. Cascading 3.0, still under development at the time of writing this, has evolved to a much deeper level, making a new promise to developers that they can write data-oriented applications once, and with little effort can adapt to new models and infrastructure.

What shouldn't come as a surprise is that Cascading has also grown to become its own ecosystem. It supports nearly every type of data source and has been ported to multiple JVM-based programming languages, including Python (Jython), Ruby (JRuby), Scala (via Scalding), and Clojure (via Cascalog). Cascading has a vibrant community of developers and users alike. Having been adopted by companies, such as Twitter, Etsy, eBay, and others, Cascading is the foundation for many advanced forms of analytics from machine learning, genomics, to being the foundation of new data-oriented languages, DSLs, and APIs. It is also the foundation of many commercial products that advertise Hadoop compatibility.

I am very enthusiastic about this book. Here, at Concurrent, we see the need for this book because it consolidates so much information in one place. This book provides details that are not always well documented or can be difficult to find. It contains many concrete coding examples, "how-to" tips, systems integration strategies, performance and tuning steps, debugging techniques, and advice on future directions to take. Also included is a real-life, end-to-end application that can serve as a reference architecture for development using Cascading. This book contains much that is valuable to developers, managers, and system administrators.

Chris K. Wensel

CTO, Concurrent, Inc.

About the Authors

Michael Covert, CEO, Analytics Inside LLC, has significant experience in a variety of business and technical roles. Michael is a mathematician and computer scientist and is involved in machine learning, deep learning, predictive analytics, graph theory, and big data. He earned a bachelor's of science degree in mathematics with honors and distinction from The Ohio State University. He also attended it as a PhD student, specializing in machine learning and high-performance computing. Michael is a Cloudera Hadoop Certified Developer.

Michael served as the vice president of performance management in Whittman-Hart, Inc., based in Chicago, and as the chief operating officer of Infinis, Inc., a business intelligence consulting company based in Columbus, Ohio. Infinis merged with Whittman-Hart in 2005. Prior to working at Infinis, Michael was the vice president of product development and chief technology officer at Alta Analytics, and the producer of data mining and visualization software. In addition to this, he has served in technology management roles for Claremont Technology Group, Inc., where he was the director of advanced technology.

I would like to thank the editors of Packt Publishing who guided us through this writing process and made significant contributions to what is contained here. I would also like to thank Bernie, Allen, and Supreet who expended tremendous effort through many hours of technical review, and in doing so, helped to ensure that this book was of the highest quality.

More than anyone else, I would like to thank my wife, Kay, for her support while writing this book, and more so, throughout my entire adult existence. Without her, most of the good things that have occurred in my life would not have been possible. I also would like thank my dogs, Ellie and Josie, who served as constant, faithful companions through all of this. Lastly, I would like to thank my coauthor, business partner, and most of all, my friend, Victoria Loewengart. She has not only helped make all this possible, but working with her also made it fun and rewarding.

Victoria Loewengart, COO, Analytics Inside LLC, is an innovative software systems architect with a proven record of bringing emerging technologies to clients through discovery, design, and integration. Additionally, Victoria spent a large part of her career developing software technologies that extract information from unstructured text. Victoria has published numerous articles on topics ranging from text analytics to intelligence analysis and cyber security. Her book *An Introduction to Hacking & Crimeware: A Pocket Guide* was published by IT Governance, UK, in January 2012. Victoria earned a bachelor's degree in computer science from Purdue University and a master's degree in intelligence studies from the American Military University.

I am indebted to the editors of Packt Publishing who did a fantastic job in making sure that this book sees the light of day. Also, I would like to thank our reviewers Bernie, Allen, and Supreet for putting a lot of time and effort into making sure that this book addresses all the necessary issues and does not have technical errors.

On a personal note, I would like to thank my wonderful husband, Steven Loewengart, for his never-ending love, patience, and support through the process of writing this book. I would also like to thank my parents, Boris and Fanya Rudkevich, for their encouragement and faith in me. I am grateful to my daughters, Gina and Sophie, for keeping me young and engaged in life. Finally, I would like to thank my coauthor, friend, and business partner, Mike Covert, for his wisdom and mentorship, and without whom, this book would have not happened.

About the Reviewers

Allen Driskill holds a BS in computer science from Murray State University and an MS in information science from The Ohio State University, where he has also been an instructor.

Since 1974, Allen has been a software developer in various fields and guises. He has developed business systems on a variety of small and large platforms for NCR, Burroughs, IBM, online information delivery systems, search and retrieval, hierarchical storage and management, telecommunications, imbedded systems for various handheld devices, and NLP systems for chemical information analysis.

He is currently employed by Chemical Abstracts Service in Columbus, Ohio, as a senior research scientist. In this capacity, he is currently using a large Hadoop cluster to process chemical information from a variety of massive databases.

Bernie French has over 20 years of experience in bio and cheminformatics. His interests are in the field of graph-based knowledge and analytic systems. He has developed analytic solutions within the Hadoop ecosystem using MapReduce, Cascading, and Giraph. He has also created analytic solutions using Spark and GraphX technologies. Bernie has a PhD in molecular biology from The Ohio State University and was an NIH Fellow at the The Wistar Institute, where he specialized in molecular and cellular biology. He was also an NIH hematology/oncology Fellow at The Ohio State University's Comprehensive Cancer Center.

Supreet Oberoi is the vice president of field engineering at Concurrent, Inc. Prior to this, he was the director of big data application infrastructure for American Express, where he led the development of use cases for fraud, operational risk, marketing, and privacy on big data platforms. He holds multiple patents in data engineering and has held executive and leadership positions at Real-Time Innovations, Oracle, and Microsoft.

www.PacktPub.com

Support files, eBooks, discount offers, and more

For support files and downloads related to your book, please visit www.PacktPub.com.

Did you know that Packt offers eBook versions of every book published, with PDF and ePub files available? You can upgrade to the eBook version at www.PacktPub.com and as a print book customer, you are entitled to a discount on the eBook copy. Get in touch with us at service@packtpub.com for more details.

At www.PacktPub.com, you can also read a collection of free technical articles, sign up for a range of free newsletters and receive exclusive discounts and offers on Packt books and eBooks.

https://www2.packtpub.com/books/subscription/packtlib

Do you need instant solutions to your IT questions? PacktLib is Packt's online digital book library. Here, you can search, access, and read Packt's entire library of books.

Why subscribe?

- Fully searchable across every book published by Packt
- Copy and paste, print, and bookmark content
- On demand and accessible via a web browser

Free access for Packt account holders

If you have an account with Packt at www.PacktPub.com, you can use this to access PacktLib today and view 9 entirely free books. Simply use your login credentials for immediate access.

Table of Contents

Preface

Big data is the new "must have" of this century. Suddenly, everyone wants to manage huge amounts of data and find patterns in it, which they did not see before. The problem, however, is that big data is not one, but a whole slew of technologies, which work together to produce the desired outcome. New technologies are emerging, and existing ones are evolving very quickly. The design and development of big data systems is very complex, with an incredibly steep learning curve and not a whole lot of prior experience and best practices to rely on. This is where Cascading comes in. Cascading sits on top of the core big data frameworks and makes design and development of big data applications intuitive and fun! Cascading significantly simplifies and streamlines application development, job creation, and job scheduling. Cascading is an open source software, and many large organizations prefer to use it to manage their big data systems over more complicated solutions, such as MapReduce.

We discovered Cascading after our applications started to get to the level of complexity when pure MapReduce turned into a blood-pressure-raising nightmare. Needless to say, we fell in love with Cascading. Now, we train other developers on it, and evangelize it every chance we get. So, this is how our book came about. Our vision was to provide a book to the Cascading user community that will help them accelerate the development of complex, workflow-based Cascading applications, while still keeping their sanity intact so that they can enjoy life.

This book will teach you how to quickly develop practical Cascading applications, starting with the basics and gradually progressing into more complex topics. We start with a look "under the hood", how Cascading relates to core big data technologies, such as Hadoop MapReduce, and future emerging technologies, such as Tez, Spark, Storm, and others. Having gained an understanding of underlying technologies, we follow with a comprehensive introduction to the Cascading paradigm and components using well-tested code examples that go beyond the ones in the open domain that exist today. Throughout this book, you will receive expert advice on how to use the portions of a product that are undocumented or have limited documentation. To deepen your knowledge and experience with Cascading, you will work with a real-life case study using Natural Language Processing to perform text analysis and search large volumes of unstructured text. We conclude with a look to the future, and how Cascading will soon run on additional big data fabrics, such as Spark and Tez.

Cascading has rapidly gained popularity, and obtaining development skills in this product is a very marketable feature for a big data professional. With in-depth instructions and hands-on practical approaches, *Learning Cascading* will ensure your mastery of Cascading.

What this book covers

Chapter 1, *The Big Data Core Technology Stack*, introduces you to the concepts of big data and the core technologies that comprise it. This knowledge is essential as the foundation of learning Cascading.

Chapter 2, *Cascading Basics in Detail*, we will begin our exploration of Cascading. We will look at its intended purpose, how it is structured, how to develop programs using it base classes, and how it then manages the execution of these programs.

Chapter 3, *Understanding Custom Operations*, is based on the newly acquired Cascading knowledge. We will learn more advanced Cascading features that will truly unleash the power of the Cascading API. We will concentrate on an in-depth discussion about operations and their five primary types.

Chapter 4, *Creating Custom Operations*, will show you how to actually write a custom operation for each type of operation. This is done after we've completely explored and understood the anatomy of operations in the previous chapter.

Chapter 5, *Code Reuse and Integration*, introduces you to learning how to assemble reusable code, integrating Cascading with external systems, and using the Cascading instrumentation effectively to track and control execution. Specifically, we will discuss how Cascading fits into the overall processing infrastructure.

Chapter 6, Testing a Cascading Application, provides in-depth information on how to efficiently test a Cascading application using many techniques.

Chapter 7, Optimizing the Performance of a Cascading Application, provides in-depth information on how to efficiently optimize a Cascading application and configure the underlying framework (Hadoop) for maximum performance.

Chapter 8, Creating a Real-world Application in Cascading, takes everything we learned and creates a real-world application in Cascading. We will use a practical case study, which could be easily adapted to a functional component of a larger system within your organization.

Chapter 9, Planning for Future Growth, provides information that will allow you to continue to advance your skills.

Appendix, Downloadable Software, provides information that will allow you to download all the code from the book.

What you need for this book

Software:

- Eclipse 4.x (Kepler, Luna, or beyond) or other Java IDE
- Java 1.6 or above (1.7 preferred)
- Cascading 2,2 or above (2.6.2 preferred)
- Hadoop Virtual Machine is optional, but it'll be nice to have (Cloudera or Hortonworks are preferred)

OS:

- If you have a Hadoop Virtual Machine: Windows 7 or above
- If no Hadoop Virtual Machine: Linux (CentOS 6 and above preferred)
- Hadoop version 2 (YARN) running MapReduce version 1 is preferred. Hadoop MapReduce (0.23 or beyond) will also work

Who this book is for

This book is intended for software developers, system architects, system analysts, big data project managers, and data scientists.

The reader of this book should have a basic understanding of the big data paradigm, Java development skills, and be interested in deploying big data solutions in their organization, specifically using the Cascading open source framework.

Conventions

In this book, you will find a number of text styles that distinguish between different kinds of information. Here are some examples of these styles and an explanation of their meaning.

Code words in text, database table names, folder names, filenames, file extensions, pathnames, dummy URLs, user input, and Twitter handles are shown as follows: "A key script, such as hadoop-env.sh, is needed in instances where environment variables are set."

A block of code is set as follows:

```
public class NLPUtils
{
  /* Parse text into sentences
   * @param text - document text
   * @return String
   */
  public static String[] getSentences(String text)
  {
    String sentences[]=text.split("[.?!]");
    for (int i=0; i< sentences.length; i++)
    {
      sentences[i]=sentences[i].trim();
    }
    return sentences;
  }
}
```

When we wish to draw your attention to a particular part of a code block, the relevant lines or items are set in bold:

```
Tap docTap = new FileTap (inputScheme, args[0]);
Tap sinkTap = new FileTap(outputScheme, args[1],
  SinkMode.REPLACE );
Pipe inPipe = new Pipe("InPipe");
Pipe pipeTextProcess = new SubAssemblyExample(inPipe);
Flow flow = new LocalFlowConnector();
```

Any command-line input or output is written as follows:

```
hadoop jar myjob.jar com.ai.jobs.MainJob data/input data/output
```

New terms and **important words** are shown in bold. Words that you see on the screen, for example, in menus or dialog boxes, appear in the text like this: "Right-click on the project and navigate to **DebugAs | DebugConfigurations....**"

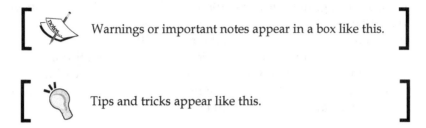

Warnings or important notes appear in a box like this.

Tips and tricks appear like this.

Reader feedback

Feedback from our readers is always welcome. Let us know what you think about this book—what you liked or disliked. Reader feedback is important for us as it helps us develop titles that you will really get the most out of.

To send us general feedback, simply e-mail feedback@packtpub.com, and mention the book's title in the subject of your message.

If there is a topic that you have expertise in and you are interested in either writing or contributing to a book, see our author guide at www.packtpub.com/authors.

Customer support

Now that you are the proud owner of a Packt book, we have a number of things to help you to get the most from your purchase.

Downloading the example code

You can download the example code files from your account at http://www.packtpub.com for all the Packt Publishing books you have purchased. If you purchased this book elsewhere, you can visit http://www.packtpub.com/support and register to have the files e-mailed directly to you.

Downloading the color images of this book

We also provide you with a PDF file that has color images of the screenshots/diagrams used in this book. The color images will help you better understand the changes in the output. You can download this file from https://www.packtpub.com/sites/default/files/downloads/8913OS_ImageBundle.pdf.

Errata

Although we have taken every care to ensure the accuracy of our content, mistakes do happen. If you find a mistake in one of our books—maybe a mistake in the text or the code—we would be grateful if you could report this to us. By doing so, you can save other readers from frustration and help us improve subsequent versions of this book. If you find any errata, please report them by visiting http://www.packtpub.com/submit-errata, selecting your book, clicking on the **Errata Submission Form** link, and entering the details of your errata. Once your errata are verified, your submission will be accepted and the errata will be uploaded to our website or added to any list of existing errata under the Errata section of that title.

To view the previously submitted errata, go to https://www.packtpub.com/books/content/support and enter the name of the book in the search field. The required information will appear under the **Errata** section.

Piracy

Piracy of copyrighted material on the Internet is an ongoing problem across all media. At Packt, we take the protection of our copyright and licenses very seriously. If you come across any illegal copies of our works in any form on the Internet, please provide us with the location address or website name immediately so that we can pursue a remedy.

Please contact us at copyright@packtpub.com with a link to the suspected pirated material.

We appreciate your help in protecting our authors and our ability to bring you valuable content.

Questions

If you have a problem with any aspect of this book, you can contact us at questions@packtpub.com, and we will do our best to address the problem.

1
The Big Data Core Technology Stack

This chapter will introduce the reader to the concepts of big data and the core technologies that comprise it. This knowledge is essential as the foundation to learn Cascading. Cascading provides a comprehensive framework that definitely eases many of the verbose and mundane tasks associated with writing Hadoop, and in the future, many other types of big data jobs. However, as with all complex subjects, an understanding of how Hadoop works is required to gain a full understanding of how to best use Cascading.

Reviewing Hadoop

Hadoop is very complex and has many low-level details and nuances that require a significant amount of documentation and explanation to cover. This chapter is a high-level overview of the Hadoop system and is not intended to be sufficient for anything other than laying the groundwork that you will need to begin Cascading programming. For a deeper dive into Hadoop, we recommend *Hadoop Explained* by Aravind Shenoy.

Hadoop is designed to provide massively parallel (often referred to as "embarrassingly parallel"), fault-tolerant, and high-performance computing. Hadoop is intended to solve one specific problem — how to reduce the duration of time that is required to read a very large amount of data from disk sequentially. We see that with most physical (mechanical spinning) disks, the amount of time to read a block of data is in the order of 2 ms-10 ms, depending on the characteristics of the disk. If we do a simple calculation using a disk that can read 25 MBps, we see that reading 1 TB of data sequentially will require 40 seconds. However, if this data were spread across multiple disks, say 20 of them, we could read this data parallelly in 2 seconds! This is the key element of Hadoop — using parallel I/O to improve performance.

We must also note that disk performance improvements have lagged far behind compute improvements. While disk performance (measured in megabytes per second) has only moderately increased, compute performance (such as instructions per second or other benchmark metrics) has improved by orders of magnitude, growing at an average rate of 50 percent annually since 1986, and a modern day processor now runs 1000 times faster than one of a 1986 vintage. This disparity between I/O and compute provides the basis for the invention of Hadoop. Hadoop provides compute parallelism through its **MapReduce (MR)** subsystem. It provides I/O parallelism through its **Hadoop Distributed File System (HDFS)** subsystem.

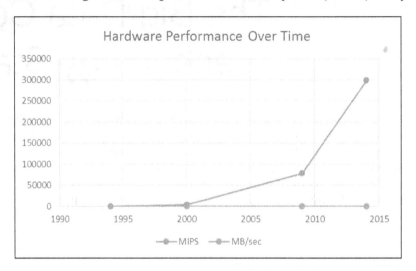

Hadoop itself is a very large system comprised of over approximately 2.4 million lines of code as of the current version. There is much to learn, and much of this knowledge is used daily. As a result, the learning curve is a steep one. One must become quite proficient at library structures, performing I/O in a cluster, accessing shared objects, Hadoop serialization, and a large number of specific classes that one must write to interact with execution and I/O subsystems. For instance, as we shall see in detail later in this chapter, just to do a multifield sort in MapReduce requires that five separate Java classes be written.

Some required knowledge is arcane, such as how to effectively process time ranges where files have been partitioned by date range, or how to only read portions of a file. After initially working with MapReduce, one can find that an enormous amount of code has been written, and that without careful planning, reusing the code is difficult to obtain. One typically ends up with many, many packages, hundreds of classes, and a significant amount of code overlap (this includes classes with minor variations that are rewritten using copied code).

Hadoop is almost universally deployed on Linux operating systems. However, it can be made to run on OS/X, many flavors of Unix, BSD, and now Microsoft Windows as well. It is also very amenable to Cloud deployment and can support a variety of Cloud-based file systems. Hadoop requires Java 1.6 or above. Versions that exist now support Java 1.7 and 1.8 as well.

Hadoop is inherently a batch processing system. Work is packaged into a job. The job is submitted and is run at the discretion of the Hadoop scheduler. The amount of time between starting the job and having results returned is not under the control of the issuer, and, in general, is difficult to use for any sort of processing where there is a desire to bound the time of execution. For instance, it is very difficult to connect a web server user request to a Hadoop job and then to wait for it to return results to achieve some service-level objective.

Hadoop itself is made more difficult to understand largely because of its history of growth and change. It now has three full versions, each with significantly different semantics. Initially, the first release of Hadoop used the class package prefix of `mapred`. It was superseded by a newer release that used the class package prefix of `mapreduce`. Later, we will see that the newest version, YARN, is now significantly different.

Hadoop is controlled by several XML configuration files. On a Linux system, these files generally reside within `/etc/hadoop/conf`, but the location of these files is actually dependent on the installation (and vendor, if you choose this route). Three primary files are used to control Hadoop:

- `core-site.xml`: It contains basic parameters, such as server port numbers, location of servers, and so on

- `hdfs-site.xml`: It contains information that controls the Hadoop Distributed File System, such as locations on local disk where data is to be stored

- `mapred-site.xml`: It contains information about the MapReduce execution framework, such as the number of threads to use

A typical configuration file looks similar to this:

```
<?xml version="1.0"?>
<?xml-stylesheet type="text/xsl" href="configuration.xsl"?>
<configuration>
  <property>
    <name>hadoop.tmp.dir</name>
    <value>/tmp/hadoop-${user.name}</value>
  </property>
  <property>
    <name>fs.default.name</name>
```

```
      <value>hdfs://server-name:54310</value>
   </property>
   <property>
     <name>mapred.job.tracker</name>
     <value>hdfs:// server-name:54311</value>
   </property>
   <property>
     <name>dfs.replication</name>
     <value>3</value>
   </property>
   <property>
     <name>mapred.child.java.opts</name>
     <value>-Xmx512m</value>
   </property>
 </configuration>
```

Additionally, several shell scripts are needed. A key script, such as `hadoop-env.sh`, is needed in instances where environment variables are set. Some important environment variables are:

- `JAVA_HOME`: It sets the location of the default Java implementation
- `HADOOP_HOME`: It sets the location of the Hadoop implementation
- `HADOOP_CONF_DIR`: It specifies where the Hadoop configuration files are located

Often, the `hadoop-env.sh` script is placed into `/etc/profile.d`, so that it will be executed automatically at login. However, sometimes, they are placed in the user's local shell startup script, so this may be different for you.

Hadoop architecture

At its most basic level, Hadoop is a system that processes records represented as key-value pairs. Every record has an associated **key** field. This key need not be unique and is accompanied by a **value** field. This value field may be composite, so that it can be decomposed into multiple subfields. While this may sound limiting at first, especially when one is used to using a relational database where multiple indexes are available, we will see that this mechanism is sufficient to do most of the processing that one may require. We will also see that this simplified approach is fundamental to the performance gains that are required to process big data.

In a nutshell, Hadoop MapReduce processing can be visualized in the following diagram:

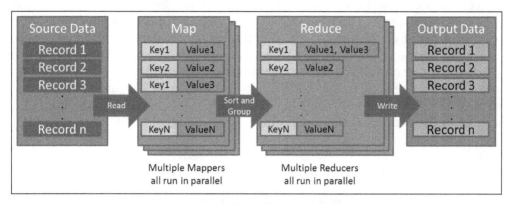

Figure 1.1 – Hadoop processing flow

While the flow does look simplistic, in this diagram, we can see some underlying similarities to how a relational database processes standard SQL queries. The **Read** phase looks a lot like SELECT *, retrieving all the records. The **Map** process is then capable of applying the WHERE criteria. The **Sort and Group** step applies both to GROUP BY and an ORDER BY. The **Reduce** process can then apply processing logic, such as COUNT, MIN, MAX, and so on. Lastly, the **Write** phase persists this data back to the disk.

One of the most interesting concepts behind Hadoop is that its data is **schema-on-read**. This means that while the data does have some sort of format, this format is not imposed until the data is read. This is in sharp contrast to the philosophy of a **relational database management system (RDBMS)**, where the schema is defined long before any data can be placed in it. Schema-on-read facilitates faster development times, since no lead times are required to define the schema, prepare the **data definition language (DDL** — the CREATE TABLE statement), execute it, load the data, and correct records with errors. In Hadoop, all data, regardless of type or format, can be copied into its storage and processed.

Downloading the example code

You can download the example code files for all Packt books you have purchased from your account at http://www.packtpub.com. If you purchased this book elsewhere, you can visit http://www.packtpub.com/support and register to have the files e-mailed directly to you.

What this means is that the interpretation of the input record itself, its key and value, is entirely dependent on the programmer. In one case, the key may be something that we would think of as an actual key, such as a name, SSN, order number, and so on. In other cases, the key may be nothing more than the record number, or maybe even the offset within the input file. This is also true of the value field. It could be a single value, such as a line of text, or it could be somehow parsable into smaller parts through some sort of record offset, or maybe just by performing a `split()` against some sort of delimiter character. Additionally, Hadoop provides many file formats that make handling data easier by supplying metadata to parse a record. Some examples of these formats are SequenceFile, Avro, and others. With these types of file structures, the actual format of the record is encoded into the dataset itself, and when the record is read, it is returned in a decomposed, record-like format, where fields can be retrieved by offsets or even by name.

The Hadoop architecture is relatively complex. It consists of two major subsystems — one that manages data and files, and the other that manages execution. The Hadoop system itself does much of the work for you, but the developer is still required to write a lot of code to perform the work.

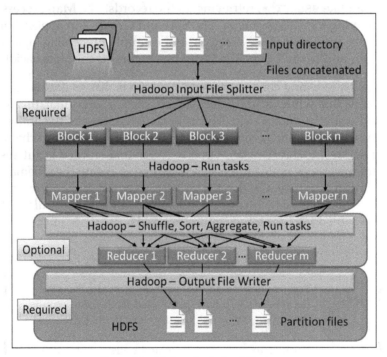

Figure 1.2 – Hadoop logical architecture

The basic tasks that Hadoop performs are as follows:

- Hadoop manages files in a familiar directory structure. However, these files are replicated in a cluster for fault tolerance and performance.

  By default, each file of data is replicated three times. This is a tunable parameter that can be set at the file, directory, or global level.

- Hadoop treats a directory of files as a single file. The files are concatenated together and then *split* into large blocks for consumption by executing tasks.

  - The block size is a file-level parameter. The default size is 64 MB, but sometimes this size is even further increased. The rationale here is to provide each task that runs in the cluster a sufficiently large amount of data so that the ratio of task startup time (consisting mainly of transferring executable code to the target system and then starting the Java Virtual Machine) to program execution time is *small*.

  - **Parallel** tasks are created in the cluster, and each is given data to process. These processes run simultaneously, and the purpose here is to improve execution speed by processing these blocks in parallel. Hadoop tasks are divided into mapper tasks and reducer tasks.

    - **Mapper** tasks process records from the input that is supplied to it. Each mapper task is assigned one block of data to process, and it is handed one record of data from its assigned block. The mapper implements three basic method calls. Only map() actually needs to be defined.

      ```
      void setup(Context c)
      throws IOException, InterruptedException
      void map(<KEYIN> key,<VALUEIN> value,
         Context context)
      throws IOException, InterruptedException
      void cleanup(Context c)
      throws IOException, InterruptedException
      ```

      setup() is used to perform one-time processing that occurs before any data is sent to the mapper. Then, map() is called repeatedly for each record. The context object passed to the map() call, and contains methods to output data that is the result of its processing. Finally, after all records are processed, cleanup() is called once to allow the user any final processing that may be required.

Note that in Hadoop, only mappers are required. The number of mappers used will be (total-bytes-processed/block-size).

Additionally, note that Hadoop methods should be able to throw IOException if an I/O error occurs, and also an InterruptedException if they are somehow stopped by any one of many types of cluster-wide interruptions that could occur.

○ Reducer tasks receive data that has been outputted by the mappers. Each mapper task processes records from its assigned block and then outputs a result. The result is sent to one reduce task for final processing. Note that, as shown in Figure 1.1, each record may be sent to a different reducer. We will discuss this in a minute.

Unlike what we saw with mappers, the number of reducers to use is specified by the programmer. This allows total control of parallelism during the final stage of aggregation. The assumption here is that the developer has some idea of the data itself and is, therefore, able to determine the degree of parallelism that is needed. It is important to note that the reducer can become a major bottleneck. For instance, if only one reducer is used, all the data generated by all the mappers will flow through it sequentially. Additionally, if one reducer receives significantly more data than others, a bottleneck will also occur.

Similar to a mapper, a reducer has the following method calls:

```
void setup(Context c)
throws IOException, InterruptedException
void reduce(<INKEY> key, Iterable<INVALUE> values,
   Context context)
throws IOException, InterruptedException
void cleanup(Context c)
throws IOException, InterruptedException
```

Reducer tasks receive data sent by the mappers that have been grouped by the Hadoop framework. This a record that consists of the grouping key followed by an Iterable<> object, containing every processed record that pertains to this key. Hadoop does this grouping for you through a **Shuffle and Sort** process that occurs after the mapper has sent records to the reducer(s).

Now, how does a mapper know which reducer should receive the record? This decision is made by a **partitioner**. A partitioner analyzes each record and determines the reducer that should process it. A partitioner has one method call that must be implemented:

```
void configure(Context c)
int getPartition(<KEY> key, <VALUE> value,
   int numReduceTasks)
```

Note that the partitioner passed a parameter telling it how many reducers it has to use. It must then return a value between 0 and `numReduceTasks`, and 1 to its caller (that is, the Hadoop framework). Hadoop will then handle the routing of this record to this reducer. The default partitioner simply looks at the key of the record and uses a `modulo` function, based on the number of reducers that have been defined to route it.

```
return key.hashCode() % numReduceTasks;
```

Hadoop allows for another component to be defined as well, and this is the **combiner**. When data is sent from the mappers to the reducers, a tremendous amount of data can be generated and sent across the wire. In some cases, bandwidth could be conserved if some preprocessing were to occur on the mapper side. This is precisely what a combiner does. It is a sort of "mini-reducer" that runs on the mapper side. It allows records to be combined (hence its name), and a consolidated record to be sent to the reducer. Care must be taken when using it, since mathematical operations that it performs should be both commutative and associative.

- Hadoop manages all these tasks, allowing them to run, pass data to each other. Data flows forward from the mappers to the reducers. In order for the reducers to receive the input that they expect, Hadoop performs sorting and aggregation/consolidation to create the composite record.

- Job execution is monitored and managed. Progress is reported back from the job so that it can be tracked for completion.

- During job execution, various errors or transient conditions may occur that hinder the job's progress. In these cases, Hadoop will attempt to keep the job running and may take corrective actions:

    ° Failing jobs may be restarted.

    ° Slow running jobs may be restarted as well.

    ° The same tasks may be run multiple times using what is called **speculative execution**. When this occurs, Hadoop starts multiple copies to see which one will finish first. This typically occurs when Hadoop determines that some sort of performance delay is occurring on one of the tasks. In this case, the task finishing first is used and the loser is unceremoniously terminated.

Most typically today, Hadoop configurations consist of a set of physical or virtual nodes, which are complete standalone systems running some version of the Linux operating system, an installed version of the Java JDK, and are all networked together with high speed Ethernet (such as InfiniBand) connectivity. Nodes are then divided into the following types:

- **Head nodes**: These are the controlling systems that contain the servers required to submit jobs, manage data, monitor a system, provide error recovery, failovers, and software distribution.

- **Slave nodes**: These are the nodes that do the actual work. They contain local disk storage (usually a lot of it), and run programs that perform the work required. They report the status of the work performed back to several of the head nodes.

- **Boundary nodes**: These are the nodes where users submit units of work to a cluster. Typically, these nodes are not part of an actual cluster, but have networked access to it. These nodes are also sometimes referred to as gateway nodes.

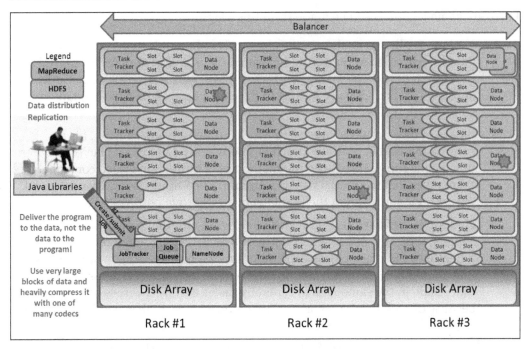

Figure 1.3 – Hadoop cluster physical architecture

Figure 1.3 shows a typical Hadoop cluster. The user sits at a boundary node system and creates/submits jobs to the cluster. The **JobTracker** server receives a request and places it into its **Job Queue**. Later, the **JobTracker** will schedule the job for execution and distribute it to one or more **Task Tracker** servers to start the **Java Virtual Machine (JVM)** and execute the program. **Task Trackers** are configured with *slots*, which represent the number of job components that they are allowed to start.

In the above diagram, the following points about the cluster should be noted.

- The **JobTracker** and **NameNode** reside on a head node that manages the execution of the jobs.

- Every other node shown is a slave node.

- Typically, many more head nodes are used than the single one shown in the preceding figure.

- Note that there are asymmetric nodes that have differing numbers of slots (and maybe even different hardware configurations, such as number of processor cores, and so on). While this is possible, it is discouraged, since it will lead to another level of diagnostics when analyzing performance delays.

There are some key points to be made from this diagram:

- Hadoop replicates its data in the cluster. The default is that every block of data is written three times (the replicated block is shown in red). This aids in redundancy, performance, and scheduling. This is a definable parameter and is controlled globally by specifying `dfs.replication` in the Hadoop configuration files.

- Blocks of data are very large with the default size being 64 MB. This size is controllable and is typically much larger, usually 128 MB and beyond. Often, this data is compressed, and the method of compression is also controllable. Remember that we have a massive amount of compute at our disposal, and we are trying to address the I/O latency to improve performance.

- Hadoop is "rack aware." A **rack** is a hardware unit that contains multiple servers, typically, in a single container (a rack). HDFS, when replicating data will attempt to place blocks on different racks, if possible. The rationale is that should an entire rack fail, no data will be lost, and I/O across servers that reside in the same rack is generally faster than I/O across different racks, because of rack-level network optimization (that is, high speed backplanes).

 Note that the definition of a rack is a manual task. A rack number must be defined for a node. It is not automatically detected.

- Hadoop jobs are Java or Java-based programs. They are packaged in Java JAR files (Java Archives). The JAR files are delivered to the data. The rationale here is simple: it is less costly to move the relatively smaller JAR file to where the data lives, rather than transfer it through the network to an executing program. It is often said that "moving computation is cheaper than moving data."

- Being rack aware, the **JobTracker** can be smarter about the node it uses to dispatch a task. Its first choice is to pick a node with a free slot where the data resides locally. Its second choice is to use a node with a free slot where data exists on the same rack. Its third and final choice is to use any node that has a free slot.

HDFS – the Hadoop Distributed File System

Hadoop comes with its own form of file storage called the Hadoop distributed file system (HDFS). HDFS is designed to do several things:

1. Provide a namespace that can control, read, write, update, and delete actions performed on files using a POSIX style of file system. A typical HDFS file locator (a URI) for a file named `file.tsv`, owned by a user named `mcovert`, is of the `hdfs://users/mcovert/data/file.tsv` form.

2. Provide redundancy so that losing a small section of data will not *break the cluster*.

3. Provide high speed and parallel access to data, thereby *feeding* the execution framework with data as quickly as possible.

4. Provide utilities (the **balancer**) that can rectify any imbalances that may exist in the cluster. For instance, if a node fails, typically all of its blocks will be lost, but the balancer will assign new nodes where these missing blocks can be copied from the surviving two nodes.

HDFS is implemented in the form of several server processes that handle I/O requests for data stored in the cluster. These server processes are explained in the next section.

The NameNode

The **NameNode** is where information about the data in the cluster is stored. It represents a catalog of all the files and directories that are managed by the cluster. The NameNode is a very complex server process. It is memory-intensive, since it caches most file metadata. Also, note that a file that resides in HDFS is spread across data nodes in the cluster, and also that each block of the file is replicated, so that the data catalog tends to be very large for even a moderate sized system.

The NameNode itself is a Java server. Hadoop provides an application programming interface (API) to access data and to perform various file management tasks. When a program runs, it is assigned a block of data to process, and the NameNode is queried to find the location of the server (see DataNode in the *DataNodes* section that follows) where the data resides, and also to obtain various metadata about the file and the data block. When data is written back into HDFS, the NameNode is notified, so that it can record the block metadata into its catalog, and to subsequently handle replication as well. Later, when we discuss the DataNode, we will complete this understanding.

The secondary NameNode

The secondary NameNode is where a backup copy of NameNode data is stored. This server provides recoverability in case of catastrophic failures. While the mechanics of catastrophic recovery are beyond the intentions of this discussion, there are two modes of recovery that can be configured. A basic mode of recovery can occur when the NameNode fails (for instance, due to a hard drive error), and then the redundant copy of the NameNode metadata is used to restart the failed NameNode. In this case, the cluster itself fails, and all running jobs are lost and must be rerun. A more sophisticated capability exists, called **High Availability (HA)**, where the secondary NameNode assumes control of HDFS storage. In this case, the cluster will continue to run, and active jobs generally can be completed without requiring a restart.

DataNodes

Every node in the cluster that is assigned the task of handling data runs a **DataNode**. The DataNode performs local I/O, which means that when a block of data belonging to a file in the cluster has been requested, the NameNode finds it, and then assigns the DataNode that owns the data block to deliver it to the requesting program.

The DataNode is largely unaware of the activities of the NameNode and is only responsible for storing data locally. It is not stored by the actual file name though. The DataNode stores blocks as files that are spread across directories. This prevents a directory from becoming *overloaded* and makes the time required to open files occur faster. The DataNode is only responsible for passing this information back to the NameNode so that it can be stored in the catalog.

MapReduce execution framework

MapReduce jobs are orchestrated by two primary server types—the **JobTracker** and the **TaskTracker**. There is one JobTracker, and it uses one or more TaskTrackers running on slave nodes where it distributes the work (the mappers and reducers).

The JobTracker

The JobTracker is the manager of all the jobs that are submitted to Hadoop and it performs many tasks. It queues jobs into an input queue, and then determines the order they are allowed to run in. Hadoop starts with a very basic approach here, which is to run jobs in the order in which they are received, or first come first served (FCFS). Clearly, this can be very inefficient, so Hadoop allows this to be customized by providing several other types of schedulers that take into account system capacity, assigned job priority, assigned job class, and so on.

The TaskTracker

The TaskTracker is the manager of all the tasks that are started by the JobTracker. A TaskTracker is responsible for a lot of things:

- It physically manages the JVM container that will run the task.
    - Note that typically, a JVM requires a few seconds to initialize. Therefore, Hadoop provides a, `mapred.job.reuse.jvm.num.tasks` parameter, that can be used to *reuse* an existing JVM. Its default value is 1.

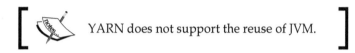 YARN does not support the reuse of JVM.

- It starts the mapper or reducer that it has been assigned.
- It handles I/O mapping for its assigned task.
- It reports *progress* back to the JobTracker.

The TaskTracker also provides a "heartbeat" back to the JobTracker. This is a message sent by default every 3 seconds. It is configurable through the `dfs.heartbeat.interval` parameter.

Hadoop jobs

Every job that executes on the Hadoop cluster is represented by a `Job` object. Through this object, the job also has access to a `Configuration` object that can be used to pass information to its tasks as they execute. This object is essentially a HashMap of keys and values, where the key represents the parameter name, and the value represents the value of the parameter. In a job, you create this object, set values on it, and then use it to first create the `Job` object, which is then submitted to the cluster:

```
import org.apache.hadoop.conf.Configuration;

Configuration conf = new Configuration();
conf.set("parm", "value");
// Set other configuration items
Job job = Job.getInstance(conf);
// Set up your job
job.setJarByClass(MRJob.class);
job.setJobName("MRJob");
```

```
FileInputFormat.setInputPaths(job, new Path(args[0]));
FileOutputFormat.setOutputPath(job, new Path(args[1]));
job.setMapperClass(MRMapper.class);
job.setReducerClass(MRReducer.class);
job.setPartitionerClass(MRPartitioner.class);
job.setSortComparatorClass(MRComparator.class);
job.setMapOutputKeyClass(org.apache.hadoop.io.Text.class);
job.setMapOutputValueClass(org.apache.hadoop.io.Text.class);
job.setOutputKeyClass(Text.class);
job.setOutputValueClass(Text.class);
job.setNumReduceTasks(1);

int return_code = (job.waitForCompletion(true)) ? 1 : 0;
return return_code;
```

Distributed cache

One important thing to remember is that when your job is run and it submits your work, it will run on a boundary machine, but the components of your job (its mappers and reducers) will run on nodes within the cluster. Therefore, local files that can be accessed at the time the job is submitted are not automatically available to the actual running job. In these cases, in order for your job to run on the Hadoop cluster, there needs to be some way for these external files to be copied to the cluster. This is true when:

- Additional JAR files are required to be in CLASSPATH
- Various other files are needed, containing parameters, lookup data, and so on

Clearly, it would be possible to just copy these files to every node, but this quickly becomes unwieldy. The files could also be copied to HDFS, but this makes versioning difficult since a using job must know what file name to use. To solve this problem, Hadoop provides a facility called **distributed cache**, which allows these files to be automatically copied to wherever the task will run.

The distributed cache component allows one to specify various files that should be copied to nodes that will run our tasks. This includes JAR files, regular files, and compressed files (such as ZIP files that contain multiple files organized into directories). In order to use the DistributedCache, the following lines of code can be used:

```
URI parms = new URI("parms.txt#parms");
DistributedCache.addCacheFile(parms, job);
DistributedCache.addCacheArchive(new URI("map.zip", job);
DistributedCache.addFileToClassPath(new Path("lib.jar"), job);
```

Note, the movement of `parms.txt` into a distributed cache and the strange `#parms` syntax at the end. This causes Hadoop to copy this file to each node where processes will run, and then to symbolically link it to a simple file name of `parms`, which can then be opened and read typically in a `setup()` method. This is powerful because it frees our tasks from needing to know the real file name. We could easily send a `newparms.txt` file call by only changing our job code, and then the underlying mappers and reducers would never need to know this.

When dealing with multiple JAR files, there is another technique, which is often used, called a **FAT JAR**. This is a single JAR file where all the required JAR files are unpacked and repacked. This can even include the required Cascading JAR files. While unwieldy, this is still a very useful technique, and it can save you debugging time when you get the dreaded `java.lang.ClassNotFound` exception.

Counters

Hadoop also provides instrumentation: the ability to define **counters** that can be used for debugging, performance assessment, and general visibility into the workload being processed. Here, we must note that jobs that run in a cluster are largely out of your control. They cannot use typical development techniques, such as debugging breakpoints. Additionally, since there are a lot of them running simultaneously, even using the ubiquitous `System.out.println` function is problematic, since so many output consoles are being captured. Counters are easy to use, as shown in the following example:

```
public enum COUNTERS {
   RECORDS_WITH_ERRORS
}
```

Then in a mapper, reducer, and so on:

```
context.getCounter(RECORDS_WITH_ERRORS).increment(1L);
```

And later in our job:

```
System.out.printf("Errors: %d\n",
   counters.findCounter(COUNTERS.RECORDS_WITH_ERRORS).getValue());
```

YARN – MapReduce version 2

As can be seen in the architecture, the JobTracker is a single point of failure. Additionally, it performs a tremendous amount of work. It handles job submission, job scheduling (including finding and allocating *slots* where the parallel parts of each job run), and also tracking the progress of the job itself. It became a major bottleneck over time. As a result, version 2 of Hadoop now splits job scheduling and job execution into separate components.

In YARN, jobs are submitted to the **Resource Manager**. This server tracks all active nodes and their resources (such as CPU, memory, disk, and so on). When a job is to be dispatched, the job itself gives an indication of the resources it would like to use. This is a negotiation though, and the job is given what can be made available to it, in the form of a set of nodes where its tasks can run and some other guidance for what it can use. Then, the Resource Manager starts an Application Master. This process runs on a slave node and manages the entire job. It dispatches the mappers and the reducers. It also receives progress notifications. Each mapper and reducer runs inside a JVM container.

So, we can see that the old JobTracker is now split into Application Master and Node Manager. The **Application Master** offloads the management of the running job. This reduces the points of failure, since the failure of an Application Master will only kill its tasks.

One other significant aspect of YARN is that it does much more than just run MapReduce. In fact, YARN was designed to run arbitrary frameworks. For instance, both Spark and Tez can run on YARN.

What we are seeing here is the emergence of an application stack. YARN now forms the basis for resource management and scheduling/dispatching functions. Frameworks, such as MapReduce, Tez, Spark, and others, provide an application execution framework. After this, application development frameworks, such as Cascading, run within the application execution environment. It is this separation of concerns that is driving innovation, reducing the complexity of development, and providing upward compatibility by freeing the tight coupling that the original MapReduce imposed.

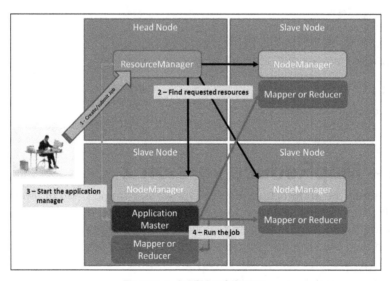

Figure 1.4 – YARN architecture

Make no mistake, YARN is more complicated. However, frameworks are also emerging to aid developers. Additionally, existing MapReduce jobs can run without change on YARN. So, the addition of YARN, has provided a major enhancement to Hadoop. It allows scalability far beyond what version 1 could achieve. It has all but eliminated the single points of failure, and it now provides consideration for the resources that are being requested by the job. Also, YARN is being adopted rapidly. First, adopters chose it to build infrastructure that required persistent servers and better scalability. For instance, Spark and Tez (see the *Beyond MapReduce* section that follows) can now run on top of YARN. Given that YARN can seamlessly support legacy MapReduce applications, its adoption is now occurring at the application level.

A simple MapReduce job

Let's take a look at a simple MapReduce job. Let's look at a simple task. We are going to compute a weighted average of prices for some products. We will have data that represents price changes over time for some set of products. This is how the data looks:

```
product-id,date,price
1,1/1/2014,10.00
1,6/1/2014,11.00
1,11/26/2014,9.99
1,12/31/2014,11.99
```

Product number 1 has gone through several markups and markdowns. We seek to determine the average price over the low date and high date within the data for each product. In order to compute our average, we will need records that arrive at our reducer and are sorted both by the product ID date. For this, we will use the following classes:

- `MRJob`: This is a program that submits a job to the Hadoop cluster for execution

- `MRMapper`: This is a mapper that handles each data split and formats the data, in such a way that reducers can perform counting

- `MRReducer`: This is a reducer that performs a summary

- `MRPartitioner`: This is a class that ensures that all identical keys get routed to the same reducer

- `MRComparator`: This is a class that compares the correct portions of the composite keys so that they can be sorted correctly

Let's start by looking at a job that will submit work to Hadoop. This job is provided with command-line arguments that specify input and output directories, as well as any other parameters that may be required:

```
// Package and import statements omitted
public class MRJob extends Configured implements Tool {
  /**
   * @param args  input_directory_name   (required, HDFS)
   *              output_directory_name (required, HDFS)
   */
  public static void main(String[] args) throws Exception {
    int rc = ToolRunner.run(new MRJob(), args);
    System.exit(rc);
  }
  @Override
  public int run(String[] args) throws Exception {
    Configuration conf = getConf();
    Job job = Job.getInstance(conf);
    job.setJarByClass(MRJob.class);
    job.setJobName("MRJob");
    FileInputFormat.setInputPaths(job, new Path(args[0]));
    FileOutputFormat.setOutputPath(job, new Path(args[1]));
    job.setMapperClass(MRMapper.class);
    job.setReducerClass(MRReducer.class);
    job.setPartitionerClass(MRPartitioner.class);
    job.setMapOutputKeyClass(org.apache.hadoop.io.Text.class);
    job.setMapOutputValueClass(org.apache.hadoop.io.Text.class);
    job.setOutputKeyClass(Text.class);
    job.setOutputValueClass(Text.class);
    job.setNumReduceTasks(8);
    int rc = (job.waitForCompletion(true)) ? 1 : 0;
    return rc;
  }
}
```

We can make a few notes here now. The job itself looks much like the standard Java program by implementing a static `main()` method. It is passed `String args[]`, containing the parsed command line. Only two parameters are specified: the input directory and the output directory. Both are assumed to be HDFS by default. However, this class implements the `Tool` interface, and uses a static `ToolRunner` call to start execution. Use this form to save yourself a lot of trouble. `ToolRunner` implements a lot of good functionalities, and specifically, it is responsible for handling generic command-line arguments. These are specialized parameters that can specify additional JAR files that must be placed into the Java CLASSPATH. Other files and compressed archives should also be copied there, and also various parameters that are placed directly into the Hadoop `Configuration` container. The actual job submission then occurs in the `run()` method of this class. We can see that this is where each class is defined and will be used as mappers, reducers, partitioners, and so on.

First, let's look at a mapper. Note the usage of `LongWritable` as the key. This effectively passes the record offset as the key of the data record being processed.

```
// Package and import statements omitted
public class MRMapper extends Mapper<LongWritable,Text,Text,Text>
  {
  private static String INSEP = ",";
  private static String OUTSEP = "#";
  private Map<String, String> recordMap;
  @Override
  void map(LongWritable key, Text value, Context context)
  throws IOException, InterruptedException {
    // Field 0 is product ID, field 1 is date, field 3 is price
    String[] fields[] = value.toString().split(INSEP);
    // Our KEY is product-ID#date
    // Our VALUE is date,price
    context.write(new Text(fields[0] + OUTSEP + fields[1]),
                  new Text(fields[1]+ INSEP + fields[2]));
  }
}
```

 This input definition and supplying the record offset as the key is the default behavior of the `FileInputFormat` setting in the job. Different input formats can be used to change this behavior.

Now, let's look at a reducer. It will receive a single product key with an iterator of all the date, price values that are sorted by increasing the date:

```
// Package and import statements omitted
public class MRReducer extends Reducer<Text,Text,Text,Text> {
    // Allocate our objects once and reuse them!
    Text outKey = new Text();
    Text outText = new Text();
    int sum;
    @Override
    void reduce(Text key, Iterable<Text> values,
                Context context)
        throws IOException, InterruptedException {
            // Split our composite key to get just the product ID.
            String[] prodDef = key.toString().split(SEP);
            double average_price;
            // Compute the weighted average of prices based on number of
            // days difference between sorted records
            for (Text v : values) {
            // Computation of weighted average
        }
        outKey.set(prodDef[0]);
        outText.set(new Text(Double.toString(average_price)));
        context.write(outKey, outText);
    }
}
```

Next, let's look at the partitioner. It will route records based just on the product number so that all identical products arrive at the same reducer together to be group:

```
// Package and import statements omitted
public class MRPartitioner extends Partitioner<Text,Text>
implements Configurable
{
    @Override
    public int getPartition(Text key, Text value, int
      numReduceTasks) {
        private static String SEP = "#";
        String[] partStr = key.toString().split(SEP);
        int prodNum = Integer.parseInt(partStr[0]);
        return prodNum % numReduceTasks;
    }
}
```

Lastly, we have the comparator. This compares two composite keys. If the product numbers are different, it performs just like a normal compare. If they are the same, it compares their date fields so that the results will be sorted by the date:

```
// Package and import statements omitted
public class MRComparator implements RawComparator<Text> {
  private static String SEP = "#";
  @Override
  public int compare(byte[] b1, int s1, int l1,
                     byte[] b2, int s2, int l2)
  {
    return WritableComparator.compareBytes(b1, s1, l1, b2, s2,
      l2);
  }

  /**
   * Compares the two objects
   */
  @Override
  public int compare(Text o1, Text o2) {
    String s1[], s2[];
    s1 = o1.toString().split(SEP);
    s2 = o2.toString().split(SEP);
    int prod1 = Integer.parseInt(s1[0]);
    int prod2 = Integer.parseInt(s2[0]);
    if(prod1 == prod2) {
      return MRUtil.compareDates(s1[1], s2[1]);  // See code
    }
    if (prod1 < prod2)
      return -1;
    else
      return 1;
  }
}
```

Whew! This is a lot of code to do something that seems pretty easy. There must be a better way! Cascading provides us with a mechanism that will greatly simplify these tasks.

Beyond MapReduce

With Hadoop, there are really only two primary job types that are supported by the framework: mapper-only jobs and mapper/reducer jobs. This has become limiting as we attempt to maximize performance within a cluster. During many of the Hadoop phases of processing, files are written to disk and then immediately reread. This is inefficient. Also, all job structures usually exist as Map -> Reduce -> Map -> Reduce .... Every job must start with a mapper, even if it's `IdentityMapper` that simply reads a record and writes the same record. In this case, the only purpose that the mapper actually serves is to perform the file split.

 Other job sequences do exist that allow Map -> Map -> ... -> Map -> Reduce, but discussion of these is beyond the scope of this book. See the `ChainMapper` class for more information on this.

As a result, some new systems are seeking to become replacements for Hadoop, or at the very least, to become part of the "plumbing" that Hadoop provides. There are many of these, but two are noteworthy; they're gaining adoption and are proving to provide major performance improvements. We provide a very brief description of these here:

- **Apache Tez** is a new architecture that follows the basic paradigm of MapReduce, but allows for more generic processing than simple mapper and reducer functionalities, and it also provides finer grained control over how data is interchanged and persisted.

- **Apache Spark** is also a new paradigm that is a total replacement for MapReduce. It has its own controlling framework of servers that are *persistent*, that is, they can remain operational and wait for new data when it becomes available. It provides very generic processors, and includes in-memory computing through its **resilient distributed datasets (RDD)**. Interestingly enough, Spark now can run using YARN as its resource manager. Spark is written in Scala, a very powerful programming language that runs in a JVM.

The Cascading framework

Now let's look very briefly at Cascading. Cascading provides a much higher-level API in addition to MapReduce, and as we shall soon see, many other types of big data "fabrics," such as Tez, Spark, and Storm. Additionally, Cascading provides an abstraction that insulates our code from the underlying fabric and the data source type and protocol. It also gives us an integrated **orchestration layer** that allows us to build sophisticated sequences of jobs, and it provides rich out-of-the-box functionalities. MapReduce programmers have realized very quickly that much of the code that write is dedicated to some very basic things, such as preparing the sort keys and handling the comparisons for the sort. As we saw previously, MapReduce is verbose! Even such a simple task requires five classes and well over 100 lines of code.

Fundamentally, in this code, little is actually occurring other than key preparation, partitioning, sorting, and counting. Cascading handles this by assigning the input and output sources and destinations, creating the sort keys, performing the sort, and then performing the counting. It accomplished all this in a single class with an astonishing 20 lines of code! We need to know a little bit more about Cascading, so after we gain this understanding in a later chapter, we will look at this code in detail and then return to compare the differences, outlining the efficiency gains.

To a large degree, Cascading hides much of the complexity of MapReduce and of many big data programming complexities in general. Now, to be perfectly clear, Cascading has its own set of complexities. It also provides a standardized approach that has a *smaller surface area* than all of Hadoop. Cascading is, in fact, a **domain-specific language** (**DSL**) for Hadoop that encapsulates map, reduce, partitioning, sorting, and analytical operations in a concise form. This DSL is written in a fluent style, and this makes coding and understanding of the resulting code line much easier.

A **fluent interface** (also sometimes known as a **builder pattern**) is one in which each call to a class returns an object (called its context) through which the method operates. This functional style allows for concise code to be written where the resulting lines of code resemble a "scripted language," as shown here:

```
Company company = new Company("XYZ Corp");
company.setAddress("Company Address")
.setPhone("123-456-7890")
.addEmployee("Jim")
.addEmployee("Sue");
```

The execution graph and flow planner

When Cascading executes its job code, it is really preparing an execution graph. This graph has as its vertices every process that must be performed. These are things, such as reading and transforming records, performing sorts, performing aggregations, and writing results. Its edges are in the form of all of the data exchanges that occur between these processing steps. After this graph is prepared, Cascading plans how it will be executed. The planner is specific to the underlying framework. In the preceding example, we use `HadoopFlowConnector` to do this. Herein lies the beauty of Cascading. There are other connectors.

`LocalFlowConnector` can run the job without needing Hadoop at all. It is simply run as a connected set of Java programs. Using this connector, a developer can test their code in isolation. This is very valuable for a developer.

In future, you can see how `TezConnector`, `SparkConnector`, and others can be created. So, what we've seen is that we can write one code line and then execute it on differing frameworks. We have magically freed our code from being frozen in place! We've now gain the ability to move to newer, more performant, and more feature-rich big data frameworks without requiring expensive rewrites.

How Cascading produces MapReduce jobs

After the execution graph is produced, the creation of MapReduce jobs is relatively easy. Most everything that we tell Cascading is translated into mappers, reducers, partitioners, and comparators. The lower-level semantics of performing record mapping, multifield sorts, and so on are handled for us.

Additionally, as we shall soon see, Cascading provides a rich set of high-level functions to do basic ETL work, such as regular expression parsing, data transformation, data validation, error handling, and much more.

Summary

We have now learned what drives the need for big data technology. We have also learned about Hadoop, its components, how it is used, and how it differs from other traditional relational database systems. We have discussed what the future holds for similar technologies, and the problems that exist with Hadoop and MapReduce Lastly, we took a brief look at Cascading and discussed how it addresses many of these problems, how Cascading can help preserve our investment in development, and how it can help us adapt to rapidly moving technological innovation that is evident in big data frameworks.

In the next chapter, we will take a much closer look at Cascading, its architecture, and how it can be used to solve typical problems in data processing.

2
Cascading Basics in Detail

In this chapter, we will begin our exploration of Cascading. We will look at its intended purpose, its structure, developing programs using it base classes, and managing the execution of these programs.

Understanding common Cascading themes

Cascading is an application development and a data processing framework that makes Hadoop development simpler and more durable over time. It does this by reducing the number of lines of code that are required to perform most tasks, and durability comes through its seamless support of Hadoop and other big data frameworks.

Hadoop application development with MapReduce and other frameworks is a difficult task with a very steep learning curve, as you have seen in the previous chapter. Cascading significantly simplifies this process with an intuitive high-level abstraction over Hadoop application development, job creation, and job processing. With Cascading, developers can create reusable components and pipe assemblies, which are reliable and scalable.

Data flows as processes

Imagine a plumbing system, a water filtration system, or a brewery—anything that uses a stream of some kind to be processed and is ultimately used. The system usually starts with some source—maybe a tank with some gray liquid to be filtered and modified in a particular way to be ultimately turned into a delicious beverage. The final beverage itself at the end will be deposited into another container (a sink) from which it will be dispensed to happy customers. All the modifications from gray liquid to a delicious beverage take place in pipes. Different pipes perform different operations: some filter the liquid, and some apply procedures to modify the liquid in many different ways. Pipes merge to combine different parts of the liquid, and they split to carry away filtered out residue. Imagine this seamless flow that hides a plethora of complexity from those who operate it and those who enjoy the final results. Now, imagine many of these flows running simultaneously, creating a magnificent cascade that simultaneously produces one or many useful products, and utilizing one or many "gray liquid" sources.

Figure 2.1 – Beer brewery to illustrate a Cascading system. Picture released to public domain by Lila Frerichs. Downloaded 1/23/2015 from http://www.publicdomainpictures.net/view-image. php?image=57925&picture=beer-brewery

A plumbing/liquid processing model is a logical paradigm for the data processing model, because each data processing step draws an input from the output of the previous step. Thus, the Cascading data processing paradigm resembles the preceding system. Our gray liquid is the data input, the delicious beverage ready for consumption is the output data, and pipes are where the input data is processed and transformed into the output data. The Cascading processing model is based on data streams (using the metaphor of pipes) and data operations, which include filters, functions, assertions, aggregators, and buffers (described later in this book). Furthermore, the Cascading API allows the developer to assemble pipe assemblies that split, merge, group, or join streams of data while applying operations to each data record or groups of records.

Our liquid processing system in this example (the image shows a beer brewery) could be represented in this way:

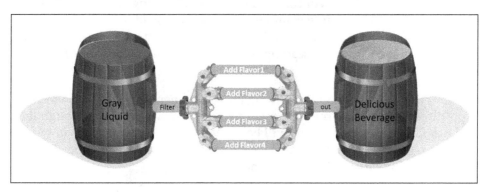

Figure 2.2 – Example of the Cascading system described in the code

It can be pseudo-coded in Cascading in this way:

```
// Set up the source container with gray liquid
Scheme grayLiquidScheme = new TextDelimited( new Fields( "grayLiquid"
), true, "," );
Tap sourceContainer = new FileTap( grayLiquidScheme,
sourceContainerPhysicalLocation );

// Set up the output "sink" container which will receive the resulting
beverage
Scheme deliciousBeverageScheme = new TextDelimited( new Fields(
"deliciousBeverage" ), true, "," );
Tap outputContainer = new FileTap(deliciousBeverage,
sinkContainerPhysicalLocation );

/* Set up the pipe assembly to filter, flavor and finalize the
beverage. Note that the final pipe contains the result of all the
previous pipes*/
```

```
Pipe pipe = new Each(pipe, new Filter());
Pipe topPipe = new Each(pipe, new AddFlavor1());
Pipe midPipe1 = new Each(pipe, new AddFlavor2());
Pipe midPipe2 = new Each(pipe, new AddFlavor3());
Pipe bottomPipe = new Each(pipe, new AddFlavor4());
Pipe outPipe = new Merge(topPipe,midPipe1,midPipe2,bottomtPipe);
/* Now connect the source container with the pipe assembly and the
output container and create the flow which converts gray liquid into
delicious beverage! As simple as that! */
Flow flow = new LocalFlowConnector().connect(sourceContainer,
outputContainer,outPipe );
flow.complete();
```

As you can see, the code closely follows the actual physical process of the preceding "brewery" example. The great advantage of using Cascading is that it is easy to mimic even a very high-level concept of a big data processing system without being exposed to the underlying complexity of big data (Hadoop/MapReduce, for example) implementation. This code will become clearer after we define Cascading terminology and learn about Cascading objects, which are the basic blocks of a Cascading application.

Throughout this book, we will be defining terms pertinent to a specific concept or concepts discussed in the current chapter or section. As we progress through this book, the definitions of these terms will be refined, and the new terms will be defined to reflect newly acquired knowledge. We will start with these basic concepts. These concepts are explained in detail later in the book:

- **Tuple** is a data record. Cascading represents all data as tuples.

- **Tuple stream** is a series of tuples passing through a pipe branch or assembly.

- **Pipe** is a data stream upon which operations are performed. Typical operations are data transformations, filtering, computations, summarizations, and aggregations.

- **Branch** is a simple chain of pipes without forks or merges.

- **Pipe** assembly is an interconnected set of pipe branches.

- **Taps** are data sources and data sinks. Data sources supply data that is to be read. Data sinks produce data that is persisted to disk. Taps must be bound to pipe assemblies. Data source taps should be bound to the beginning of a pipe assembly as inputs, and data sink taps should be bound to the tail of a pipe assembly as outputs.

- **Groups** are collections of records that have something in common, such as items in an order or information records about a single customer. Cascading has a variety of simplified methods that group records, allowing various operations, such as aggregation (sums, averages, counts, and so on) to be performed.

- **Flow** is a system of taps and pipe assemblies, in which one or more datasets *flow* forward to be compared, combined, or otherwise manipulated to produce result.

- **Cascade** is a collection of flows. Multiple flows can be grouped together and executed as a single process. In this context, if one flow depends on the output of another, it is not executed until all of its data dependencies are satisfied.

Understanding how Cascading represents records

Now that you have gotten a glimpse of how you can implement a data processing system using Cascading, let's dive into the internals of it. In this section, we will learn how to define and structure data streams for Cascading processing.

Using tuples and defining fields

The idea of a tuple is very similar to that of a record in a database.

Tuples (`cascading.tuple.Tuple`) provide storage for a vector or a collection of values, addressed by offset that can be associated with specific object types and names. A tuple can have data objects of different types. A series of tuples make a tuple stream. A simple example of a tuple is [`String name, Integer age`]. A tuple has a large set of methods to get, set, append, and remove fields.

Strictly speaking, a tuple stores data in positional columns, such that each column is accessed by its ordinal position. Each element is assumed to represent a single data element, and all are assumed to be of a standard Java-defined `Object` data type (that is `String`, `Integer`, `Long`, `Object`, and so on). We shall see later that these elements can be automatically converted to a desired format. For instance, data stored as `String` can be converted to `Integer` automatically. However, we will also see that we must be aware of problems that may arise if the data is invalidly formatted, which will cause the conversion to fail.

Some of the most useful methods are shown as follows:

- The `size` method returns a new `Tuple` instance of the given size with nulls as its element values:

  ```
  public static Tuple size(int size)
  ```

  For example, `Tuple result = Tuple.size(3)` will create a tuple named `result` of the size of three objects.

Note that `Tuple.size()` uses a different creation paradigm to the typical Java new method that we are used to using.

- Method `getObject` returns the element at a given position. This method will perform no type coercion on the element:

```
public Object getObject(int pos)
```

For example, `tuple.getObject(0)` will return an object at the position zero of a tuple.

Similarly, to get tuple elements of a specific type, use these methods:

```
public boolean getBoolean(int pos)
public int getString(int pos)
public float getFloat(int pos)
public double getDouble(int pos)
public integer getInteger(int pos)
```

However, how do we know the kind of data inside a tuple and how to access it? For this, we use another Cascading class called `Fields`.

Fields (`cascading.tuple.Fields`) provide storage for field metadata—names, types, comparators, and type coercion. This class represents the field name in tuple or it can also reference values in a tuple as a selector. A tuple field may be a literal `String` value, representing a name, or it may be a literal `Integer` value, representing a position, where positions start at position 0. A `Fields` instance may also represent a set of field names and position. They can either be strings (such as city or country), or integers indicating the position of a field (starting with 0 for the first position or -1 for the last position). Field values are also comparable, and this allows them to be sorted.

 Comparators are needed for data elements, because at some point in time, it may be necessary to sort all records using this field. `Comparator` is a Java class that implements a method called `compare()`. This method is passed two values to compare and it returns an int that tells the caller whether the two values are equal, less than, or greater than each other.

Here is an example of the code instantiating a `Fields` object:

```
Fields people = new Fields( "first_name" , "last_name");
```

Once again, fields are metadata over the tuple; during tuple operations this metadata can be used to select or constrain the values used for the operations on a tuple. Note also that the same field within a tuple may be known by multiple *names* during its lifetime if different fields metadata are supplied.

The `Fields` object is very flexible and there are many things can be done when the names, types, or even the number of fields are not known, and this is an essential part of Cascading. The `Fields` object provides the preceding metadata, but more importantly, it is also used to control and map data elements as they are processed.

Using a Fields object, named field groups, and selectors

Fields in a tuple, when the tuple is consumed or produced by operations, can be *constrained* or selected in two basic ways. One way is to simply describe the `Tuple` values as a `Fields` object:

```
Fields selectedFields = new Fields("name", "address", "phone");
```

Another way is to use specially predefined constants that select `Fields`, representing `Tuple` values/columns, based on their meaning in reference to Cascading.

There are sets or substitutions that provide convenient wild cards for field declarations. These wild card manipulations are often referred to as **field algebra** for the fields stored in tuples, using `Fields` sets.

Field sets are most typically used to control how tuples are passed from one processing step to another. Later, we will see how this occurs. The most useful field sets are:

- `Fields.ALL`: The `cascading.tuple.Fields.ALL` constant is a wildcard that represents all the current available fields.

- `Fields.UNKNOWN`: The `cascading.tuple.Fields.UNKNOWN` constant is used when `Fields` must be declared, but it's not known how many fields or what their names are. This allows processing tuples of arbitrary length from an input source or a given operation.

- `Fields.ARGS`: The `cascading.tuple.Fields.ARGS` constant is used when `Fields` are supplied as input arguments to an operation are to be selected.

- `Fields.RESULTS`: The `cascading.tuple.Fields.RESULTS` constant is used when `Fields` are produced as results by an operation are to be selected.

- `Fields.GROUP`: The `cascading.tuple.Fields.GROUP` constant is used when `Fields` that have been grouped (through `GroupBy`, for example), are to be selected.

There are other predefined field sets. They are: VALUES, REPLACE, and SWAP. For an in-depth coverage of these field sets, please refer to the JavaDoc Cascading. Some of these sets are covered later in this chapter with the appropriate examples.

Fields are used as both declarators and selectors. A **declarator** declares that a given Cascading operation or a process returns a specific set of values, which are the size of the given Fields instance. A **selector** is used to select given referenced fields from a tuple.

Data typing and coercion

Sometimes, it is necessary to implicitly specify the data type of a field. Coercion can be used to handle implicit conversions. It means that one data type can be converted to another. For example, parsing the "100" Java string to the 100 integer is coercion. Cascading supports primitive type coercions natively through the cascading. tuple.coerce.Coercions class. The type information, if specified, is propagated downstream. Here is one way to coerce a string field to a number of type long:

```
pipe = new Coerce(new Fields("timestamp"), Long.class);
```

Another way to do it is by simply specifying a data type when declaring Fields. Please note that this simple version only works when a single field is specified:

```
Fields simple = new Fields ("age", Long.class);
```

Working with multiple fields in a tuple can be handled by using an array of fields, shown in the example in the *Defining schemes* section.

The coercion discussion would not be complete without mentioning the TupleEntry coercion methods. Later in this chapter, we will discuss TupleEntry in detail. In a nutshell, TupleEntry objects are used to encapsulate fields associated with schemes and a single tuple of data. It is possible to implicitly invoke coercions through the cascading.tuple.TupleEntry interface by requesting a Long or String representation of a field, via TupleEntry.getLong() or TupleEntry.getString(), respectively. The example here will return the third element of TupleEntry as a string:

```
String label = tupleEntry.getString(2);
```

Defining schemes

A tuple is described by a **scheme**. A scheme contains field definitions. For example, a scheme describing a person may include fields for a person's first name, last name, and age.

Fields are named, so this is how the code for a scheme defining a person tuple may look:

```
Scheme personScheme = new TextLine( new Fields(
  "first_name","last_name", "age") );
```

The types associated with fields are metadata about the types used in the tuple. Fields do not need to have a data type, but they can, as we saw earlier. This example shows how to coerce all the fields at once into the types we want:

```
Fields longFields = new Fields("age", "height", Long.class);
```

Keep in mind that the types are not *typing* the fields themselves, they're just providing the metadata for the field.

If we want to type several fields, we have to use an array of `Fields` and `Types`:

```
Fields[] nameFields = new Fields[] {new Fields("name"),
  new Fields("age")};
Type[]typeFields = new Type[]{ String.class, Integer.class };
Scheme personScheme = new TextLine(new Fields(nameFields,
  typeFields));
```

We also have one other way to type a given field, and that is to use a fluent interface method defined in the `Fields` class:

```
Fields inFields = new Fields("name", "address", "phone", "age");
inFields.appplyType("age", long.class);
```

This is just a *spoiler* for the later discussion on a fluent interface.

Many types of preexisting scheme exist, as follows:

- `NullScheme` – It is used as a placeholder when a scheme is needed. It does nothing but allow a scheme argument to be supplied when one is needed.

- `TextLine` – It is broken into simples *lines* (such as CR, CR LF, or NL).

- `TextDelimited` – It breaks delimiter characters. It can also skip headers. This is useful for processing comma-separated (`.csv`) or tab-separated (`.tsv`) files.

- `SequenceFile` – It is a Hadoop SequenceFile of binary key/value pairs.

Schemes in detail

Schemes are used to not only read data, but also to parse and convert/transform it. The data that is read is often referred to as **source data**. When data is converted to some other format, or otherwise transformed, what is produced is referred to as **sink data**.

The `TextLine` class is used to read and write text files. `TextLine` returns tuples that contains two fields: a line number or byte offset as the first field (named `offset`), and the line of the text as the second field (named `line`). When `TextLine` is used to write tuples, all the values are converted to a Java `String`, in which these two fields are delimited by a TAB (`\t`) character. By default, `TextLine` uses the `UTF-8` character set. This can be overridden on the appropriate `TextLine` constructor. A separate `TextLine` scheme exists for local and Hadoop modes.

Here are the most commonly used `TextLine` constructors. For the full set of constructors, please refer to Cascading JavaDoc for `TextLine()`. See *Chapter 9, Planning for Future Growth* for more information.

```
TextLine(Fields sourceFields)
```

- `sourceFields` – the source fields for this scheme
- If `sourceFields` has one field, only the text line will be returned in the subsequent tuples

```
TextLine(Fields sourceFields, Fields sinkFields)
```

- `sourceFields` – the source fields for this scheme
- `sinkFields` - the sink fields for this scheme
- If `sourceFields` has one field, only the text line will be returned in the subsequent tuples

```
TextLine(Fields sourceFields, Fields sinkFields, String
    charsetName)
```

- `sourceFields` – the source fields for this scheme
- `sinkFields` – the sink fields for this scheme
- `charsetName` – It is of the `String` type

The `charsetName` argument could be `DEFAULT_CHARSET` or one of the following:

Charset	Description
`US-ASCII`	This is a seven-bit ASCII, also known as ISO646-US, and the Basic Latin block of the Unicode character set
`ISO-8859-1`	This is the ISO Latin alphabet No. 1, also known as ISO-LATIN-1
`UTF-8`	This is an eight-bit UCS transformation format
`UTF-16BE`	This is a sixteen-bit UCS transformation format, and a big-endian byte order
`UTF-16LE`	This is a sixteen-bit UCS transformation format and a little-endian byte order
`UTF-16`	This is a sixteen-bit UCS transformation format, and the byte order is identified by an optional byte-order mark

Also, the Java `StandardCharsets` class defines constants for each of the standard charsets.

Here is a code example using `TextLine()`:

```
/* Create a basic test line scheme */
Scheme textLine = new TextLine();
/* Create a text line scheme using custom fields */
Fields fields= new Fields ("city", "country");
Scheme textLine = new TextLine(fields);
```

`TextDelimited` is a scheme that breaks on delimiter characters, such as CSV (comma-separated variables) and TSV (tab-separated variables). This scheme also allows to skip headers and can use quoted text. When written to, all tuple values are converted to strings and joined with the specified character delimiter. The `TextDelimited` class is a subclass of `TextLine`.

It is assumed that if the sink/source fields are set to either `Fields.ALL` or `Fields. UNKNOWN` and `skipHeader` or `hasHeader` is true, the field names will be retrieved from the header of the file and used during planning. The header will be parsed with the same rules as the body of the file. By default, headers are not skipped. This form is very useful for `.csv` and `.tsv` files, since it allows field names to be defined from the data. In other words, since the file itself contains a header with field names, it will be used. The file becomes self-describing.

`TextDelimited` may also be used to write a header in a file. The fields' names for the header are taken directly from the declared fields. Or, if the declared fields are `Fields.ALL` or `Fields.UNKNOWN`, the resolved field names will be used, if any.

By default, headers are not written. If `hasHeaders` is set to true on a constructor, both `skipHeader` and `writeHeader` will be set to true. This scheme works for both local and Hadoop modes.

Here are the most commonly used `TextDelimited` constructors. For the complete list of `TextDelimited` constructors, please see the Cascading JavaDoc:

```
TextDelimited()
```

The `TextDelimited` Constructor creates a new `TextDelimited` instance, sourcing `fields.UNKNOWN`, sinking `Fields.ALL`, and using `TAB` as the default delimiter:

```
TextDelimited(boolean hasHeader, String delimiter)
TextDelimited(boolean hasHeader, String delimiter, String quote)
TextDelimited(Fields fields)
TextDelimited(Fields fields, boolean skipHeader, boolean
  writeHeader, String delimiter)
TextDelimited(Fields fields, boolean skipHeader, boolean
  writeHeader, String delimiter, String quote)
```

Here is an example of code using the `TextDelimited` scheme:

```
/* No header and TAB delimited */
Scheme textDlmLine = new TextDelimited();
/* Has a header and is comma delimited */
Scheme textDlmLine = new TextDelimited(true, ",");
```

`SequenceFile` is a very efficient file format to use with Hadoop. It is a binary file, and it consists of sets of key/value pairs. This file format can only be read on a Hadoop platform. Note that other similar file formats exist, such as Avro, RCFile, etc.

The `SequenceFile` constructor is shown here:

```
SequenceFile(Fields fields)
```

This creates a new `SequenceFile` instance, which stores the given field names:

```
Scheme seq = new SequenceFile(fields);
```

`WritableSequenceFile` reads and writes Hadoop writable objects (such as key and/or value). This class is helpful if you have sequence files created by other applications. On writing, key and/or values are serialized into the sequence file. On reading, key and/or value objects are wrapped in a `Tuple` Cascading and passed to the pipe assembly. This class is only available for a Hadoop platform.

There are two constructors for the `WritableSequenceFile` class. These are:

- `WritableSequenceFile(Fields fields, Class<? extends Writable> valueType)`
- `WritableSequenceFile(Fields fields, Class<? extends Writable> keyType, Class<? extends Writable> valueType)`

The `WritableSequenceFile` class is a subclass of `SequenceFile` that reads and writes values of the given `writableType` class, instead of tuple instances used by default in `SequenceFile`. This example shows how to use `WritableSequenceFile` for a `Tap` sink:

```
Tap tapValue=new Hfs(new WritableSequenceFile(new
  Fields("line"),Text.class),getOutputPath("value"),
SinkMode.REPLACE);
```

TupleEntry

We have briefly introduced `TupleEntry` earlier. The `TupleEntry` class allows a tuple instance and it declares a `Fields` instance to be used as a single object. In other words, `TupleEntry` provides a map from a textual field name to its ordinal position within a tuple.

Once `TupleEntry` is created, its `Fields` cannot be changed, but the `Tuple` instance it holds can be replaced or modified. The managed tuple should not have elements added or removed, as this will break the relationship, which is stored internally as `Map<String, Integer>`, with the associated `Fields` instance.

`TupleEntry` allows access to a tuple using field names. `Fields` encapsulated by a `TupleEntry` play an important role in Cascading. These `Fields` form the metadata for `Tuple`. In other words, they define the name of a column and its data type. `Fields` are also used to select data out of a tuple, as the tuple flows through its stages of data processing. We have already seen how selectors are used, and we will look at this aspect some more, in the section entitled *Default output selectors*.

Here is a code example of `TupleEntry`:

```
Fields selector = new Fields("name","ssn");
Tuple tuple = Tuple.size(2);
TupleEntry tupleEntry = new TupleEntry(selector, tuple);
```

`TupleEntry` is generally useful to have when we need the field metadata wrapped in with the tuple. For example, `TupleEntry` is useful for most operations, which will be described in more detail along with examples in the next chapter.

Understanding how Cascading controls data flow

Now, we know what the Cascading *record* looks like. How do we process these records? How do we move and manipulate data? Cascading provides us with the concept of pipes. Pipes control how data is managed during the processing segment.

Using pipes

Pipes are things that *do stuff*. The Cascading API allows the developer to assemble pipe assemblies that split, merge, group, or join streams. As data moves through pipes, streams may be separated or combined for various purposes:

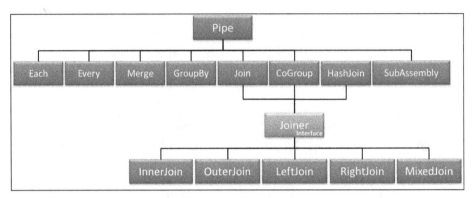

Figure 2.3 – Pipe definition

Some pipes, such as `Merge`, `GroupBy`, and the `Join` classes, perform single actions on entire Tuple streams. Others, such as `Each` and `Every` require an operation to be attached to them. It is the operation code that performs the desired task. We will look at operations briefly in this chapter, though *Chapter 3, Understanding Custom Operations* will explore them in detail.

Creating and chaining

Pipes are created through both declaration and instantiation, and by *chaining* them together. Pipes specify input and output tuple information.

A **branch** is a chain of pipes that are without merges or splits. Several connected, merged, or split pipe branches make a pipe assembly, and a stream of tuples processed by pipes is referred to as a **tuple stream**.

Pipe operations

Specific types of pipes allow various data operations to occur as individual records or sets of records flow through them. An operation is, therefore, an executable piece of code that the pipe calls, passing it one or more tuples that the pipe is processing. Later, when we look at the `Each` and `Every` pipes, we shall see how these operations are used. The following list shows the operation types that Cascading uses:

- **Filter** – It discards unwanted records, based on some specified criteria.
- **Function** – It performs transformations or calculations on the data.

- **Aggregator** – It summarizes data across sets of records. An aggregator is notified when a new group of records is being processed, and also when the last record of a group is being processed. It is called once with each record in the group. In this manner, the aggregator can perform various counting, summing, or other arithmetic operations on the group of records.

- **Count** - It counts grouped records and is an example aggregator.

- **Buffer** – It operates on a set of records in a manner similar to an aggregator, though a buffer is given to all the grouped records at once.

- **Assertion** – It imposes asserted conditions on the records that fail if they're not met. It is similar in usage to `Java assert()`.

This is just a brief introduction to operations. They will be discussed in more detail in the next chapter.

The following code shows a simple example of pipes that use operations:

```
/* Create a pipe named main */
Pipe firstPipe = new Pipe("main");
/* Chain a specific pipe type to it and perform a function on it
*/
Pipe eachPipe = new Each(firstPipe, new MyFunction());
/* Chain a specific pipe type to it and perform a filter on it */
eachPipe = new Each(firstPipe, new MyFilter());
```

`MyFunction()` is a function to be applied to each tuple in the tuple stream, and `MyFilter()` is a filter to be applied to each tuple in the tuple stream. For now, `MyFilter()` and `MyFunction()` are defined outside this example, but we will have a detailed discussion on how to apply filters and functions in the next chapter.

Each

You may have noticed that we used the `Each` construct to create the last two pipes in our code example. The `Each` pipe is the simplest. It flows tuples one at a time through its processing chain. It applies the operation that has been connected to it on each record. An `Each` pipe is allowed to use either a `Filter` or a `Function` operation.

In this example, we have a payroll data stream, which includes name, division, and salary of an employee. For each employee, we calculate his or her raise using the `calc_raise()` function. `Function` is created outside this example. The next chapter will address creating custom functions.

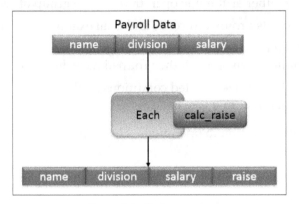

Figure 2.4 – Each example

The following code illustrates the example used in this diagram:

```
Pipe payroll =Pipe("payroll");
payroll = new Each(payroll, new calc_raise(), new
    Fields("name","division","salary","raise"));
```

Note that the pipe is reused. The `Each` pipe actually maintains an internal state and builds a structure that manages all the operations applied to it.

Splitting

Splitting a pipe is easy: just create new "downstream" pipes using the prior pipe.

In this example, we are splitting the HR data into developers and managers, applying the `GetDevelopers()` and `GetManagers()` filters to each tuple:

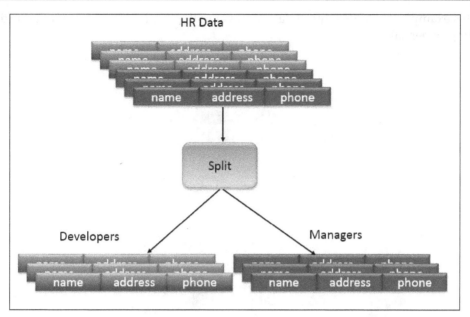

Figure 2.5 – Split example

This code illustrates the example used in the diagram:

```
Pipe hrdata = new Each("hrdata", new
   Fields("name","address","phone"));
Pipe developers = new Each(hrdata, new GetDevelopers());
Pipe managers = new Each(hrdata, new GetManagers());
```

> It should be noted here that the format of the new Each()
> statement shown in the preceding code takes a previous Pipe
> as its first parameter. You will frequently see constructs where
> a declared Pipe variable is reused by placing the newly
> created Pipe reference in it. By inference, we can see that
> Pipe is actually a sort of linked list that has its predecessor
> and successor stored as internal fields. We shall look at this in
> much more detail soon.

GroupBy and sorting

A GroupBy pipe is used to perform groupings on sets of tuples, and can also be
used to perform secondary sort operations. The emitted sequence of tuples will
be grouped by the designated fields. No secondary sorting is provided by default,
although it can be specified.

In this example, we have payroll data, and we will grouping it by division name and sorting as per salary:

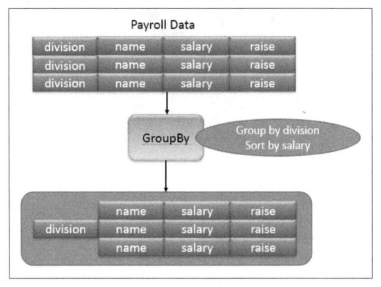

Figure 2.6 – GroupBy example

This code illustrates the example used in the diagram:

```
Pipe payroll = new Each("payroll", new Fields("division", "name",
  "salary", "rise"), new Identity());
// Group by division, sort by salary
Fields groupFields = new Fields( "division");
Fields sortFields = new Fields( "salary" );
Pipe assembly = new GroupBy( payroll, groupFields, sortFields );
```

 As we saw in the last chapter, this secondary sort capability saves us a lot of coding when using Hadoop.

Every

An `Every` pipe operates on groups of records. It is produced by the `GroupBy` or `CoGroup` pipes. Different kinds of operations, such as an aggregator or buffer, can be applied to these groups. These operations will be discussed in the next chapter. For the time being we are using the `Calc_totals()` aggregator, which is hypothetically defined outside this example.

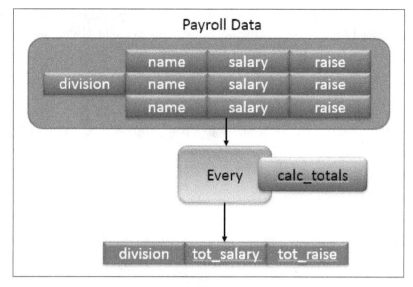

Figure 2.7 – Every example

This code illustrates the example used in the diagram:

```
// group by assembly pipe is calculated in the previous example
Pipe totals = Every(assembly, new Calc_totals(), new
    Fields("division", "tot_salary", "tot_raise"));
```

Merging and joining

It is often necessary to combine data from several data streams into a single data stream, and the data from different data sources into one compiled output. Cascading provides several pipe types to handle data joining and merging.

A merge is performed by passing two or more pipe instances to a Merge or GroupBy pipe.

A join combines data from two or more streams that have different fields, based on common field values (analogous to a SQL join). This is done by passing two or more Pipe instances to a HashJoin or CoGroup pipe.

The Merge pipe

The Merge pipe merges (hence its name) multiple streams into a single stream. The streams must have identical fields in order for merge to work. This is similar to SQL Union.

In this example, we will merge **HR Data** and **HR Data Update** into a single stream. Note that duplicates may occur in the output stream. We will discuss eliminating duplicates in *Chapter 3, Understanding Custom Operations*.

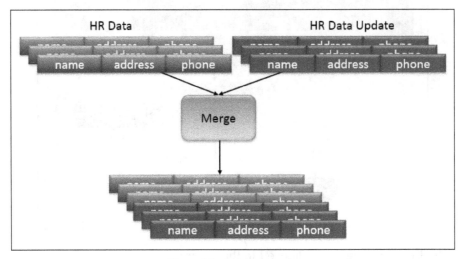

Figure 2.8 – Merge example

This code illustrates Merge:

```
Pipe lhs = new Each("hrdata", new Fields("name", "address",
  "phone"), new Identity());
Pipe rhs = new Each("hrdataupdate", new Fields("name", "address",
  "phone"), new Identity());
Pipe merge = new Merge(lhs, rhs);
```

The join pipes – CoGroup and HashJoin

As seen with SQL, join types are available and invoked by providing various joiner classes. These are as follows:

- **Inner** – It is the standard inner join where the resultant dataset must have elements in both joined sets

- **Outer** – It is the outer join where data is included, whether data on the left and right-hand side match or not

- **Left** – It refers to the left inner and right outer join

- **Right** – It refers to the left outer and right inner join

- **Mixed** – Here, three or more tuple streams are joined using a small Boolean array to specify each of the join types to be used

CoGroup

CoGroup is the basic join pipe. CoGroup accepts two or more input streams and groups them in one or more specified keys, and performs a join operation on equal key values. It is similar to a JOIN SQL. The default is an inner join, but it maintains all the fields within each joined dataset and the resulting tuple.

In this example, we will join **HR Data** and **Payroll Data** through a name to produce a record that contains an address, phone, division, and salary:

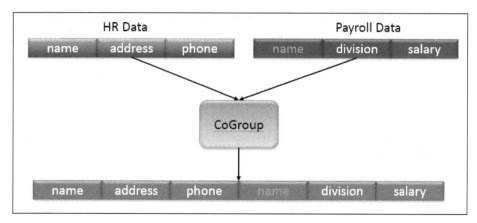

Figure 2.9 – CoGroup example

It would seem that a logical way to write code for this example would be as follows:

```
Pipe lhs = new Each("hrdata", new Fields("name", "address",
  "phone"), new Identity());
Pipe rhs = new Each("payrolldata", new Fields("name", "division",
  "salary"), new Identity());
Fields common = new Fields( "name" );
Pipe join = new CoGroup( lhs, common, rhs, common);
```

However, this code is incorrect and will throw an error, because the output will contain two distinct fields, both named name. This is not allowed. The correct way is to supply a "declared field" that renames the two instances of name to a separate name. Remember, fields are just metadata and it can be changed without altering the underlying tuple values. The mapping between the algebra field and the tuple is fluid and changeable, and you, the developer, have control over it.

The correct code is shown as follows:

```
Pipe lhs = new Each("hrdata", new Fields("name", "address",
  "phone"), new Identity());
Pipe rhs = new Each("payrolldata", new Fields("name", "division",
  "salary"), new Identity());
```

```
Fields common = new Fields( "name" );
/* Rename the second "name" to "name2" */
Fields declared_fields = new Fields("name", "address", "phone",
   "name2", "division", "salary");
Pipe join = new CoGroup( lhs, common, rhs, common,
   declared_fields);
```

HashJoin

`HashJoin` is a highly optimized join. It keeps the entire right-hand side stream in memory. Care must be taken here, because if this condition is not met then the right stream will probably spill to disk and a memory error may occur.

If these conditions are met, this join will outperform `CoGroup`, which is usually significantly.

 In Hadoop, if the full dataset can fit into memory, `HashJoin` is a map-side join!

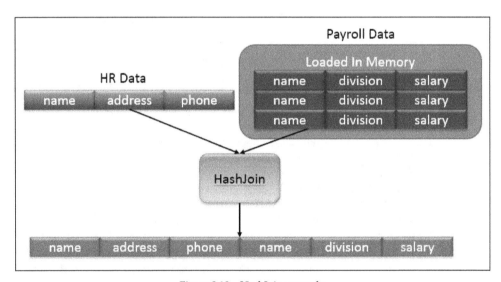

Figure 2.10 – HashJoin example

This code describes the use of `HashJoin`:

```
Pipe lhs = new Each("hrdata", new Fields("name", "address",
   "phone", "effective_date"), new Identity());
Pipe rhs = new Each("payrolldata", new Fields("name", "division",
   "salary"), new Identity());
Fields common = new Fields( "name" );
```

```
/* The payrolldata is smaller than the hrdata, so it is specified
  on the right hand side */
Fields declared_fields = new Fields("name", "address", "phone",
  "name2", "division", "salary");
Pipe join = new HashJoin( lhs, common, rhs, common,
  declared_fields);

// Spill parameters can also be set
SpillableProps props = SpillableProps.spillableProps()
.setCompressSpill( true )
.setMapSpillThreshold( 50 * 1000 );
props.setProperties( join.getConfigDef(), ConfigDef.Mode.REPLACE
  );
```

Spill parameters control the behavior of the Hadoop sort process that lies between mappers and a single reducer. When the data sent to a reducer by one or more mappers exceeds the given buffer size, it will be "spilled" to disk. This data that is written to disk can be compressed to reduce the I/O read/write time. Each spilled buffer is sorted before it is written. Later, all spill files can be "sort merged" to create the final sorted file.

Default output selectors

Cascading itself does a lot of work before the job is generated and submitted. One thing it does is to implement a "fail fast" mechanism, whereby, if the data flow has any sort of logical mismatch, the job will fail during compilation so that a wasted execution does not occur. Typically, a mismatch most frequently occurs when expected data elements (Fields) are missing, and to detect this Cascading ensures that the number of input fields exactly matches the expected number of input fields specified by an operation.

The following code fragment creates an Every pipe using a custom buffer operation. When specified this way, the default input and output Fields are used:

```
pipe = new Every(pipe, new GraphBuffer());
```

At some point in time, if you insist on using defaults, it is likely that you will receive the dreaded resolved wrong number of arguments error:

Caused by: cascading.pipe.OperatorException:

[InPipe] [com.ai.MyClass.<init>(MyClass.java:15)] resolved wrong number of arguments: [{1}:'name'], expected: 2

This indicates that the input expected by a pipe or its operation did not match the output delivered by the preceding pipe.

If this occurs, it is important to understand how Cascading determines the default output selectors that will be used. These defaults are a bit more complex than one might expect, in that they depend on both the pipe type (that is, whether it is a grouped pipe or a singleton pipe) and the operation that is being used.

The following table shows how all this comes into play. In most cases, where combinations of pipe types and operations are allowed, the default is simply `Fields.ALL`. This means that everything that comes in goes out. This makes a lot of sense for a filter, since this is exactly what we expect. However, functions by default output only their results, such as `Fields.RESULTS`.

Another anomaly occurs when we see that an `Every` pipe, which uses an aggregator, outputs all the group variables as well as any new results. However, if an `Every` pipe is connected to a buffer, the default again reverts to all.

	Default	Filter	Function	Aggregator	Buffer
Each	-	ALL	RESULTS	-	-
Every	-	ALL	-	GROUP + RESULTS	ALL
CoGroup	ALL	-	-	-	-
GroupBy	ALL	-	-	-	-
Merge	ALL	-	-	-	-
HashJoin	ALL	-	-	-	-

Figure 2.11 – Field sets table

In general, we recommend specificity. When writing your code, define exactly what the output at the pipe level will be. Use a field array of names. Leave no doubt and stay away from defaults. It will make you code easier to debug and maintain. So, how do we correctly use output selectors to prevent this mismatch? Output selectors can specified as parameters to operations. They tell Cascading that `Fields` that will be generated and outputted by an operation. Although you will have to define the actual `Fields` that are *expected* to be received by an operation, the definition of what it produces occurs through this specification:

```
pipe = new Every(pipe,
    new Fields( "graph", "node", "list"),
    new GraphBuffer(),
    new Fields( "graphnum", "nodes", "links", "connected"));
```

Using taps

Pipe assemblies are specified independently of the data source they process. So, before a pipe assembly can be executed, it must be bound to taps, that is, data sources and sinks. Taps abstract integration logic from business logic. A Tap type allows access to data that is described by a Scheme and is used for the following purposes:

- Source taps provide data to consumers
- Sink taps persist data
- A tap can be both a source and a sink, but this is not commonly used

The following image visually describes how taps are connected to pipes:

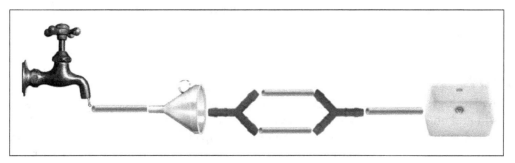

Figure 2.12 – Example of taps

Several common Tap types are provided here:

- Hfs is the tap that accesses Hadoop files, either local or remote. These files are usually named hdfs://users/vnl/datafile.

- Lfs (which is a subclass of Hfs) accesses local files. These are files that are stored in the Hadoop cluster, but are accessed by their local file name, not their HDFS name. This class is typically not used.

- Dfs (which is a subclass of Hfs) accesses HDFS files. In general, you will use the Hfs tap type instead of this one.

- FileTap is the tap that accesses purely local (that is, not Hadoop) files. These files are normal files named something, such as /tmp/datafile (for Linux or UNIX) or C:\data\datafile.txt (for Windows).

This code shows how to define schemes and attach them to taps:

```
// define source and sink Taps.
Scheme sourceScheme = new TextLine( new Fields( "line" ) );
Tap source = new Hfs( sourceScheme, inputPath );
Scheme sinkScheme = new TextLine(new Fields("department","salary"
  ));
Tap sink = new Hfs( sinkScheme, outputPath, SinkMode.REPLACE);
```

`SinkMode` can be specified to handle the disposition of the output data. Proper usage of it can prevent data overwrites from occurring using the KEEP option. To control how output files are managed to allow or prevent overwriting, the types of `SinkMode` that can be used are:

- KEEP – It will fail if the file exists
- REPLACE – It replaces the file
- UPDATE – It will attempt to reuse the file, if allowed by the filesystem

 Note that in Hadoop, REPLACE is a full directory delete, followed by a reallocation of all the files created by it. Also, in Hadoop, UPDATE is not allowed. Remember, HDFS files are immutable!

Flow

Flow is a logical unit of work. In our "brewery" example, a flow begins with a grey liquid and ends with a consumable beverage. In more precise technical terms, the result of binding one or more pipe assemblies to taps is a flow, which is executed on a computer or cluster using the Hadoop framework. A flow compiles to one or more MapReduce jobs, and in the future, will work with many other underlying fabrics, such as Tez, Spark, and so on.

After we have created a set of pipes, defined their schemes, and attached them to sources and sinks, a flow is used to actually execute the defined process. A flow is a sequence of manipulations performed on the pipes of tuple streams.

A flow creates an execution graph. An execution graph, as we previously discussed in *Chapter 1, The Big Data Core Technology Stack*, is a set of processors (that is, pipes with attached operations) and connections, which represent the forward flow of data. An execution graph must be a "directed acyclic graph", which means that each connection between two pipes can allow data to flow in only one direction, and also, no connection can flow *backwards* to create a loop in the graph.

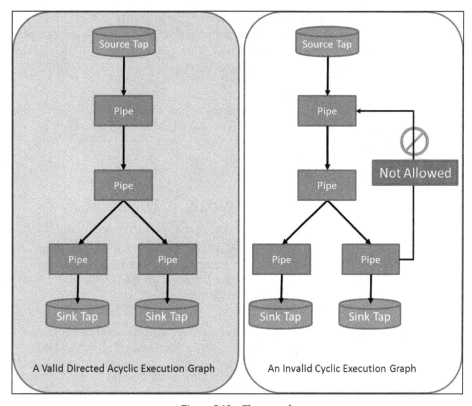

Figure 2.13 – Flow graph

A flow can have multiple inputs and outputs. Each Tap produces or receives a set of tuples, each in the same format.

FlowConnector

FlowConnectors are Cascading classes that convert execution graphs into executable jobs that run on various platforms. We have already seen that jobs can be run purely locally, or they can be run on a Hadoop cluster. This gives rise to the three main types of FlowConnector:

- LocalFlowConnector
- HadoopFlowConnector
- Hadoop2TezFlowConnector – new in Cascading 3

In the following example, we will use `FlowConnector` to create our `FlowDef`, and then we will execute the job. You may have noticed that this is another example of the fluent interface. The arguments are defined in a `FlowDef` object, which in turn is passed to the `Flow` connector:

```
// Create a local flow connector
FlowConnector flowConnector = new LocalFlowConnector();
// connect the taps, pipes, etc., into a flow
FlowDef flowDef = FlowDef.flowDef()
.addSource( copyPipe, inTap)
.addTailSink( copyPipe, outTap );
// run the flow
flowConnector.connect( flowDef ).complete();
```

> In version 3.0 of Cascading, new `FlowConnector` types are being added. The first was a `TezFlowConnector`, which allows jobs to be run against Tez/YARN-based clusters. In the future, it is expected that Spark too, will be supported.

`FlowConnector` uses a very specific `FlowPlanner` to build the execution graph. The flow planner is specific to the requested underlying platform, that is local, Hadoop, Tez, and so on.

Flows are very important and useful because they promote reusing code. Additionally, you can encapsulate MapReduce code (or even Hive code, though it's not discussed in this book) in Cascading flows and develop a complex end-to-end data flow built with heterogeneous technologies.

Cascades

A **cascade** is a connected series of flows. It allows multiple flows to be executed as a single logic unit. A Cascade is useful when a single flow becomes too large and performs too many tasks. Using a series of flows instead of one flow promotes modularity and reusability.

Flows should be connected through sink and source `Tap` file locations. Please note that no automatic cleanup of intermediate files is performed.

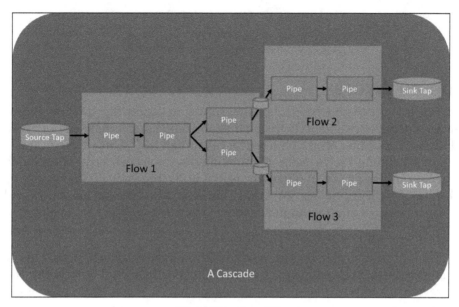

Figure 2.14 – A cascade

Here is the example code for a cascade:

```
// First flow has a final Tap that writes to output path 1
Flow final parseDocFlow = …
// Second flow reads from output path 1 and writes to output path 2
Flow final processParseFlow = …
// Now can use a Cascade to run the sequentially
Cascade textCascade = new  CascadeConnector()
.connect(parseDocFlow, processParseFlow);
textCascade.complete();
```

Local and Hadoop modes

Cascading jobs can be run in either a local mode or fully executed against a Hadoop cluster (MapReduce). A local mode helps developers to develop and test their Cascading code rapidly, without the complexities of managing a Hadoop cluster.

Cascading can use a wide variety of file types, such as from a local filesystem, HDFS residents, and even external filesystem (AWS S3 and others). As a result of this, you will often find pairs of identically named classes, one for Hadoop-specific processing, and the other for local file processing.

This example shows the code for Hadoop and local file processing:

```
// Hadoop mode
Tap source = new Hfs( sourceScheme, file1 );
// Local mode
Tap source = new FileTap( sourceScheme, file1 );
```

Common errors

Sometimes, things can go wrong when developing in Cascading, but luckily, and by design, Cascading does a lot to help you diagnose and correct these errors. As we stated earlier, Cascading uses a philosophy called "fail fast." This means that when Cascading is building a job execution graph, it does some basic error checking that can prevent runtime errors. In other words, if it finds things that it knows will cause the job to fail, it will not run the job at all! This saves developers a lot of time and effort, versus trying to figure out the runtime errors or incorrect results that may occur later.

Mixing Hadoop and local Java classes will result in indeterminate errors. This is a common problem, since so many classes are identically named. In general, one should review the import statements and ensure that all `Tap` and `Scheme` classes either come from `cascading.scheme.local` or `cascading.scheme.hadoop` and `cascading.tap.local` or `cascading.tap.hadoop`. In many cases, you will see an error that looks something similar to this:

Exception in thread `main cascading.flow.planner.PlannerException`: could not build flow from assembly: [`java.util.Properties cannot be cast to org. apache.hadoop.mapred.JobConf`]

This is Cascading telling you that there has been a mismatch in the underlying representation of the job. In this case, a local mode property object was expected, but it is running as a Hadoop job, which expects a `JobConf` object. When you see this, immediately look at the import statements for the mismatch and correct it to reference the proper package.

 Please note that tools such as Eclipse may auto-include classes when a reference to a class is unresolved. Sometimes, there are conflicts with standard Java class names, such as `Path`, `FileSystem`, `File`, `Pipe`, and so on. Be careful to import correct Cascading classes and not Java classes with similar names.

Data errors data errors are common. Later, in *Chapter 3, Understanding Custom Operations*, we will discuss common techniques to handle data errors. These will include handling missing or bad data, conversion errors, and even logical errors that may be detected by your job.

Duplicate field names, when they are created using `CoGroup` or `HashJoin` will cause the job to fail. In this case, a specific output selector must be used to rename the fields so that no duplication occurs.

Pipe connections and field mismatches occur when the expected number of fields supplied to a pipe is not provided. This is also a common error. We will discuss this in detail in *Chapter 3, Understanding Custom Operations*.

Putting it all together

This code illustrates how to put together a simple Cascading application, which takes inputs from two CSV (comma-separated value) files and joins them in common fields.

Here is the problem: in some organizations, employees are also published authors. We would like to compile a list of employees who are authors, and add department information to the list.

We have two CSV files: one file contains data on author's name, organization, journal title, and a keyword (the topic of their published work), and the second file contains department names and employee names. Our desired resultant list is the list of employees who are also authors, including their organization, department, journal title, and keyword. We will describe step by step how to build this application.

1. Here are the important libraries to import in order for the program to work:

    ```
    import cascading.property.AppProps;
    import cascading.scheme.Scheme;
    import cascading.scheme.local.TextDelimited;
    import cascading.scheme.local.TextLine;
    import cascading.tap.SinkMode;
    import cascading.tap.Tap;
    import cascading.tap.local.FileTap;
    import cascading.tuple.Fields;
    import cascading.flow.FlowDef;
    import cascading.flow.Flow;
    import cascading.flow.local.LocalFlowConnector;
    import cascading.operation.Debug;
    import cascading.operation.Identity;
    import cascading.pipe.CoGroup;
    import cascading.pipe.Each;
    ```

```
import cascading.pipe.GroupBy;
import cascading.pipe.Pipe;
import cascading.pipe.joiner.InnerJoin;
```

2. Next, we will create the `main` class, where the arguments are two files that need to be joined:

```
public class MyApp{
  public static void main(String[] args) {
    //application code goes here
  }
}
```

- ° `file1` has data that includes the author's name, organization, document title, and a keyword. This file has a header. This is how the data can look:

```
author,organization,document,keyword
Shoustrup Boyd C,ACT Manufacturing Inc.,Journal of
  Catalysis,Nitrogen
Kavello Stu P,3Com Corp,Journal of Catalysis,Phosphorus
Shoustrup Boyd C,Cendant Corp,Chemical
  Communications,Sulfur
Horowitz Jorge P,Cenex Harvest States Cooperatives,Journal
  of Catalysis,Boron
Horowitz Jorge P,York International Corp,Chemical
  Communications,Nitrogen
Rue Stu B,Abercrombie & Fitch Co.,Education in
  Chemistry,Neon
Kahn Luke M,ABM Industries Incorporated,Analytical
  Chemistry,Beryllium
```

- ° `file2` has data that has department names and employee names. Note that the employee name has the same data as the author name:

```
department,employee
Risk Management,Rue Stu B
Product Management,ShoustrupBoyd C
Research and Development,KahnLuke M
Quality Control,KavelloStu P
Information Technology,JhangGilbert U
Information Technology,HorowitzJorge P
```

3. Next, we will define schemes to represent the tuples in the source and sink taps:

```
Scheme source1Scheme = new TextDelimited( new Fields(
   "author", "organization", "document", "keyword" ), true,
   "," );
Scheme source2Scheme = new TextDelimited( new Fields(
   "department", "employee"), true, "," );
```

> Note that source1Scheme represents the tuple layout of the first file, taking into account that the file has a header (true as the second parameter) and "," as the delimiter (third parameter). Similarly, source2Scheme represents the tuple layout of the second file.

4. Now, we are ready to create source (input) taps for our application. In this case, we will be using the local mode:

```
Tap source1 = new FileTap( source1Scheme, file1 );
Tap source2 = new FileTap( source2Scheme, file2 );
```

5. Similarly, we must create schemes and taps for the output. We want to create one file that is a join of file1 and file2. The sinkScheme object incorporates fields from both sourceScheme1 and sourceScheme2:

```
Scheme sinkScheme = new TextDelimited( new Fields(
   "organization", "department", "employee", "document",
   "keyword"), true, "," ));
Tap sink = new FileTap( sinkScheme, outputFile,
   SinkMode.REPLACE );
```

Please note that SinkMode.REPLACE means that the data in the output file will be replaced each time the Tap sink is written, so existing files will be overwritten.

6. For a flow with more than one source Tap, or more than one sink Tap, it is possible to create HashMap so that all the taps of the same kind can be referred to by just one object.

One way to do it is shown here:

```
Map<String, Tap> sources = new HashMap<String, Tap>();
sources.put("lhs", source1);
sources.put("rhs", source2);
```

However, the preceding code is longer than the preferred method. A better way to do it is to use a fluent interface. This is the code that is used in our example:

```
// Do the same thing using the FlowDef fluent interface
FlowDef flowDef = FlowDef.flowDef()
                        .addSource(lhs, source1)
                        .addSource(rhs, source2)
                        .addTailSink(someTailPipe, sink);

// Tail pipe is described a little later below
```

7. It is time to create the actual data streams or pipes. Since we have two data streams, we will create two pipes: `lhs`, the left-hand pipe and `rhs`, the right-hand pipe:

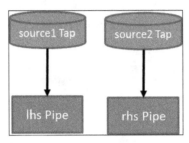

Figure 2.15 – Multiple sources

Please notice the `Debug()` filter, which is applied to the `Each` pipe. `Debug()` will dump the *contents* of the pipe, and it is very helpful for testing and… you guessed it—debugging! `Debug()` is, in fact, a filter that allows all data to pass through (that is, it is a filter that does not filter anything!):

```
Pipe lhs = new Pipe("lhs");
lhs = new Each(lhs, new Debug());
Pipe rhs = new Pipe("rhs");
rhs = new Each(rhs, new Debug());
```

8. Finally, we are going to join our two data streams to get the resultant product. In our case, `author` in `file1` and `employee` in `file2` are both people's names; these are identical common fields, and these are the fields we are going to do an inner join on. We only want the data on the employees who are also authors. Just a reminder: inner join means that only tuples from `file1` and `file2` that match each other by `author`/`employee` names will be kept in the resultant output file.

    Notice that we are creating a `CoGroup` pipe named join. We are joining the `lhs` pipe using common fields, such as `common1` (which is `author`) and `rhs` pipe using fields, such as `common2` (which is `employee`) via `InnerJoin()`, as discussed earlier.

In the last line of code, we are refining our join pipe so that each outgoing tuple encompasses the fields that we want. Please note, the `Identity()` function. `Identity()`, as used here, means that the outgoing fields are the same as the incoming fields. The `Identity()` function will be described in the following chapter:

```
Fields common1 = new Fields( "author" );
Fields common2 = new Fields( "employee" );
Pipe join = new CoGroup(lhs, common1, rhs, common2,
  new InnerJoin());
join = new Each(join, new Fields( "organization",
  "department", "employee", "document", "keyword"),
  new Identity());
```

9. At the end, we need to create the flow and connect all the parts. You may recall that we have several sources, and we can pass them as a single argument, because we showed how to encapsulate these sources into a `HashMap`:

```
Flow flow = new LocalFlowConnector().connect( sources,
  sink, join );
```

However, since a fluent interface is our preferred method, we can do this:

```
FlowDef flowDef = FlowDef.flowDef()
                       .addSource(lhs, source1)
                       .addSource(rhs, source2)
                       .addTailSink(join, sink);
Flow flow = new LocalFlowConnector().connect(flowDef);
```

Notice that we finished this application with the `flow.complete()` function. This function notifies any external application that the Cascading flow execution is completed:

```
flow.complete();
```

10. The entire application will look like this. This application will run locally. Please note that in this application, we replaced `file1`, `file2`, and output with `args[]`. `args[0]`=Input File Name1, `args[1]`=Input File Name2, and `args[2]`=Output File Name:

```
import cascading.property.AppProps;
import cascading.scheme.Scheme;
import cascading.scheme.local.TextDelimited;
import cascading.scheme.local.TextLine;
import cascading.tap.SinkMode;
import cascading.tap.Tap;
import cascading.tap.local.FileTap;
import cascading.tuple.Fields;
import cascading.flow.FlowDef;
```

```
import cascading.flow.Flow;
import cascading.flow.local.LocalFlowConnector;
import cascading.operation.Debug;
import cascading.operation.Identity;
import cascading.pipe.CoGroup;
import cascading.pipe.Each;
import cascading.pipe.GroupBy;
import cascading.pipe.Pipe;
import cascading.pipe.joiner.InnerJoin;

// Use these classes if you want to go the HashMap route
//import java.util.HashMap;
//import java.util.Map;

public class MyApp {
  public static void main(String[] args) {
    // define source and sink Taps.
    Scheme source1Scheme = new TextDelimited(
      new Fields( "author", "organization", "document",
      "keyword" ), true, "," );
    Scheme source2Scheme = new TextDelimited( new Fields(
      "department", "employee"), true, "," );
    Tap source1 = new FileTap( source1Scheme, args[0] );
    Tap source2 = new FileTap( source2Scheme, args[1] );
    Scheme sinkScheme = new TextDelimited(
      new Fields( "organization", "department", "employee",
      "document", "keyword"), true, ","  );
    Tap sink = new FileTap( sinkScheme, args[2],
      SinkMode.REPLACE );

    Pipe lhs = new Pipe("lhs");
    lhs = new Each(lhs, new Debug());
    Pipe rhs = new Pipe("rhs");
    rhs = new Each(rhs, new Debug());

    Fields common1 = new Fields( "author" );
    Fields common2 = new Fields( "employee" );
    Pipe join = new CoGroup(lhs, common1, rhs, common2,
      new InnerJoin());
    join = new Each(join, new Fields( "organization",
      "department", "employee", "document", "keyword"),
      new Identity());

    FlowDef flowDef = FlowDef.flowDef()
                          .addSource(lhs, source1)
```

```
                        .addSource(rhs, source2)
                        .addTailSink(join, sink);
    Flow flow = new LocalFlowConnector().connect(flowDef);
    flow.complete();
  }
}
```

It is advisable to create and run your Cascading application in local mode while testing and debugging. After testing and debugging is completed, it is very easy to modify your application to run on a Hadoop cluster.

11. To make the preceding example executable on a Hadoop cluster, make the following changes:

   ○   Replace:

```
import cascading.scheme.local.TextDelimited;
import cascading.scheme.local.TextLine;
import cascading.tap.local.FileTap;
import cascading.flow.local.LocalFlowConnector;
```

   With:

```
import cascading.scheme.hadoop.TextDelimited;
import cascading.scheme.hadoop.TextLine;
import cascading.tap.hadoop.Hfs;
import cascading.flow.hadoop.HadoopFlowConnector;
```

   ○   Replace:

```
Tap source1 = new FileTap( source1Scheme, args[0] );
Tap source2 = new FileTap( source2Scheme, args[1] );
Tap sink = new FileTap( sinkScheme, args[2],
  SinkMode.REPLACE );
```

   With:

```
Tap source1 = new Hfs( source1Scheme, args[0] );
Tap source2 = new Hfs( source2Scheme, args[1] );
Tap sink = new Hfs( sinkScheme, args[2],
  SinkMode.REPLACE );
```

   ○   Replace:

```
FlowDef flowDef = FlowDef.flowDef()
                        .addSource(lhs, source1)
                        .addSource(rhs, source2)
                        .addTailSink(join, sink);
Flow flow = new LocalFlowConnector().connect(flowDef);
```

With:

```
Properties properties = new Properties();
AppProps.setApplicationJarClass(properties,
                                <package.MyApp>.class);
FlowDef flowDef = FlowDef.flowDef()
                        .addSource(lhs, source1)
                        .addSource(rhs, source2)
                        .addTailSink(join, sink);
Flow flow = new
   HadoopFlowConnector(properties).connect(flowDef);
```

After all replacements are done, your application will be runnable on a Hadoop cluster. The `Properties` and `AppProps` classes will be explained later in this book.

Summary

In this chapter, you learned the basics of the Cascading API and the elements of a Cascading application. We started with the most basic building blocks of a Cascading application, such as tuples, fields, pipes, and simple pipe assemblies. We learned how to read and write data using taps and define data types using schemes. Later in the chapter, we learned how to create more complex pipe assemblies by joining separate datasets together, and showed you how to merge, spit, group, and sort data. We touched on operations as a lead-in into the next chapter. We introduced you to flows and learned how to assemble them into Cascades. Finally, we touched on data handling and how to use Cascading in both local and Hadoop modes. We concluded with our first fully functional Cascading application. This chapter gave us a foundation for a deeper immersion into Cascading in the consequent chapters.

In the next chapter, we will learn how to extend Cascading and make it transform data and also perform computations on it. We will discuss using built-in and custom developed operations, which are used by pipes. We will do this by diving into software development, so that after this chapter, you will be prepared to write a real, fully-functioning Cascading application.

3
Understanding Custom Operations

As we saw previously, creating custom operations form the foundations of data processing in Cascading. Many of these operations exist already and quite a bit can be accomplished without resorting to this level of programming, but to fully enable Cascading it is almost always necessary to create these lower-level building blocks to perform various custom functionalities.

In this chapter, we will concentrate on an in-depth discussion about operations and their five primary types. We will focus on understanding how they work, their "life cycle", and what method calls must be implemented to create a custom operation of the designated type. In the next chapter, we will actually write them!

Understanding operations

Operations form the basis for most things that can be done to data as it passes through a pipe. They are connected to the appropriate type of a `Pipe` instance.

There are several classes of operations:

- **Filter**: It discards unwanted records.
- **Function**: It performs transformations.
- **Aggregator**: It summarizes data across sets of records.
- **Buffer**: It operates on a set of records.
- **Assertion**: It imposes asserted conditions on the records that fail if they're not met. Assertions are specific to single tuples (that is, `Each`), pipes, and grouped tuples (that is, `Every`) pipes. As we shall see later, assertions are special and follow a slightly different set of rules than the other four preceding operations listed.

Using operations is easy. An operation is just a class. They are instantiated as objects using new, and then are *attached* to pipes by passing them as parameters when Pipe is created. Then, the pipe passes tuples to the attached operation where they are processed. The following example shows how this is done using various types of operations:

```
// Each (single Tuple) pipes
// Invoke a custom Function assuming that inPipe has already been
declared
inPipe = new Each(inPipe, new MyFunction());
// Invoke a custom Filter
inPipe = new Each(inPipe, new MyFilter());
// Invoke a custom ValueAssertion
inPipe = new Each(inPipe , AssertionLevel.STRICT,
                        new MyValueAssertion() );


// Every (grouped Tuple) pipes
// Invoke a custom Aggregator
inPipe = new Every(inPipe, new MyAggregator());
// Invoke a custom Buffer
inPipe = new Every(inPipe, new MyBuffer());
// Invoke a custom GroupAassertion
inPipe = new Every (inPipe , AssertionLevel.STRICT,
                        new MyGroupAssertion() );
```

The base interface definition for all operations is Operation. Other specific interfaces derive from this interface. It is this interface implementation that defines the specific type of Operation. Other interfaces, such as Filter, Function, Aggregator, and Buffer all extend this interface.

BaseOperation provides a concrete implementation that must be subclassed. All Operation types use this base class (or for assertions, a subclass of this base class), and it provides a lot of the routine plumbing, which allows Cascading to invoke the operation.

Operations and fields

When an operation is attached to a pipe as shown earlier, it can be made aware of the input tuples that it needs to process. Refer to *Chapter 2, Cascading Basics in Detail*, and the section called *Using a Fields object, named field groups, and selectors* that describes field constants. Fields supplied to the Operation by default use Fields.ALL. Another form allows just one or more specific Fields to be passed. Let's look at a couple of ways that this can be done:

```
// Attach a Function to a pipe and tell it to use all of the
   Fields
inPipe = new Each(inPipe, Fields.ALL, new MyFunction());

// Attach a Function to a pipe and tell it to use specific of the
   Fields
inPipe = new Each(inPipe, new Fields("name", "address"),
   new MyFunction());
```

Similarly, an operation typically also produces data in the form of a tuple, and through the TupleEntry, this data is bound to field names. The output of an operation is referred to by the Fields.RESULTS constant. Here, it would be good to refer back to the *Chapter 2, Cascading Basics in Detail* section, titled *Default output selectors*, to review how tuples produced by Operation types are used by the Each and Every pipes. Let's look at a couple of ways that this can be done:

```
// Attach a Function to a pipe and tell it to emit all of the
   Fields
inPipe = new Each(inPipe, new MyFunction(), Fields.ALL);

// Attach a Function to a pipe and tell it to emit just the
   RESULTS Fields
inPipe = new Each(inPipe, new MyFunction(), Fields.RESULTS);

// Attach a Function to a pipe and tell it to emit specific of the
   Fields
inPipe = new Each(inPipe, new MyFunction(), new
   Fields("name", "address"));
```

The Operation class and interface hierarchy

Operations implement a rather complicated set of interfaces and classes. The following diagram shows how these are laid out. Later, we will refer to this diagram again as we discuss each `Operation` type. It will be important to fully understand how these classes and interfaces relate to each other to help you get past some common errors that may not very obvious to correct.

Note also that operations are typed in a manner similar to a Java generic class. This type defines a `Context` object that is used during the invocation of `Operation` by `Pipe` to which it is attached. The `Context` is a generic type parameter that specifies the type of object that is stored in the `Operation` class. It could have been easily called `<T>`, which is how these type parameters are generally referred to in Java documentation. In other words, there is no `Context` object. There is only the class that is provided by the user that is a generic parameter to operations methods. We will describe this in detail soon.

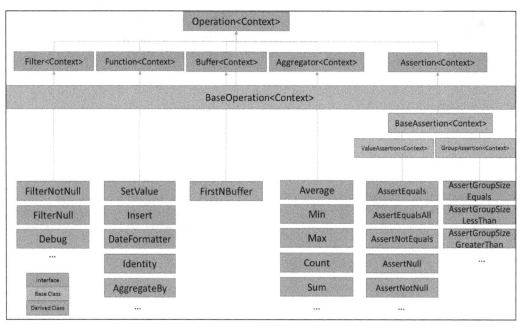

Figure 3.1 – The Operation class and interface hierarchy

The basic operation lifecycle

Operations, regardless of type, follow a sort of life cycle. The pipe to which the operation is attached creates it, then calls a `prepare()` method to allow it to initialize. After this, the calls become type-specific (meaning each `Operation` type defines its own `operate` method semantics to process tuples), but these calls are all made by the pipe, to allow the operation to process the tuples that the operation has passed. Finally, when the tuples from the data have all been processed, the operation's `cleanup()` method is called to allow it to do any post-processing that may be required (such as freeing memory, closing files, and so on).

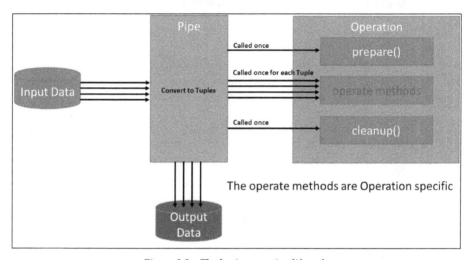

Figure 3.2 – The basic operation lifecycle

When each `Operation` is called, there are some specific data structures (classes) that are passed to all the `Operation` methods. These classes package the information that `Operation` needs to access. Let's start by looking at the call signatures of the `Operation` interface. We will define what each method does soon:

```
void prepare(FlowProcess flowProcess,
        OperationCall<Context> operationCall)

void cleanup(FlowProcess flowProcess,
        OperationCall<Context> operationCall)

void flush(FlowProcess flowProcess,
        OperationCall<Context> operationCall)

int getNumArgs()

Fields getFieldDeclaration()

boolean isSafe()
```

Contexts

Operation calls use objects that are called **contexts**. These are static object classes that allow states to be persisted through all calls. Contexts are just user-defined classes that are allocated by a single Operation, and then this object is passed to every Operation call. In this manner, a context provides a place to store state information across all calls.

Operations are generically typed to specify their context type. Interface subclasses are defined to mark specific operation types. There is no class or interface called context. Its definition is totally controlled by the developer.

In many cases, the context will simply be a tuple of the appropriate size, as specified by the number of output fields. This tuple then becomes a reusable object that can be cleared and reset at every call. The reason to do this is to reduce the number of object instantiations and frees (garbage collection) that occur. In other cases, it may be necessary to create a more complex object.

Many Cascading objects are made type-safe by supplying this user-defined context object as their specific type. For instance, if a function operation used a Map<String, String> object as its context to look up and translate strings, it would be declared as follows:

```
class SomeFunction<Map<String, String>> extends
   BaseOperation<Map<String, String>> implements
   Function<Map<String, String>>
```

Note how in this declaration type safety is ensured through the usage of the Java generic type specifier, how the class is *marked* as a function using an interface definition, and how BaseOperation is subclassed to handle many of the functionalities that would otherwise need to be implemented.

We should also note here that in some cases, context objects are simply not required to perform the necessary function. In this case, it is okay to just use the untyped base classes (such as BaseOperation, OperationCall, and so on) and not supply the type-safe generic specifications.

A context is specific to an instance of the enclosing Pipe and Operation. In other words, when Hadoop is being used, there will be many of these context objects, each running in a particular mapper or reducer with each of these job segments running on one or more nodes in the cluster.

FlowProcess

The first object that we encounter in the `Operation` methods is the `FlowProcess` object. `FlowProcess` allows `Operation` to access many elements associated with the underlying processing system. What this means is that if we are running in a local mode, we can get to various property values, but if we are running in Hadoop mode, we can gain access to all the Hadoop classes that are encapsulated in its `JobConf` object. `FlowProcess` is created by the Cascading system and is passed to our `Operation` methods. It allows us access to system counters and other Cascading specific identifiers and resources. `FlowProcess` does not have to be typed.

OperationCall<Context>

Next, we see the `OperationCall<Context>` object. This object encapsulates all the parameters that were specific to this `Operation`, as it is called by the pipe to do its processing. The `OperationCall<Context>` object allows us to gain access to the user supplied `Context` object where it can store state that will last from one processing call to the other. It also allows us to access any parameters that are supplied to `Operation`.

Note that each `Operation` type has its own interface that is derived from `OperationCall<Context>`. For instance, filters have `FilterCall<Context>`, functions have `FunctionCall<Context>`, and so on. These interfaces allow us to access other necessary objects. One is the `TupleEntryCollector`, also referred to as just `OutputCollector`. This is the object that allows us to output tuples to be processed as an output from this `Operation`. This is accessed using the `getOutputCollector()` method. Similarly, these specific interfaces allow us to get input arguments with `getArguments()`, any declared `Fields` (see *Chapter 2, Cascading Basics in Detail*) using `getDeclaredFields()`, and if the operation is grouped, `getGroups()`. As we shall see later, buffers get a set of data passed in, and so they need an iterator, which is accessed through the `getArgumentsIterator()` call. The following table shows you the interface each of these methods is defined in:

Interface	getContext()	setContext()	getArguments()	getDeclaredFields()	getOutputCollector()	getGroup()	getArgumentsIterator()
OperationCall	X	X					
FunctionCall			X	X	X		
FilterCall			X				
AggregatorCall			X	X	X	X	
BufferCall			X	X	X	X	X
ValueAssertionCall			X				
GroupAssertionCall			X			X	

Figure 3.3 – Interfaces and methods

An operation processing sequence and its methods

As we said before, the prepare() method is called once at the beginning of all the processing that the operation will perform. It can do many things, but typically, this method allocates a context object and stores it into the OperationCall<Context> object that it is passed as a parameter. Note here though that prepare() can do much more, such as loading data from disk, making notifications, and so on.

The cleanup() method is called when all the processing is done. Typically, it frees the Context object and any allocated storage that it might contain.

 Note that in reality, prepare() can be called multiple times, depending on circumstances that occur within the cluster. However, prepare() will never be called twice in a row without an intervening call to cleanup(). Therefore, knowing this, design your method calls such that they expect that this type of behavior may occur.

Operational parameters can also be obtained. These methods are already provided by the BaseOperation class, so nothing needs to be done to enable this functionality. The getFieldDeclaration() call returns the Fields object, containing information about all Fields created by this operation. The getNumArgs() call returns an integer with the number of input fields that the operation expects.

The isSafe() method needs some elaboration. It is used to tell Cascading that this operation can safely operate on the same value (that is, the exact same tuple) multiple times without fear of unwanted side effects. In some rare cases, Cascading will *redo* tuples. Returning true from this method call tells Cascading that the operation is *idempotent*, which means that it can be called as many times as required with the same data.

Operation types

Operations fall into two broad categories: those that operate on a stream of single tuples, and those that operate on groups of tuples. This naturally means that the former operations are associated with Each pipes, and the latter are associated with Every pipes. We are now going to look at all the Operation types grouped together by the pipe types that can use them.

Each operations

`Each` pipes process a single tuples. `Each` pipes can have specific operation types attached that process one tuple at a time.

Filters

A **filter** is the simplest of all operations. It is called with a single tuple and it returns a Boolean, indicating whether the tuple is to be removed from the pipe. It needs only one method to be implemented, `isRemove()`, which is passed a tuple and returns true if this tuple should be removed from the data stream.

Filter calling sequence

The sequence in which filters are called is shown in the following diagram. Just like we've mentioned earlier, the `prepare()` and `cleanup()` methods and the filter implements `isRemove()` as its operation-specific method. The arrows show the flow of tuples, and one of the following tuples is removed from the stream by the filter:

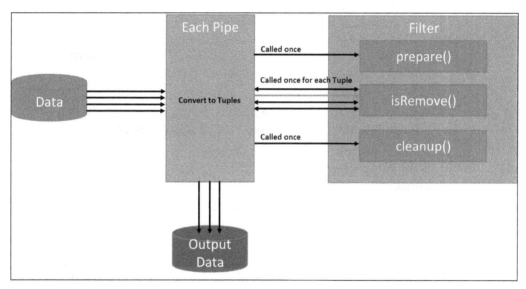

Figure 3.4 – Filter calling sequence

The following code shows the class definition and method signature used by filters:

```
public class SomeFilter extends BaseOperation<Context> implements
    Filter<Context>

public boolean isRemove(FlowProcess flowProcess,
    FilterCall<Context> filterCall)
```

Built-in filters

There are several useful built-in filters that contain a very high number of prebuilt functionalities to do common tasks. Here is a list of some of the most useful ones:

- `ExpressionFilter` – It passes an expression string, compiles the string, binds incoming tuples by name or position, and executes it, returning the Boolean result of the expression. This uses the Janino compiler.

    - The **Janino** compiler is a small (minimum of 1 MB), lightweight Java compiler that converts Java programs coded as text strings into Java bytecode, and then executes this code by binding variable names to values. It implements a rich set of features, but not everything that you can perform in Java. It attempts to maintain compatibility with Java 1.5. In particular, certain varargs, annotations, and type safe enums are not fully implemented.

- `RegexFilter` – It passes a regular expression to its constructor, concatenates every tuple value together using a `TAB` delimiter, and returns true if the regular expression matches this string. Optionally, it supplies the `removeMatch` parameter, it can be made to filter all nonmatches. Additionally, by supplying the `matchEachElement` parameter, each `Tuple` field is individually matched (that is, they are not concatenated).

- `Sample` – It passes a sample fraction (as a double between 0. and 1.0), and it outputs approximately this fraction of records. Optionally, a seed value can be passed to it to initialize the random number generator function.

- `ScriptFilter` – It passes a set of expression strings delimited by semicolons, compiles the string, binds incoming tuples by name or position, and executes it, returning the Boolean result of the expression. This uses the Janino compiler.

- `Debug` – It prints each tuple to `STDOUT`. It always returns true as a filter result (that is, so that it actually filters nothing). Also, `STDERR` can be specified as an output.

- `FilterNotNull` – It filters out any tuples that do not contain null values in the supplied fields.

- `FilterNull` – It filters out any tuples that contain null values in the supplied fields.

- `And` – It passes an array of filters; this filter returns the logical AND of all of them, so if any supplied filter returns false, the record will be removed.

- `Or` – It passes an array of filters; this filter returns the logical OR of all of them, so if any supplied filter returns true, the record will be not be removed.

- `Not` – It passes a filter on its constructor, and will negate the outcome of this filter.

- `Xor` – It passes a set of filters (typically, just a pair of them) on its constructor; it will return the exclusive OR (XOR) of these two filters. More generally, it will XOR a full set of filters, returning false if all the filters return true or false.

Let's look at some example lines of code that can show how to use some of these built-in filters:

```
// Remove all Tuples from the in the data stream where the word
   SAVE is not present in at least one field
inPipe = new Each(inPipe, new RegexFilter("SAVE"));

// Extract 20% of all Tuples in the data stream
inPipe = new Each(inPipe, new SampleFilter(0.2));

// Filter on an expression
inPipe = new Each(inPipe, new ExpressionFilter("$0 + $1 <=
   100000"));

// Or use field names, and only pass these fields
inPipe = new Each(inPipe, new Fields("salary", "raise"), new
   ExpressionFilter("$salary + $raise <= 100000"));

// Write all Tuples to STDOUT
inPipe = new Each(inPipe, new Debug());

// Check multiple filters and allow records where one of the
   passes
inPipe = new Each(inPipe, new Or(new MyFilter1(), new MyFilter2(),
   new MyFilter3()));

// Check multiple filters and allow records where all of them pass
inPipe = new Each(inPipe, new And(new MyFilter1(), new
   MyFilter2(), new MyFilter3()));
```

Function

Functions emit tuples based on sets of input (such as one tuple and a set of parameters). Functions are very general purpose. They process one tuple at a time and generally perform a calculation or transformation on it, then emit one or more resulting tuples.

Function calling sequence

The sequence in which functions are called is shown in the following diagram. Functions use the `operate()` method as their specific `Operation` call.

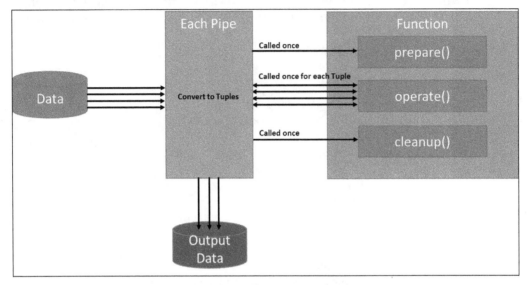

Figure 3.5 – Function calling sequence

The following code shows the class definition and method signatures used by functions:

```
public class SomeFunction extends BaseOperation<Context>
    implements Function<Context>

public void operate(FlowProcess flowProcess, FunctionCall<Context>
    functionCall)
```

Built-in functions

As seen before with filters, there are many built-in functions that can perform various common tasks without requiring a custom filter to be written:

- `Identity` – It does nothing other than write its input tuple to its output collector.

- `DateFormatter` – It converts Java timestamp fields to a Java string. It must be passed in a format string that conforms to the Java `SimpleTimeFormat` convention, and it can optionally be passed as `Timezone` and a `Locale` object as well.

- `DateParser` – It converts `String` fields to a Java `Timestamp` object. It must be passed in a format string that conforms to the Java `SimpleTimeFormat` convention, and it can optionally be passed as `Timezone` and a `Locale` object as well.

- `RegexParser` – It passes a regular expression match string to its constructor, and it parses values out of a string based on a match string.

- `RegexReplace` – It passes a regular expression match string and a replacement string to its constructor, and it replaces values in the string when the match string is found.

- `RegexSplitGenerator` – It passes a regular expression match string, a single tuple will be split into multiple tuples and output for every match that is found.

- `RegexSplitter` – It passes a regular expression delimiter; a single tuple will be split into multiple tuples and output for every delimiter that is found.

- `ExpressionFunction` – It passes an expression string; this function will compile the string to bytecode, and then execute it by binding fields names (or tuple positions) and outputting the result of the expression. This function uses the Janino compiler.

- `ScriptFunction` – It passes a more complex set of expression strings, each delimited by a semicolon; this function will compile the strings to bytecode, and then execute it by binding fields names (or tuple positions), and outputting the result of the expression. This function uses the Janino compiler.

- `FieldJoiner` – It joins designated fields into a single field separated by an optional delimiter (the default is `TAB`).

- `FieldFormatter` – It joins designated fields into a single field using a format string.

- `SetValue` – It passes a field name, filter, "true" replacement value, and a "false" replacement value; it sets the value of a field based on the Boolean outcome of this filter. This acts much like the Java expression `? true_value : false_value` statement.

- `UnGroup` – It passes a group field selector and an array of value field selectors; it will output a separate tuple for each value field selector (also containing all the `Fields` group).

- `Insert` – It passes an array of field names and a list of literal values, and emits a tuple with each field set to its corresponding (by position) literal value.

- `XPathParser` – It extracts values from a field (which is assumed to be a valid XML document) using an `XPath` expression. As many tuples will be output as the `XPath` matches.

- `TagSoupParser` – It converts HTML into valid XHTML (that is, by creating XML end tags for most HTML single tags) using the tag soup parser engine.

Let's look at some example lines of code that can show you how to use some of these built-in functions:

```
// Insert a value into a Tuple Field
inPipe = new Each(inPipe, new Insert(new Fields("data_source"),
  "HR DATA"));

// Concatenate three fields into one
inPipe = new Each(inPipe, new FieldJoiner(new Fields("last_name",
  "first_name", "middle_initial"), " "));

/* Split a Tuple using UnGroup. The result for the following data:
 * first_name,last_name,salary,raise
 * Jim,Jones,75000,7500 -> Jim,Jones,75000
 *                         Jim,Jones,7500
 * Note that UnGroup in Hadoop is a Map only process (unless a
 * subsequent GroupBy is specified.
 */
inPipe = new Each(inPipe,new UnGroup(new Fields("first_name",
  "last_name"), new Fields[] { new Fields("salary"),
  new Fields("raise")}));

// Compute a new value for new_salary based on salary and raise
inPipe = new Each(inPipe, new ExpressionFunction(new
  Fields("new_salary"), "$salary + $raise", Long.class));
```

Every operations

The `Every` operation is called by an `Every` pipe after some sort of grouping has been applied to the tuples. Typically, this is through a `GroupBy` pipe. The `Every` operation processes multiple tuples from a group. These multiple tuples can be processed one at a time (aggregator) or all at once (buffer). We shall see how these two styles differ, and how we can chose between one or the other.

Aggregator

Aggregators perform aggregations (such as sum, average, and so on) on groups of tuples and emit a single value. Aggregators are notified when a new group is starting, and then they are called with each tuple in the group to perform their aggregation. Then, when the last tuple in the group has been processed, the aggregator is notified so that it can emit its result.

Aggregator calling sequence

The sequence in which aggregators are called is shown in the following diagram. Aggregators have three operation specific method calls: start(), aggregate(), and complete(). These methods allow the aggregator the ability to process entire groups of tuples one at a time, and tell it when a new group starts and ends.

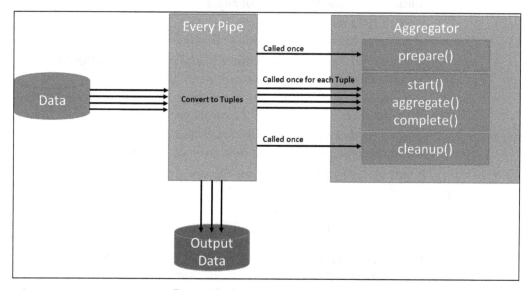

Figure 3.6 – Aggregator calling sequence

The following code shows the class definition and method signature used by aggregators:

```
public class SomeAggregator extends BaseOperation< Context>
    implements Aggregator< Context>

public void start( FlowProcess flowProcess,
    AggregatorCall<Context> aggregatorCall)

public void aggregate( FlowProcess flowProcess,
    AggregatorCall<Context> aggregatorCall )

public void complete( FlowProcess flowProcess,
    AggregatorCall<Context> aggregatorCall )
```

Built-in aggregators

There are several useful built-in aggregators that perform many SQL-like summarizations based on a grouped set of records:

- `First` – It outputs only the first record of any group
- `Last` – It outputs only the last record of any group
- `Min` – It passes a field name to its constructor, and outputs the record of any group that contains the minimum value of this field
- `Max` – It passes a field name to its constructor, and outputs the record of any group that contains the maximum value of this field
- `Average` – It passes a fields array to its constructor, and outputs a record that contains the sum of each specified field over its group
- `Sum` – It passes a fields array to its constructor, and outputs a record that contains the average of each specified field over its group
- `Count` – It outputs a record that contains the count of the number of tuples in a group

> The usage of many of these aggregators is slowly changing in Cascading. The `Min` and `Max` aggregators are now formally deprecated (but still work). Subassemblies called `MinBy` and `MaxBy` are their replacements. `MinBy` and `MaxBy` use a class called `AggregateBy` as their base class. The other classes too have companion subassemblies that end in By (`FirstBy`, `AverageBy`, `SumBy`, and `CountBy`). In Hadoop, this `AggregateBy` performs map-side performance optimizations that are similar to a MapReduce `Combiner` class. To do this, `AggregateBy` automatically inserts `GroupBy` into the stream that will perform the reducer function. We will discuss these subassemblies in more detail in *Chapter 4, Creating Custom Operations*.

Let's look at some example lines of code that can show how to use some of these built-in aggregators:

```
// Count records in a group
inPipe = new GroupBy(inPipe, new Fields("name"));
inPipe = new Every(inPipe, Fields.ALL, new Count(new Fields(
  "total_records")), Fields.ALL );

// Sum records in a group
inPipe = new GroupBy(inPipe, new Fields("name"));
inPipe = new Every(inPipe, new SumBy(new Fields(new Fields(
  "bonus_amounts"), new Fields("sum_of_bonuses"), Long.class));
```

```
// Find the minimum person's age in a department
// Group by department, sort by age, take the first one
// Note, you can also do this with the MinBy subassembly (chapter
  4)
inPipe = new GroupBy(inPipe, new Fields("department"),
  new Fields("age"));
inPipe = new Every(inPipe, new First());
```

Buffers

Buffers allow operations on a "window" of data tuples. A buffer is similar to an aggregator, but it is passed all the tuples in the group at the same time, rather than individually. So, when data has been grouped, a buffer can be used to process every tuple in the group at the same time. This grouping is generally defined by a GroupBy or CoGroup pipe. The buffer's operate() method is passed an iterator over the constituent TupleEntries.

Buffer calling sequence

The sequence in which buffers are called is shown in the following diagram. A buffer, like a function, only uses one operation method, operate(). This method is passed a set of all tuples that it will operate on.

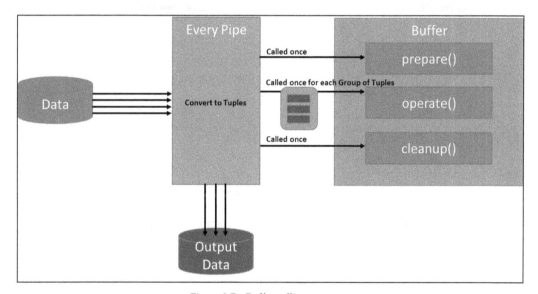

Figure 3.7 – Buffer calling sequence

The following code shows the class definition and method signature used by buffers:

```
public class AverageBuffer extends BaseOperation<Context>
    implements Buffer<Context>

public void operate( FlowProcess flowProcess, BufferCall<Context>
    bufferCall)
```

Built-in buffers

Only one built-in buffer is generally available and this is `FirstNBuffer`. This buffer can be used whenever the number of tuples in a group are expected to be very large. In this case, the `FirstNBuffer` is able to just retrieve a specified number of tuples from the group. This is very similar to the SQL `SELECT TOP n` (or also usage of the `LIMIT` predicate) statement. Here is an example of how to use this buffer:

```
// Select out just the first 1000 records in each group and then
    process them with a custom function.
inPipe = new Every(inPipe, new FirstNBuffer(1000));
inPipe = new Each(inPipe, new MyFunction());
```

Assertions

Assertions are conditions that can be set, similar to a Java assert statement, that when the defined condition is not met, an exception is thrown.

> Note that, typically, this exception will be caught by a trap. We will discuss this later in *Chapter 4, Creating Custom Operations.*

Assertions are very valuable to use during testing. In many cases, they form the basis for unit testing.

Assertions are a little bit different than just being operations (and, hence, derive from `BaseOperation`). Assertions derive from `BaseAssertion<Context>`, and they implement either the `ValueAssertion<Context>` or `GroupAssertion<Context>` interface (depending on whether the assertion will be applied by an `Each` or an `Every` pipe).

For the `Each` used version and its `ValueAssertion<Context>` interface, there is only one method call that needs to be implemented, which is `doAssert()`.

ValueAssertion calling sequence

The sequence in which `ValueAssertions` are called is shown in the following diagram. `ValueAssertions` primarily use the `doAssert()` method to perform their work. The `getTrace()` method is a convenience method that may be used to provide additional information about the call that caused the assertion to fail, if so required.

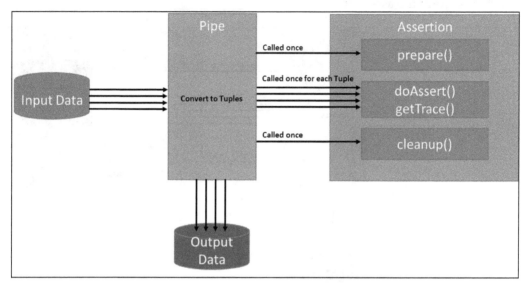

Figure 3.8 – ValueAssertion calling sequence

For the `Every` version, and its `GroupAssertion<Context>` interface, one must implement `start()`, `aggregate()`, and `doAssert()`. The `start()` method indicates to the assertion that a new group is being processed. Then, each tuple in the group is passed to `aggregate()` where computations can be performed similar to those in an aggregator. Finally, when the last tuple in the group has been processed with the `aggregate()` call, `doAssert()` is called.

GroupAssertion calling sequence

The sequence in which GroupAssertions are called is shown in the following diagram. GroupAssertions follow the method design pattern of an aggregator. They implement a start() method that is called when a new group starts. Then aggregate() is called with every tuple in the group, and finally, doAssert() is called to perform the assertion.

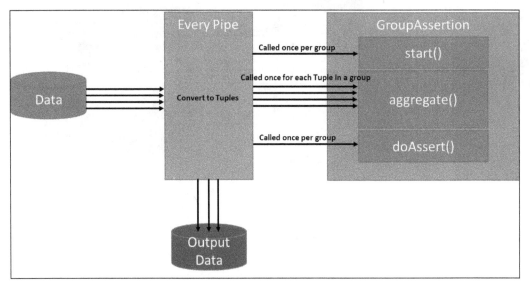

Figure 3.9 – GroupAssertion calling sequence

AssertionLevel

Assertion levels can be set on all assertions. They are really just descriptors that can aid during development by allowing one to specify whether the assertion is part of a test environment or if it is used for some sort of production control. The following assertion levels can be used:

- AssertionLevel.STRICT is used to designate assertions that are used by a production job.

- AssertionLevel.VALID is used to designate assertions that are used during testing.

- AssertionLevel.NONE can be used to turn off all assertions at various levels of granularity within a Cascading job. See *Chapter 6, Testing a Cascading Application* for more information on how to do this.

Assertions can be used to check many things, and there are a lot of built-in assertions (see the following *Built-in assertions* section) that perform several types of tests. You can also easily write your own assertions to do more complex or business logic-specific tests such as:

- Number of arguments passed
- Size of tuples
- Elements in a group
- Null or not null arguments (or tuple values)
- Expressions
- Other custom conditions

Here is an example of the method signatures for the Each style, ValueAssertions:

```
public class SampleValueAssertion extends BaseAssertion<Context>
   implements ValueAssertion<Context>

public void doAssert( FlowProcess flowProcess,
   ValueAssertionCall<Context> assertionCall)
```

Here is the method signature information for the Every style, GroupAssertions:

```
public class SampleGroupAssertion extends BaseAssertion<Context>
   implements GroupAssertion<Context>
```

The start() method is called when a new group is being processed. Note that unlike other operations, this start() method is where Context objects should be created, initialized, and saved into the GroupAssertionCall using its setContext() method. The very first time that this start() method is called, the Context will be null, and so if one is needed, it should be allocated and set here:

```
public void start( FlowProcess flowProcess,
   GroupAssertionCall<Context> assertionCall )
```

The aggregate() method is called for each tuple in the group. In this method, GroupAssertion can do any required functionality. For instance, if GroupAssertion is checking for some sort of sum, it can be accumulated in each of these calls:

```
public void aggregate( FlowProcess flowProcess,
   GroupAssertionCall<Context> assertionCall )
```

The doAssert() method is called once for each group to actually check the condition that is being asserted as true. In the preceding example, a sum would have been accumulated and stored in the context, and in this method it would be checked for validity:

```
public void doAssert( FlowProcess flowProcess,
   GroupAssertionCall<Context> assertionCall )
```

There are also some convenience methods and functionalities that will make your life easier. In the constructor, you can supply a text message that will be used if the assertion fails:

```
public SampleAssertion(){
   super( "argument '%s' failed Sample Assertion, in tuple: %s" );
}
```

There is also a convenience method called `fail()` that is called when the assertion you write fails the test:

```
Void fail( Object fieldValue, Object tuple.print())
```

Using assertions

The following code segment shows how to use the preceding `SampleValueAssertion`:

```
public class TestAssertion {
public static void main(String[] args)
{
// define source and sink Taps.
Scheme scheme = new TextDelimited(new Fields( "name","address","phone"
),
                                              true, "," );
Tap source = new FileTap( scheme, args[0] );
Tap sink = new FileTap( scheme, args[1], SinkMode.REPLACE );
Pipe inPipe = new Pipe("InPipe");
inPipe = new Each(inPipe, new Debug());
inPipe = new Each(inPipe, AssertionLevel.STRICT, new
SampleValueAssertion());
Flow flow = new LocalFlowConnector().connect( source, sink, inPipe );
flow.complete();
 }
}
```

Built-in assertions

There are many handy built-in assertions that can be easily used, as shown here. The presence of `Group` indicates that the assertion is used with an `Every` pipe:

- `AssertEquals` – It is passed a tuple on its constructor, and it then verifies that all processed tuples passed as arguments containing the same number of entries. These should be position-by-position equal using `.equals()`.

- `AssertEqualsAll` – It is passed a tuple on its constructor and it then verifies that all the processed tuples are passed as arguments containing the same number of entries. These should be position-by-position equal using value equality.

- `AssertExpression` – It is passed an expression string and it then verifies that all processed tuples, when substituted into this expression, evaluate to TRUE. Note that this class uses the Janino compiler.

- `AssertGroupBase` – This is a base class and is not used, except when it is subclassed by custom assertions.

- `AssertGroupSizeEquals` – It is passed a long `size` parameter on its constructor, and it asserts that the number of tuples in the group match the specified size. Note that a regular expression string can be passed and will be matched against the grouped fields, such that this assertion is only applied to these tuples.

- `AssertGroupSizeLessThan` – It is the same as `AssertGroupSizeEquals`, but uses "less than" (that is, <) to determine its validity.

- `AssertGroupSizeMoreThan` – It is the same as `AssertGroupSizeEquals`, but uses "more than" (that is, >) to determine its validity.

- `AssertMatches` – It joins all the fields in the tuple into a single string, with each field separated by a TAB character, and then applies a regular expression match to determine the validity.

- `AssertMatchesAll` – It applies a regular expression match against every element of the tuple individually to determine its validity.

- `AssertNotEquals` – It passes a tuple on its constructor and then verifies that all processed tuples that are passed as arguments are position-by-position not equal using `.equals()`.

- `AssertNotNull` – It asserts that all processed tuples elements are not null.

- `AssertNull` – It asserts that all processed tuples elements are null.

- `AssertSizeEquals` – It is passed as an integer `size` parameter on its constructor, and asserts that all processed tuples elements are of this exact size.

- `AssertSizeLessThan` – It is passed as an integer `size` parameter on its constructor, and asserts that all processed tuples elements are of a length less than this exact size.

- `AssertSizeMoreThan` – It is passed as an integer `size` parameter on its constructor, and asserts that all processed tuples elements are of a length greater than this exact size.

Let's look at some example lines of code that can show how to use some of these built-in assertions:

```
// Verify that all fields in each Tuple is not null
inPipe = new Each(inPipe, AssertionLevel.STRICT,
  new AssertNotNull());

// Verify that all Tuple are of length 5
inPipe = new Each(inPipe, AssertionLevel.STRICT,
  new AssertSizeEquals(5));

// Verify that the first two fields sum to 10
inPipe = new Each(inPipe, AssertionLevel.STRICT,
  new AssertExpression("$0 + $1 == 10L", Long.class));

// Verify that the two fields named "salary" and "raise" sum to
  less than 100,000
inPipe = new Each(inPipe, AssertionLevel.STRICT, new
  AssertExpression("$salary + $raise < 100000L", Long.class));

// Verify that there are two or more 2 Tuples in each group
inPipe = new Every(inPipe, AssertionLevel.STRICT,
  new AssertGroupSizeMoreThan(1));
```

A note about implementing BaseOperation methods

All the BaseOperation methods are available for every Operation type. However, there is a trick to using prepare() and cleanup() that may not be obvious at first. The issue here has to do with the (BaseOperation) base class, versus the interfaces (such as filter, function, aggregator, buffer, and assertion).

Whenever a new operation is created, you must implement specific methods for the Operation type. The filter that is required is isRemove(), and functions and buffers require operate(). Also, aggregators require start(), aggregate(), and complete(), and assertions require doAssert(). Each of these methods are supplied as parameters for FlowProcess, and are also a subclass of OperationCall<Context>, specifically FilterCall<Context>, FunctionCall<Context>, AggregatorCall<Context>, BufferCall<Context>, and ValueAssertionCall<Context> or GroupAssertionCall<Context>, respectively.

However, BaseOperation is where prepare() and cleanup() are actually implemented (again, as empty methods). Therefore, when a subclass that you create uses these methods, they will be declared with the @Override decorator as such:

```
@Override
public void prepare(FlowProcess flowProcess,
    OperatorCall<Context>)

@Override
public void cleanup(FlowProcess flowProcess,
    OperatorCall<Context>)
```

Since BaseOperation is where prepare() and cleanup() are actually implemented, note that the second parameter is typed as OperatorCall<Context>. Here, one may be tempted to use a subtype of OperatorCall<Context>, such as FilterCall< Context > or FunctionCall< Context >. If you do this, it will not work! If you do this and use @Override, the Java compiler will complain that no such method exists in the super-type (because it doesn't exist with this exact signature in BaseOperation). If you are then tempted to remove @Override, it will compile but never be called! The effect here will probably be null pointer exceptions later, if this is where you allocate your context. So, the correct way to do this (using a filter as an example) is in this way:

```
public class MyFilter extends BaseOperation<Context> implements
Filter<Context> {

    public void prepare(FlowProcess flowProcess, OperationCall<Context>
operationCall) { … }

    public void cleanup(FlowProcess flowProcess, OperationCall<Context>
operationCall) { … }

    public boolean isRemove(FlowProcess flowProcess,
FilterCall<Context> filterCall) { … }
}
```

Summary

In this chapter, we learned about the Operation class hierarchy, how operations are marked by interfaces, and also about operation lifecycle and calling sequences. We also looked at how Tuple and TupleEntry objects are supplied by pipes and used by operations, and how operations can use Context objects to store a state. Lastly, we looked at the isSafe() method and how it is used to prevent the same record from being processed more than once.

In the next chapter, armed with our current understanding of operations, we will learn how we can extend our Cascading application's functionality by creating custom operations.

4

Creating Custom Operations

Cascading provides you with the degrees of freedom to do complex things. One very useful capability of Cascading is allowing the developer to create custom operations if the pre-defined operations do not fit the bill. So now, after we have fully explored and understood the anatomy of an operation in the previous chapter, we will show you how to actually write a custom operation of each type.

Writing custom operations

We have now seen the function signatures for each of the custom operations. We also know that an operation is generically typed. Its type defines the `Context` class that it will use. Let's look in detail at how we actually write these extensions. There are several things that we must discuss first though.

As we have seen, operations are attached to pipes. When tuples of data flow through the pipes, these operations are called to process them. Remember that tuples are accessed only by position, so really they are vectors of data. But we know that tuple positions are also defined as `Fields`.

How is this managed inside of an operation? Well, a tuple is "wrapped" in a `TupleEntry` object. A `TupleEntry` object has method calls that allow positional elements in the tuple to be accessed by field name. It seems clear that to do this, an internal map must be kept where the textual field name can be looked up to obtain the ordinal position within the tuple. Because of this, tuples cannot be changed. In other words, new fields cannot be added, deleted, or renamed. The overall scheme of the tuple and its defining `TupleEntry` object is therefore immutable to any called operation.

We must also consider the fact that operations are going to exist in multiple places within the cluster, since ultimately they become elements of mappers and reducers. So a single operation will run many times on many machines. As a general rule, there is no facility for operations on different machines to communicate with each other. And on a single machine, an operation will likely be called many times, each receiving a distinct tuple to process.

On a single machine, there is a way for different operation calls to communicate with each other, and this is through a Context object. A Context object can be allocated, data placed into it, and then it can be accessed by every component of the operation. This effectively allows the state to be saved. Typically, a context is created and saved in an operation's prepare() method. It is usually called once. Then for each tuple, the operation's operate() method is called. Finally, when all assigned tuples are processed, the operation's cleanup() method is called.

Operation subtypes implement extended interfaces of the Operation<TYPE> interface. This allows reflection (instanceof) to be used to determine the type of the operation being used. This is necessary, because different classes of operations have different call semantics. For instance, when values are being aggregated, a grouped set of tuples will pass through the operation. Therefore the operation must be told when a new group has started and ended. Because of this, the method calls are different than those where only a single tuple should be considered. We will look at this in detail soon.

One thing that is also desirable is to somehow inform an operation of some detail that it may need to know. While this can be done in its constructor, it is also possible to pass information to it through a Configuration object. A Configuration object is really just a map.

 There is again confusion here. Several types of Configuration object exist, and the program must be aware of its environment. In local mode, the Configuration object is really just a Java Properties object. In a prior version of Hadoop, the Configuration object is a JobConf type. Now in the most recent version 1 of Hadoop, Configuration is an actual Configuration object (of which JobConf is a subclass). In Cascading, a JobConf object is still used!

Writing a filter

Earlier in this book, we discussed an operation called a filter. A filter removes tuples from the stream that meet specific conditions.

Now, we will show you how to write a simple filter operation called `SampleFilter`. It accepts tuples with two fields—line number and line text, and filters out the tuples that contain specific text passed as a parameter.

SampleFilter extends the class `cascading.operation.BaseOperation`. This class is common for all of the cascading operations, and therefore just like all of the operations, it inherits these methods:

- `cleanup()`
- `flush()`
- `getFieldDeclaration()`
- `getNumArgs()`
- `isSafe()`
- `prepare()`

`SampleFilter` also implements the `Filter` interface, so to write a very simple filter, you just need to implement `isRemove()` method. The `isRemove()` method returns a Boolean. It is true if the tuple meets conditions to be removed from the stream.

We will take you step by step through creating a custom filter. For our example, we will use an input file that looks like this:

```
line_num, line
1, This is a test
2, This is a line
```

1. The following are the classes you need to include in your code:
   ```
   import cascading.flow.FlowProcess;
   import cascading.operation.BaseOperation;
   import cascading.operation.Filter;
   import cascading.operation.FilterCall;
   import cascading.tuple.Fields;
   import cascading.tuple.TupleEntry;
   ```

2. Next, as we mentioned earlier, let's create a public class `SampleFilter` and its constructor. This class extends `BaseOperation` and implements filter:
   ```
   public class SampleFilter extends BaseOperation implements Filter
   {
     static Fields fieldInputs = new Fields( "line_num",
       "line");
     String filterWord="";

     public SampleFilter(String word)
   ```

```
{
    // expects 2 field arguments, fail otherwise
    super(2);
    filterWord=word;
}
...
    // Some code here
}
```

Several things are worth mentioning here:
- Since our tuples will consists of line number and line text, we can create a field definition for `fieldInputs` here with two fields.
- We plan to pass the text to filter by as a parameter, so we can create a `filterWord` property, which will be set in the constructor and used later in the code.
- `SampleFilter` expects 2 field arguments, otherwise it will fail.
- We are passing a text to filter by in the constructor, and we set our `filterWord` property to that text.

3. Now we are ready to write the `isRemove()` method. We will get the tuple and the corresponding fields into `TupleEntry`, so we can access arguments by position.

Generally, it is advisable to access arguments by position when the exact position of each argument is known in advance. Otherwise it is easier to access arguments by name.

4. We will return true if a `TupleEntry` instance contains our `filterWord` value. When attached to a pipe, this filter will "throw away" all the tuples that contain `filterWord`:

```
public boolean isRemove( FlowProcess flowProcess,
    FilterCall call )
{
    // get the arguments TupleEntry
    TupleEntry arguments = call.getArguments();
    // filter out the current Tuple if the sentence contains
      a specific word
    return arguments.getString(1).contains(filterWord);
}
```

5. Here is the `SampleFilter` code in its entirety:

```
import cascading.flow.FlowProcess;
import cascading.operation.BaseOperation;
import cascading.operation.Filter;
import cascading.operation.FilterCall;
import cascading.tuple.Fields;
import cascading.tuple.TupleEntry;


public class SampleFilter extends BaseOperation implements
  Filter
{
  /* Note that fieldInputs not used. It is there just to
  show What the input looks like */
  static Fields fieldInputs = new Fields( "line_num",
  "line");
  String filterWord="";

  public SampleFilter(String word)
  {
    // expects 2 arguments, fail otherwise
    super(2 );
    filterWord=word;
  }
  public boolean isRemove( FlowProcess flowProcess,
    FilterCall call )
  {
    // get the arguments TupleEntry
    TupleEntry arguments = call.getArguments();

    // filter out the current Tuple if the sentence
    // contains a specific word
    return arguments.getString(1).contains(filterWord);

  }
}
```

> Note that in the preceding code, we are not typing the filter with a context. This is okay here since we do not need a context. For more sophisticated requirements, it is still a good idea to do so though.

6. The following is the class to test our `SampleFilter` example. Please note the schemes, and source and sink taps we have created. Also note that we used the word `test` as a filter word:

```
public class TestFilter {
  public static void main(String[] args) {

    // define source and sink Taps.
    Scheme mainScheme = new TextDelimited(
    new Fields("line_num", "line" ), true, "," );
    Tap source = new FileTap( mainScheme, args[0] );
    Tap sink = new FileTap( mainScheme, args[1],
    SinkMode.REPLACE );
    Pipe inPipe = new Pipe("InPipe");
    inPipe = new Each(inPipe, new SampleFilter("test"));
    Flow flow = new LocalFlowConnector().connect(
    source, sink, inPipe );
    flow.complete();
  }
}
```

The result will look like this (note that the line with the word `test` is removed):

```
line_num,line
2,This is a line
```

Writing a function

When we need to do a more sophisticated processing than a filter will allow, we will create a custom Cascading function. As mentioned in the previous chapter, a Cascading function operates on the `Each` pipe assembly. Just like a filter, a Cascading function extends the class `cascading.operation.BaseOperation` and therefore just like all of the operations, it inherits these methods:

- `cleanup()`
- `flush()`
- `getFieldDeclaration()`
- `getNumArgs()`
- `isSafe()`
- `prepare()`

It also implements the `operate()` method that has to be written to make a function do something. We will discuss it shortly.

A Cascading function performs some task on tuples within a pipe. You saw in *Chapter 2, Cascading Basics in Detail,* some hypothetical functions applied to pipes, such as `Pipe topPipe = new Each(pipe, new AddFlavor1());` in our "beer brewery" mock up, or `pipe = new Each(payroll, new calc_raise(), new Fields("name ","division","salary","raise"))` in our payroll example of the `Each` pipe.

Here we will write a simple function to read a text document and split the document into sentences. Then we will apply this function to a tuple stream, where each tuple represents a document. Our output will be a text file with a document name, sentence number, and a sentence on each line:

1. Let's start with a Java class that provides a method to extract sentences. We will use a "naive" method of extracting sentences. We assume that . or ? or ! will always terminate a sentence. Here is the Java code to extract sentences:

    ```java
    public class NLPUtils
    {
      /* Parse text into sentences
       * @param text - document text
       * @return String
       */
      public static String[] getSentences(String text)
      {
        String sentences[]=text.split("[.?!]");
        for (int i=0; i< sentences.length; i++)
        {
          sentences[i]=sentences[i].trim();
        }
        return sentences;
      }
    }
    ```

2. Next we need to write a Cascading function that uses the `getSentences()` function to extract sentences, as well as counts sentences within a document, and keeps track of the document name that sentences belong to. It emits tuples with the fields:

    ◦ Document name

    ◦ Sentence number

    ◦ Sentence text

3. A typical Cascading function class has methods to:

    ◦ `prepare()`: allocate context for the output tuple

    ◦ `operate()`: where function performs some action

    ◦ `cleanup()`: release memory

4. The `prepare()` and `cleanup()` methods are invoked once per thread of execution, and in the case of the Hadoop platform, only on the cluster side, never on the client.

5. Now we have all the tools to start building our sentence detection `SentFunc` function. Tell anyone who is using this function that it needs two arguments. Also make sure you declare input and output fields. Note that in `super(2, fieldOutput)` the first parameter is the number of input fields, and `fieldOutput` are all of the output fields:

```
public class SentFunc extends BaseOperation<Tuple> implements
Function<Tuple>
{
  static Fields fieldDeclaration = new Fields(
    "document","text");
  static Fields fieldOutput = new Fields(
    "document","sentnum", "sentence");

  public SentFunc () {
    super(2, fieldOutput);
  }
}
```

6. Next, we need to allocate storage for a tuple with three fields for document name, sentence number, and sentence:

```
@Override
public void prepare( FlowProcess flowProcess,
  OperationCall<Tuple> call)
{
  // create a reusable Tuple of size 3
  call.setContext( Tuple.size( 3 ) );
}
```

Now we need to write the "meat" of the function: the method `operate()`. In this method, we are going to use `call.getArguments()` to get `TupleEntry`, which represents an input tuple and its fields: `document` and `text`. The fields are accessed by their position within the `TupleEntry` scope.

7. Then we will use our custom `NLPUtils.getSentences(String)` function to extract individual sentences into a `String` array. We will use the field at position 1 in `TupleEntry`, which is the document text, as the parameter.

8. Once the sentences are extracted, for each sentence we will create a tuple and reuse the allocated tuple space via `call.getContext()`. Then we set each of the output fields as follows:

   ° `document` is the name of the document and it is the field at position 0

- ○ `sentence` is the sentence and it is the field at position 1
- ○ `sentnum` is the sentence counter and it is the field at position 2

9. The code for how to do it is as follows:

```java
public void operate( FlowProcess flowProcess,
  FunctionCall<Tuple> call )
{
  // get the arguments TupleEntry
  TupleEntry arguments = call.getArguments();
  String sentences[] = NLPUtils.getSentences
    (arguments.getString(1));
  int sentCounter=0;
  for ( String sent: sentences)
  {
    // get our previously created Tuple
    Tuple result = call.getContext();
    // First field is document name
    result.set(0,arguments.getString(0));
    // Second field is sentence number
    result.set(1,sentCounter);
    // Third field is the sentence
    result.set(2,sent);
    // return the result tuple
    call.getOutputCollector().add( result );
    sentCounter++;
  }
}
```

10. Finally, we need to release memory:

```java
@Override
public void cleanup( FlowProcess flowProcess,
  OperationCall<Tuple> call ) {
  call.setContext( null );
}
```

11. The function is completed. The following is the full code for the class `SentFunc`:

```java
public class SentFunc extends BaseOperation<Tuple>
  implements Function<Tuple> {
  static Fields fieldDeclaration = new Fields(
    "document","text");
  static Fields fieldOutput = new Fields(
    "document","sentnum", "sentence");
```

```
public SentFunc () {
  super(2, fieldOutput);
}

@Override
public void prepare(FlowProcess flowProcess,
  OperationCall<Tuple> call ){
  // create a reusable Tuple of size 3
  call.setContext( Tuple.size(3) );
}

public void operate( FlowProcess flowProcess,
  FunctionCall<Tuple> call ){
  // get the arguments TupleEntry
  TupleEntry arguments = call.getArguments();
  String sentences[] = NLPUtils.getSentences
  (arguments.getString(1));
  int sentCounter=0;
  for ( String sent: sentences){
    // get our previously created Tuple
    Tuple result = call.getContext();
    // First field is document name
    result.set(0,arguments.getString(0));
    // Second field is sentence number
    result.set(1,sentCounter);
    // Third field is the sentence
    result.set(2,sent);
    // return the result tuple
    call.getOutputCollector().add( result );
    sentCounter++;
  }
}

@Override
public void cleanup( FlowProcess flowProcess,
  OperationCall<Tuple> call ) {
  call.setContext( null );
}
}
```

12. To create a sentence splitter pipe, you need to create an `Each` pipe and apply this function as follows:

```
inPipe= new Each(inPipe, new SentFunc());
```

We will show the main program in its entirety after explaining the custom `Buffer` operation. We will show how the function and buffer operations work together.

Writing an aggregator

Cascading provides very convenient pre-built aggregators mentioned earlier in this chapter. If, however, none of these aggregators will do, you can write your own custom aggregator. The example of a custom aggregator is shown as follows.

The problem for this aggregator is as follows: we have three product types sold by several stores. Some of these products are returned back to the store. The task is to calculate the total numbers of products kept for each product (regardless of which store they are sold by). The data file looks like this:

```
store,product,sold,returned
StoreA,Product1,10,2
StoreB,Product1,20,5
StoreA,Product2,100,20
StoreB,Product2,50,1
StoreA,Product3,20,10
StoreB,Product3,10,3
```

- To accomplish this task, for each product group we need to subtract returned from sold, and sum up the results. Aggregators work on the Every pipe, which is the result of GroupBy or CoGroup pipe.

- A custom aggregator extends the class cascading.operation. BaseOperation and implements the cascading.operation.Aggregator interface. The aggregator interface defines three methods that must be implemented: start(), aggregate(), and complete(). Cascading's JavaDoc has in-depth details on the aggregator interface.

- There are two ways that a custom aggregator can be implemented: a shortcut way—implementing just the three methods just mentioned, or a classic way—implementing the prepare() and cleanup() methods similar to implementing a custom function. The following is an example of the first, shortcut way:

  1. First we start with the imports:

     ```
     import cascading.flow.FlowProcess;
     import cascading.operation.Aggregator;
     import cascading.operation.AggregatorCall;
     import cascading.operation.BaseOperation;
     import cascading.operation.Operation;
     import cascading.tuple.Fields;
     import cascading.tuple.Tuple;
     import cascading.tuple.TupleEntry;
     ```

2. Next we create a public class `SampleAggregator`, and create a `Context` class within it. You may recall from earlier in this chapter that a `Context` object provides a place to store state information across all calls. In our case, the context keeps the calculated value in the argument `Tuple` (starting with 0):

```
public class SampleAggregatorextends
BaseOperation<SampleAggregator.Context>
implements Aggregator<SampleAggregator.Context>
{
  public class Context
  {
    long value = 0;
  }
  ...
}
```

3. Then we create a constructor for `SampleAggregator`. In this case, we provide a constructor that expects two arguments and returns one field named `total_kept`. It is a good practice, however, to allow the user to override the default declared fields in order to avoid field name mismatch. Both versions of the constructor are shown in the following code:

```
public SampleAggregator()
{
  // expects 2 arguments, fail otherwise
  super(2, new Fields("total_kept"));
}

public SampleAggregator( Fields calcFields )
{
  // expects 2 arguments, fail otherwise
  super( 2, calcFields );
}
```

4. Next we write the required aggregator methods: `start()`, `aggregate()`, and `complete()`.

5. The `start()` method initializes the aggregator for every unique grouping. For our sample aggregator, we need to initialize the `AggregatorCall` context. The new instance of `Context` object will be set for each grouping. In the subsequent calls to the aggregator within the same grouping, the `Context` object will be reused:

```
public void start( FlowProcess flowProcess,AggregatorCall<Co
ntext> aggregatorCall )
```

```
{
  // set the context object,
  aggregatorCall.setContext(new Context()) ;
}
```

6. The `aggregate()` method does the calculation work for each grouping. Here we get the input `TupleEntry` arguments, calculate the difference (sold minus returned), and add the result to the `total_kept` sum for each product:

```
public void aggregate( FlowProcess flowProcess,
  AggregatorCall<Context> aggregatorCall ) {
  TupleEntry arguments = aggregatorCall.getArguments();
  Context context = aggregatorCall.getContext();
  // add the current argument value to the current sum
  context.value += (arguments.getInteger(0)-
    arguments.getInteger(1));
}
```

7. Finally, the `complete()` method is called after every `TupleEntry` instance in the grouping has been processed. The sum of the `total_kept` parameter for each product is sent to `outputCollector`:

```
public void complete( FlowProcess flowProcess,
  AggregatorCall<Context> aggregatorCall )
{
  Context context = aggregatorCall.getContext();

  // create a Tuple to hold our result values
  Tuple result = new Tuple();

  // set the sum
  result.add( context.value );

  // return the result Tuple
  aggregatorCall.getOutputCollector().add( result );
}
```

- The `SampleAggregator` code in its entirety is shown as follows:

```
import cascading.flow.FlowProcess;
import cascading.operation.Aggregator;
import cascading.operation.AggregatorCall;
import cascading.operation.BaseOperation;
import cascading.operation.Operation;
import cascading.tuple.Fields;
import cascading.tuple.Tuple;
```

```
import cascading.tuple.TupleEntry;

public class SampleAggregatorextends
BaseOperation<SampleAggregator.Context>
implements Aggregator<SampleAggregator.Context>
{
  public class Context
  {
    long value = 0;
  }

  public SampleAggregator()
  {
    // expects 2 argument, fail otherwise
    super(2, new Fields("total_kept"));
  }
  public SampleAggregator( Fields calcFields )
  {
    // expects 2 argument, fail otherwise
    super( 2, calcFields );
  }

  public void start( FlowProcess
    flowProcess,AggregatorCall<Context> aggregatorCall )
  {
    // set the context object,
    aggregatorCall.setContext(new Context());
  }

  public void aggregate( FlowProcess flowProcess,
    AggregatorCall<Context> aggregatorCall )
  {
TupleEntry arguments = aggregatorCall.getArguments();
Context context = aggregatorCall.getContext();

  // add the current argument value to the current sum
  context.value += (arguments.getInteger(0)-
    arguments.getInteger(1));
  }

  public void complete( FlowProcess flowProcess,
    AggregatorCall<Context> aggregatorCall )
  {
    Context context = aggregatorCall.getContext();
```

```
        // create a Tuple to hold our result values
        Tuple result = new Tuple();

        // set the sum
        result.add( context.value );

        // return the result Tuple
        aggregatorCall.getOutputCollector().add( result );
    }
}
```

- Now take a look at a different way to write an aggregator. This way is to follow the same pattern as writing a custom Cascading function. Compare the `SampleAggregator` code to the following code – `SampleAggregator2`. Notice the `prepare()` and `cleanup()` methods. `SampleAggegator2` is shown here in its entirety:

```
public class SampleAggregator2 extends
  BaseOperation<SampleAggregator2.Context> implements
  Aggregator<SampleAggregator2.Context>
{
  public class Context
  {
    long value = 0;
    Tuple tuple = Tuple.size(2);
  }

  public SampleAggregator2()
  {
    super(2, new Fields("total_kept"));
  }

  public SampleAggregator2( Fields calcFields )
  {
    // expects 2 arguments, fail otherwise
    super( 2, calcFields );
  }

  @Override
  public void prepare(FlowProcess flowProcess,
    OperationCall<SampleAggregator2.Context>
    aggregatorCall)
  {
    aggregatorCall.setContext(new
      SampleAggregator2.Context());
  }
```

```
@Override
public void cleanup(FlowProcess flowProcess,
  OperationCall<SampleAggregator2.Context>
  aggregatorCall)
{
  aggregatorCall.setContext(null);
}

public void start( FlowProcess flowProcess,
  AggregatorCall<SampleAggregator2.Context>
  aggregatorCall )
{
  // set the context object,
  Context context = aggregatorCall.getContext();
  context.value = 0;
  context.tuple.clear();
}

public void aggregate( FlowProcess flowProcess,
  AggregatorCall<SampleAggregator2.Context>
  aggregatorCall )
{
  TupleEntry arguments = aggregatorCall.getArguments();
  Context context = aggregatorCall.getContext();

  //add the current argument value to the current sum
  context.value += (arguments.getInteger(0)-
    arguments.getInteger(1));
}

public void complete( FlowProcess flowProcess,
  AggregatorCall<SampleAggregator2.Context>
  aggregatorCall )
{
  Context context = aggregatorCall.getContext();

  // create a Tuple to hold our result values
  Tuple result = context.tuple;

  // set the sum
  result.add( context.value );

  // return the result Tuple
  aggregatorCall.getOutputCollector().add( result );
  }
}
```

- Let's decompose `SampleAggregator2`. Notice that the `Context` class is different from the `Context` class of `SampleAggregator`. The code for this class for `SampleAggregator2` is as follows:

```
public static class Context
{
  long value = 0;
  Tuple tuple = Tuple.size(2);
}
```

- Here, in addition to initializing the value, we are creating a reusable space for the argument tuple of size 2.

- Our class constructors look the same, but now we also have a `prepare()` and `cleanup()` methods. We use these methods similarly to the way we use then in our custom Cascading function. We allocate reusable `Context` for the aggregator as shown in the following code in `prepare()`, and we release it as shown in `cleanup()`:

```
@Override
public void prepare(FlowProcess flowProcess,
    OperationCall<SampleAggregator2.Context> aggregatorCall)
{
  aggregatorCall.setContext(new
    SampleAggregator2.Context());
}

@Override
public void cleanup(FlowProcess flowProcess,
    OperationCall<SampleAggregator2.Context> aggregatorCall)
{
  aggregatorCall.setContext(null);
}
```

 Please note that the `prepare()` and `cleanup()` methods are defined in the `Operation` interface, and implemented in the `BaseOperation` class which is sub-classed by aggregator. `BaseOperation` however, only provides an empty body for these methods. They do nothing, so they must be overridden in any subclass to have them actually do anything.

Please refer to the *A note about implementing BaseOperation methods* section for more information.

- In the `start` method, in addition to initializing the `AggregatorCall` context for each grouping, we reset the value of the sum and clean up our reusable tuple for each grouping as well:

```
public void start( FlowProcess flowProcess,
  AggregatorCall<SampleAggregator2.Context>
  aggregatorCall )
{
  // set the context object,
  Context context = aggregatorCall.getContext() ;
  context.value = 0;
  context.tuple.clear();
}
```

- The rest of `SampleAggregator2` functions the same as `SampleAggregator`.

So why use the `prepare()` and `cleanup()` methods and add extra lines of code when it is possible to create an aggregator without them? The answer lies in memory usage and allocation. When we just allocate the context every time aggregator is executed, it works fine for the local mode and a relatively small number of records.

But what happens if we use Hadoop mode and billions of records? Allocating memory each time will become very costly. As these object are allocated and freed, they accumulate on the garbage collection heap, and Java will periodically run performance draining cleanups to free this memory. Because in Hadoop mode you can have billions of records, it is much better to allocate reusable storage and just clean it up after the operation on a grouping is compete. This is generally true with all operations as well, and it is a common programming paradigm within Hadoop.

- Using a custom aggregator requires some consideration. You may recall that aggregators are used on `Every` pipes, which are the result of a grouping. It is important to remember that you pass to the aggregator the argument values that you want to aggregate, not the whole tuple in that grouping. Consequently, the output will reside in the result field or fields.

- When using aggregators, try to keep them independent from actual `TupleEntry` name bindings. Do this by passing in argument values that the aggregator will use instead of the entire tuple. This will let your aggregator be reusable. Here is an example:

```
pipe = new GroupBy( pipe, new Fields( "group_on_column" )
  );
pipe = new Every( pipe, new Fields("sum_on_column"),
  new Sum( new Fields( "summed_column")), Fields.ALL );
```

- The following is the main program to call `SampleAggregator` (it works with both versions discussed earlier). Our source scheme is the structure of our input file. Our `Scheme` sink is the structure of our output file, which will have only two fields in it—the product type, and total number of products kept for this type across all stores. Here is the code:

```
public class TestAggregator {

    /* We have a list that consists of store name, product,
     * how many sold, and how many returned
     * Task to calculate how many products total are kept
     * (i.e sold and not returned)
     * Accepts two args - input file and output file
     */

    public static void main(String[] args)
    {
        // define source and sink Taps.
        Scheme sourceScheme = new TextDelimited( new
            Fields("store_name","product_name", "number_sold",
            "number_returned"), true, "," );

        Tap source = new FileTap( sourceScheme, args[0] );

        Scheme sinkScheme = new TextDelimited( new Fields(
        "product_name", "total_kept") );
        Tap sink = new FileTap( sinkScheme, args[1],
            SinkMode.REPLACE );

        // the 'head' of the pipe assembly
        Pipe assembly = new Pipe( "total" );
        assembly = new GroupBy(assembly, new
        Fields("product_name"));

        assembly = new Every(assembly, new
            Fields("number_sold","number_returned"), new
            SampleAggregator(new Fields("total_kept")),
            Fields.ALL);

        FlowConnector flowConnector = new LocalFlowConnector();
        Flow flow =
            flowConnector.connect(source,sink,assembly);
        flow.complete();
    }
}
```

- The result of our `TestAggregator` example will look like this:

```
Product1 23
Product2 129
Product3 17
```

Writing a custom assertion

Earlier in this chapter, we talked about assertions. The following code implements a simple assertion to see whether the fields in the input file are empty. This assertion is not providing a trap. This assertion simply allows the process to fail, met with the diagnostic error message when the assertion condition is met.

In our example, the input file looks like this:

```
name,address,phone
mike,123 e 4th st,123-456-7890
victoria,987 w east ave,901-234-5678
nobody,,
```

On the last line of the input file, both the `address` and `phone` fields are empty.

- Our custom `SampleAssertion` extends the class `cascading.operation. assertion.BaseAssertion` and implements the interface `cascading. operation.ValueAssertion`. The following are the imports necessary for our `SampleAssertion` example:

```
import cascading.flow.FlowProcess;
import cascading.operation.ValueAssertion;
import cascading.operation.ValueAssertionCall;
import cascading.operation.assertion.BaseAssertion;
import cascading.tuple.TupleEntry;
```

- `ValueAssertion` is used with the `Each` pipe, and the method that needs to be implemented is `doAssert()`. This method checks for the empty string in the fields of `TupleEntry` using the `private checkEmptyString()` method, which we added for that purpose. The `doAssert()` method will fail the process if any of the fields are empty.

- The following code shows the `doAssert` method:

```
@Override
public void doAssert(FlowProcess flowProcess,
  ValueAssertionCall assertionCall )
{
  TupleEntry input = assertionCall.getArguments();
  int pos = 0;
  // Check the assertion condition
```

```
    for( Object value : input.getTuple())
    {
      if( checkForEmptyString(value))
      fail( input.getFields().get(pos),
        input.getTuple().print() );
      pos++;
    }
  }
```

- The custom assertion in its entirety is shown as follows:

```java
import cascading.flow.FlowProcess;
import cascading.operation.ValueAssertion;
import cascading.operation.ValueAssertionCall;
import cascading.operation.assertion.BaseAssertion;
import cascading.tuple.TupleEntry;

// SampleAssertion checks to see if any fields are empty
public class SampleAssertion extends BaseAssertion
  implements ValueAssertion
{
  public SampleAssertion()
  {
    super( "argument '%s' failed Sample Assertion,
      in tuple: %s" );
  }

  @Override
  public void doAssert(FlowProcess flowProcess,
    ValueAssertionCall assertionCall )
  {
    TupleEntry input = assertionCall.getArguments();
    int pos = 0;
    /* Check the assertion condition */
    for( Object value : input.getTuple())
    {
      if( checkForEmptyString(value))
        fail( input.getFields().get(pos),
          input.getTuple().print() );
        pos++;
    }
  }

  private boolean checkForEmptyString(Object value)
  {
    // Check the String condition here
    if (value == null || value.toString().isEmpty())
      return true;
    return false;
  }
}
```

- The `main` program to show how to attach `SampleAssertion` to an `Each` pipe is shown as follows. Based on our sample input file with empty fields, the process will fail with the following argument `address` failed sample assertion, in tuple `['nobody', null, null]`:

```
public class TestAssertion {
  public static void main(String[] args)
  {
    // define source and sink Taps.
    Scheme mainScheme = new TextDelimited( new Fields(
      "name", "address", "phone" ), true, "," );

    Tap source = new FileTap( mainScheme, args[0] );

    Tap sink = new FileTap( mainScheme, args[1],
      SinkMode.REPLACE );

    Pipe inPipe = new Pipe("InPipe");

    inPipe = new Each(inPipe, new Debug());

    inPipe = new Each(inPipe, AssertionLevel.STRICT, new
      SampleAssertion());

    Flow flow = new LocalFlowConnector().connect( source,
      sink, inPipe );
    flow.complete();
  }
}
```

Writing a buffer

A Cascading buffer is a very useful operation. It was described earlier in this book and since there is only one built-in buffer available, you will benefit from learning how to write your own.

A buffer can be viewed as "an in-memory aggregator." Just like an aggregator, it operates on groups of tuples, but it is much more versatile because it also receives an iterator for the grouping of tuple, thus allowing us to look into the next as well as previous elements in the stream.

 It is similar to the reducer interface in MapReduce in that it is passed an iterator, and so it has already assembled all grouped records into a single call.

In the following code, we will show you how to write and utilize a custom buffer, which allows you to look ahead at the values in the data stream.

In this example, we are going to take sentences that were generated in the SentFunc example and break them down into tokens, or words. Words within our simple example sentences are separated by one or more space, colon (:), or semicolon (;) characters.

1. Here is the code for simple utility method getTokens(), which we will add to our NPLUtils class described in the *Writing a function* section:

```
public static String[] getTokens(String sentence)
{
    return sentence.split("[("["[("[ ,;:]+");
}
```

2. In our function example (SentFunc), we broke down text into sentences using a period (.), or question mark (?) or exclamation point (!). But what happens if there is an abbreviation inside of a sentence, such as Mr., or Mrs.? Our simple sentence splitter will mistakenly consider this as an end of a sentence. So we will have some of the sentences marked incorrectly.

3. The token buffer we are writing will fix this problem by looking ahead for the sentence termination symbol, and then checking if what comes directly before it is an abbreviation.

4. For our purposes, we will add some code to our helper NLPUtils class, which will define and fill up an abbreviation set. For this example, the abbreviation list is very limited:

```
static HashSet<String> abbrevs = new HashSet<String>();
static {
    loadTestData();
}
private static void loadTestData()
{
    abbrevs.add("MR");
    abbrevs.add("MRS");
    abbrevs.add("MS");
    abbrevs.add("DR");
    abbrevs.add("PHD");
    abbrevs.add("ST");
    abbrevs.add("AVE");
    abbrevs.add("RD");
}
```

5. Then we will add a simple method to check whether the token (or word) in question is indeed an abbreviation. It will return `true` if it is one of the words in our `abbrevs` list:

```
public static boolean isAbbreviation(String token)
{
  token = token.toUpperCase();
  if (abbrevs.contains(token))
    return true;
  return false;
}
```

 In real life, discerning abbreviations goes much further than just checking a list. It is a fairly complicated problem that is solved through machine learning!

6. Now the prep work is done, and we are ready to write our buffer. We want to be able for each document and each sentence within it, to check whether a word before the sentence terminator is an abbreviation. If it is, we will keep going and will merge the next sentence with the partial sentence containing an abbreviation, thus fixing erroneous sentences.

7. Our class `TokenBuffer` subclasses `cascading.operation.BaseOperation` class, and the methods that need to be implemented are defined in the `cascading.operation.Buffer` interface.

8. In this case, we are taking the document name, sentence number, and sentence as an input, and returning the document name, sentence number, word number within the sentence, and the word as an output.

9. In the following code, you see our declared and output fields, and the constructor code, which is very similar to what we saw in the custom function:

```
public class TokenBuffer extends BaseOperation implements Buffer
{
  static Fields fieldDeclaration = new Fields(
    "document","sentnum", "sentence");
  static Fields fieldOutput = new Fields(
    "documentname","sentnumber", "wordnum", "word");

  public TokenBuffer() {
    super(3, fieldOutput);
    . . .
  }
}
```

Note that we are not using a typed `Context` in the preceding example. This is permissible here since we actually do not require a context.

10. It is time to implement the `operate()` method, which is the only method that must be implemented. It is defined once for each grouping:

```
public void operate( FlowProcess flowProcess, BufferCall
bufferCall){
```

  ° In the following code, we will start with initializing the sentence counter and getting a group of arguments into a `TupleEntry` instance. You will see in the main program, shown later, that the group is created by using `GroupBy` against a document name in the input stream:

```
int sentnum = 0;
TupleEntry group = bufferCall.getGroup();
```

  ° The iterator is unique to the custom buffer operation. An argument `TupleEntry` is returned by the iterator, which is passed by `bufferCall`. This `TupleEntry` instance is returned for each value in the grouping, and it is defined by the argument selector on the `Every` pipe, which is using this buffer. It allows you to check for the next and previous values within the group. The following code shows how to invoke it:

```
// get all the current argument values for this grouping
Iterator<TupleEntry> arguments =
  bufferCall.getArgumentsIterator();
```

  ° We can iterate through every sentence within every document grouping. We check whether there are still sentences in the document—`arguments.hasNext()` will return true if there are. We write our output into the result tuple of size 4.

  ° We now break every sentence down into tokens using our `NLPUtils.getTokens()` method. We check whether this is the last token in the sentence, and whether it is an abbreviation. If this token is an abbreviation, we continue without incrementing the sentence number, and merge the next sentence with it. The code to do it shown as follows:

```
// create a Tuple to hold our result values and set its
  document name field
Tuple result = Tuple.size(4);
int token_count = 0;
```

```
while ( arguments.hasNext()) {
  Tuple tuple = arguments.next().getTuple();
  String[] tokens = NLPUtils.getTokens(tuple.getString(2));

  for (int i = 0; i < tokens.length; i++) {
    String token = tokens[i];

    if (token == null || token.isEmpty())
      continue;
    token_count++;
    result.set(0, group.getString("document"));
    result.set(1, sentnum);
    result.set(2, token_count);
    result.set(3, token);

    // Return the result Tuple
    bufferCall.getOutputCollector().add( result );

    /* See if the last token is an abbreviation.
     * If so, treat the next sentence as a continuation.
     * If not, increment our sentence number and reset the
     * word number.
     */
    if (i == tokens.length - 1) {
      if (!NLPUtils.isAbbreviation(token))
      {
        sentnum++;
        token_count = 0;
      }
    }
  }
}
}
```

11. Here is the code for the custom buffer in its entirety, including all the necessary imports:

```
import java.util.Iterator;
import com.ai.utils.NLPUtils;
import cascading.flow.FlowProcess;
import cascading.operation.BaseOperation;
import cascading.operation.Buffer;
import cascading.operation.BufferCall;
import cascading.tuple.Fields;
import cascading.tuple.Tuple;
import cascading.tuple.TupleEntry;
```

```
public class TokenBuffer extends BaseOperationimplements
  Buffer
{
  static Fields fieldDeclaration = new Fields(
    "document","sentnum", "sentence");
  static Fields fieldOutput = new Fields(
    "documentname","sentnumber", "wordnum", "word");
  public TokenBuffer() {
    super(3, fieldOutput);
  }

  public void operate( FlowProcess flowProcess,
    BufferCall bufferCall){
    int sentnum = 0;
    TupleEntry group = bufferCall.getGroup();
    //get all the current argument values for this grouping
    Iterator<TupleEntry> arguments =
    bufferCall.getArgumentsIterator();

    /* create a Tuple to hold our result values and set
     its document name field */

    Tuple result = Tuple.size(4);
    int token_count = 0;

    while( arguments.hasNext()){
      Tuple tuple = arguments.next().getTuple();
      String[] tokens =
        NLPUtils.getTokens(tuple.getString(2));

      for (int i = 0; i < tokens.length; i++){
        String token = tokens[i];
        if (token == null || token.isEmpty())
          continue;

        token_count++;
        result.set(0, group.getString("document"));
        result.set(1, sentnum);
        result.set(2, token_count);
        result.set(3, token);

        // Return the result Tuple
        bufferCall.getOutputCollector().add( result );
```

```
/* See if the last token is an abbreviation.
 * If so, treat the next sentence as a
 * continuation.
 * If not, increment our sentence number
 * and reset the word number.
 */

if (i == tokens.length - 1) {
  if (!NLPUtils.isAbbreviation(token))
  {
    sentnum++;
    token_count = 0;
  }
}

      } // for
    }// while
  }// operate
} // TokenBuffer
```

12. Finally, we can put it all together. Here is our task: given a text file similar to the following one, return a text file that will contain the document name, sentence number (within the document), word number (within this sentence) and the word itself:

```
Document text
Test1.txt This is a sample text. It can have many
  sentences.
Text2.txt This text can have ambiguous sentences, including
  names like Mr. Smith.
```

Our main program will utilize both the SentFunc function described earlier and this TokenBuffer class; args[0] is our input file, and args[1] is the output file. An interim tuple stream is created (but not saved to a file) after executing SentFunc against the Each pipe. This interim tuple stream will look something like this:

```
Test1.txt, 0, This is a sample text

Test1.txt, 1, It can have many sentences

Text2.txt, 0, This text can have ambiguous sentences, including names
like Mr

Text2.txt, 1, Smith
```

You can see that the very last sentence is incorrect. After performing the sentence extraction, we are creating a `GroupBy` pipe to group a tuple stream by document name and sort by sentence number. We are applying `TokenBuffer` against the `Every` grouping to fix the sentences, and to return the breakdown by sentences and tokens within each document. The following code shows how it is done:

```
import cascading.flow.Flow;
//import cascading.flow.hadoop.HadoopFlowConnector;
import cascading.flow.local.LocalFlowConnector;
import cascading.operation.Debug;
import cascading.pipe.Each;
import cascading.pipe.Every;
import cascading.pipe.GroupBy;
import cascading.pipe.Pipe;
import cascading.scheme.Scheme;
// import cascading.scheme.hadoop.TextDelimited;
import cascading.scheme.local.TextDelimited;
import cascading.tap.SinkMode;
import cascading.tap.Tap;
// import cascading.tap.hadoop.Hfs;
import cascading.tap.local.FileTap;
import cascading.tuple.Fields;

import com.ai.learning.SentFunc;
import com.ai.learning.TokenBuffer;

publicclass TestBuffer {

  public static void main(String[] args) {
    Fields fieldDeclarationInput = new Fields("document","text");
    Fields fieldDeclarationOutput = new Fields(
      "documentname","sentnumber","wordnum", "word");

    Scheme inputScheme = new TextDelimited( fieldDeclarationInput,
      true,"\t");
    Scheme outputScheme = new TextDelimited(
      fieldDeclarationOutput,"\t");

    // Tap docTap = new Hfs (inputScheme, args[0]);
    Tap docTap = new FileTap (inputScheme, args[0]);

    //Tap sinkTap = new Hfs(outputScheme, args[1],
      SinkMode.REPLACE );
    Tap sinkTap = new FileTap(outputScheme, args[1],
      SinkMode.REPLACE );
```

```
Pipe inPipe = new Pipe("InPipe");
inPipe= new Each(inPipe, new SentFunc());

inPipe = new GroupBy(inPipe, new Fields("document"),
  new Fields("sentnum"));

inPipe = new Every(inPipe, new
  TokenBuffer(),fieldDeclarationOutput);

/* For Hadoop -initialize app properties, tell Hadoop which
 *jar file to use
 *
 * Properties properties = new Properties();
 * AppProps.setApplicationJarClass( properties,
 *    TestBuffer.class );
 *
 * FlowConnector flowConnector = new HadoopFlowConnector(
 *    properties);
 * Flow flow = flowConnector.connect( "process", docTap,
 *    sinkTap, inPipe);
 */

// Local flow connector
Flow flow = new flowConnector.connect( "process", docTap,
  sinkTap, inPipe );

// execute the flow, block until complete
flow.complete();

    }
  }
```

 Notice in the comments the code changes/additions necessary for Hadoop mode. In the next chapter, we will talk more about local and Hadoop modes.

In the later chapters, you will learn how to create pipe subassemblies that can be called to replace several operations on pipes. These subassemblies can be reused.

The output will look similar to the output as follows:

Test1.txt, 0, 1, This

Test1.txt, 0, 2, is

Test1.txt, 0, 3, a

Test1.txt, 0, 4, sample

```
Test1.txt, 0, 5, text
Test1.txt, 1, 1, It
Test1.txt, 1, 2, can
Test1.txt, 1, 3, have
Test1.txt, 1, 4, many
Test1.txt, 1, 5, sentences
Text2.txt, 0, 1, This
Text2.txt, 0, 2, text
Text2.txt, 0, 3, can
Text2.txt, 0, 4, have
Text2.txt, 0, 5, ambiguous
Text2.txt, 0, 6, sentences
Text2.txt, 0, 7, including
Text2.txt, 0, 8, names
Text2.txt, 0, 9, like
Text2.txt, 0, 10, Mr
Text2.txt, 0, 11, Smith
```

The final sentence number has been corrected and the word `Smith` is now associated with the sentence to which it actually belongs.

Identifying common use cases for custom operations

While there are many useful built-in operations, there are several cases where writing a custom operation will be required. But let's look at our options first:

- If you need a filter or function that performs a simple comparison or calculation on one or more fields, consider using the `ExpressionFilter` or `ExpressionFunction` built-ins. These classes are very flexible and allow one to write small custom pieces of Java code that will be interpreted and executed for you. In many cases, this will be sufficient and will obviate the need for you to create a custom operation.

  However, be aware that this type of functionality uses the Janino compiler. This is a moderately large footprint "mini-Java" compiler (if not in total size, it will grow large with any sort of sophisticated code to compile). It takes as input a string that contains a Java program, compiles it to bytecode, binds input and output variables to it, and then executes it.

- A second scenario is one where some complex form of filter or function is required. While it is possible to do all of this using the `Expression` classes just mentioned, in many cases you will be better off writing this code yourself—not just because of performance, but also because of maintainability.

- Another clear use case that will require a custom operation is one where some external data file must be loaded. This is typically done in the `prepare()` method. This will be the case for several types of data-driven applications where a requirement exists for some sort of generally volatile source of data. Note that there are examples of using `HashJoin` or `CoGroup` pipes with this type of data (for instance the `StopList` functionality in the online *Cascading for the Impatient* series of articles), sometimes this is just not sufficient, and in these cases, a custom operation will allow you all of the flexibility that you need.

  Note that a new class was added in Cascading 2.6 called `cascading.hadoop.tap.DistCacheTap`. This allows files that reside in the Hadoop distributed cache to be used as a source, but not as a sink!

- Lastly, in some cases, specialized data structures or persistent classes are simply not provided by Cascading. For instance, graph processing has become quite popular, and in order to handle various graph representations, in many cases a custom operation will be required.

Putting it all together

- Operations work hand-in-hand with pipes.

- Generally, a pipe defines a single operator to perform some functionality.

- Operations fall into two broad categories, which are determined by whether they operate on a single tuple (`Each`) or a group of tuples (`Every`).

- This is then how they couple with pipes, since pipes too share this trait.

- Filters examine tuples and determine whether they are passed along.

- Assertions examine conditions that exist in the data and can generate exceptions if errors are found.

- Functions can modify data, compute new data, and insert new tuples into the stream.

- Buffers and aggregators operate on sets of tuples.

- Tuples are mutable but operations should not modify them. Operations should allocate a new copy and pass it down the pipe instead. So if you are handed a tuple, don't modify it. It will probably throw an exception if you do. Also remember that tuples can be cached elsewhere.

- Allocated memory is often reused, so make it a habit to allocate once in `prepare()`, store it in a context, free it in `cleanup()`, and reuse it in all other methods.

- On some occasions, a function will be run twice. You can prevent this by overriding its `isSafe()` method and returning `false`.

Summary

In this chapter, you learned how to write custom operations that provide the main way to extend Cascading and to perform much of the work that needs to be done. This chapter provided plentiful code examples, decomposed them into steps, and showed you how to write custom operations: filters, functions, aggregators, and buffers. Furthermore, you learned to do more sophisticated processing inside of operations, such as using `Tuple` and `TupleEntry` logic, as well as using `Context` objects to store state. You also learned from the included code how to use these operations in Cascading pipes, and how to create Cascading test projects to accomplish specific tasks.

In the next chapter, you will learn techniques to package your custom code that will aid in creating reusable modules and will also help in reducing testing and debugging cycles.

5

Code Reuse and Integration

In this chapter, you will learn how to assemble reusable code, how to integrate Cascading with external systems, and how to use Cascading instrumentation effectively to track and control execution. Specifically, we will discuss how Cascading fits into the overall processing infrastructure. You will also learn to create more complex workflows and to control intermediate files using Cascading.

Creating and using subassemblies

Code reusability is the holy grail of software development. Cascading renders itself beautifully to this concept. In Cascading it is relatively simple to create basic building blocks out of pipe assemblies. These building blocks are known as pipe **subassemblies**, which you can organize into libraries. You then pick and choose these subassemblies to create your own custom "brewery."

Cascading also generously provides us with many built-in subassemblies described in the following sections.

Built-in subassemblies

These are the built-in subassemblies:

- Coerce: `cascading.pipe.assembly.Coerce`. We briefly touched on coercing fields of one type into another type in *Chapter 2*, *Cascading Basics in Detail*. Cascading provides a built-in subassembly to do this. Using this subassembly, you can coerce fields of one type into another within a pipe assembly. For example, the following code will convert the `String` field `timestamp` into `long`:

```
pipe = new Coerce(pipe, new Fields("timestamp"),
  Long.class);
```

- Discard: `cascading.pipe.assembly.Discard` will discard specified fields from the tuple stream. All other fields will remain:

  ```
  pipe = new Discard( pipe, new Fields( "timestamp" ) );
  ```

- Retain: `cascading.pipe.assembly.Retain` will retain specified fields within the tuple stream. All other fields will be discarded:

  ```
  pipe= new Retain(pipe, new Fields( "day", "year" ) );
  ```

 Note that `Retain` and `Discard` are helpful when trimming the size of the tuple, which is important to help make the stream as efficient as possible.

- Rename: `cascading.pipe.assembly.Rename` will rename the specified field:

  ```
  pipe= new Rename( pipe, new Fields( "timestamp" ), new
    Fields( "datetime" ) );
  ```

- Unique: `cascading.pipe.assembly.Unique`, similarly to `SQL SELECT DISTINCT`, will retain unique tuples in the tuple stream based on the specified values. It uses `GroupBy` and `FirstNBuffer`. In the following example, it will retain tuples with a unique combination of year and month, while all other tuples will be discarded:

  ```
  pipe = new Unique( pipe, new Fields( "month", "year" ) );
  ```

 Please note that in order to retain tuples in a tuple Stream that are unique based on all fields, use `Fields.ALL`.

- AggregateBy: `AggregateBy` is a special subassembly that shows the power of Cascading. We are going to look at it in some detail so that we can see how such pipe constructs can be used to obtain a high degree of reusability, and how this can be leveraged to build many subtypes of assemblies.

  `AggregateBy` is written to facilitate composable aggregation operations, essentially those operations that are both commutative and associative. But `AggregateBy` is not limited just to these functions, and can therefore be used for a lot more.

  In MapReduce, `AggregateBy` allows map side optimizations that are very similar to Hadoop combiners. Since Cascading does not use combiners, `AggregateBy` allows a very similar, but optimized function to occur on the mapper. `AggregateBy` does this by using a concept known as a **functor**. A functor is a simple interface that is defined by `AggregateBy`. It has the following signature:

  ```
  public interface AggregteBy.Functor extends Serializable
  ```

```
{
  /* Retrieve the declared fields that will be aggregated
    */
  Fields getDeclaredFields();
  /* Pass a Tuple and a Context to perform the aggregation
    */
  Tuple aggregate(FlowProcess flowProc, TupleEntry args,
    Tuple context);
  /* Retrieve a Tuple with the result of the aggregation
    */
  Tuple complete(FlowProcess flowProc, Tuple context);
}
```

AggregateBy also uses an internal buffer called a **least recently used** (LRU) cache where aggregated values are stored. It is part of the context defined by AggregateBy. This LRU cache has a threshold size, and it is filled with aggregated results until it is full. After it is full, if a new aggregated group is detected, the oldest entry is emitted.

The following aggregators are subclasses of AggregateBy:

  ° MinBy: finds minimum values in a group.

  ° MaxBy: finds maximum values in a group.

  ° SumBy: finds sums of values in a group.

  ° AverageBy: finds averages of values in a group. Note that this assembly requires low values to be emitted – the average and a count!

  ° CountBy: finds a count of tuples in a group.

  ° FirstBy: finds the first value in a group. Note that there is no LastBy subassembly!

The way that an AggregateBy-derived class such as SumBy works is that it is instantiated like this:

```
Pipe mainPipe = new Pipe("aggregate_by");
/* Constructor SumBy( Pipe pipe, Fields groupingFields,
  Fields valueField, Fields sumField, Class sumType ) */
mainPipe = new SumBy(mainPipe, new Fields("employee_name"),
  new Fields("raises"), new Fields("total_raises"),
  Double.class);
/* Print all Tuples, or could also attach a Sink */
mainPipe = new Each(mainPipe, new Debug());
```

Creating a new custom subassembly

It makes sense to keep similar functionalities together, especially if they can be reused in different applications. In this section, we will show you how to create a custom SubAssembly using text processing operations. SubAssembly subclasses the cascading.pipe.SubAssembly class. We will use the example from *Chapter 4, Creating Custom Operations,* with a sentence splitter (SentFunc) and a word tokenizer (TokenBuffer). The following is the code with comments for the complete SubAssembly:

```
import cascading.operation.Debug;
import cascading.pipe.Each;
import cascading.pipe.Every;
import cascading.pipe.GroupBy;
import cascading.pipe.Pipe;
import cascading.pipe.SubAssembly;
import cascading.tuple.Fields;

public class SubAssemblyExample extends SubAssembly
{
  public SubAssemblyExample (Pipe inPipe)
  {
    // Apply SentFunc to split text into sentences
    inPipe= new Each(inPipe, new SentFunc());
    // it is a good idea to use Debug to see the interim output
    inPipe = new Each(inPipe, new Debug());
    // Prepare Tuple Stream for tokenization for each document
    // and for each sentence with in the document
    inPipe = new GroupBy(inPipe, new Fields("document"),
      new Fields("sentnum"));
    // Apply TokenBuffer
    inPipe = new Every(inPipe, new TokenBuffer(),
      new Fields( "documentname","sentnumber", "wordnum",
      "word"));
    inPipe = new Each(inPipe, new Debug());
    // The resultant tail pipe
    setTails(inPipe);
  }
}
```

This code looks very similar to some of the code in the main class in the example of TokenBuffer in *Chapter 4, Creating Custom Operations.* In this SubAssembly in the constructor, we passed in the pipe assembly that we wanted to work against:

```
public SubAssemblyExample (Pipe inPipe)
```

After the work is done, we returned the result of the SubAssembly example by using the setTails() method.

But what would happen if we would like to return more than one pipe assembly from a subassembly? With Cascading, we have the capability to create a split subassembly.

Let's rewrite the preceding subassembly so it returns two separate pipe assemblies: one with just sentences and one with the word tokens:

```
public SubAssemblyExampleTails (Pipe inPipe)
{
  // New pipe to handle sentence split based on the input pipe
  Pipe pipeSent = new Pipe( "pipeSent", inPipe );
  // Apply SentFunc to split text into sentences
  pipeSent = new Each(pipeSent, new SentFunc());

  // New pipe to handle tokenizer based on the sentence pipe
  Pipe pipeTok = new Pipe( "pipeTok", pipeSent );

  // Prepare Tuple Stream for tokenization for each document
  // and for each sentence with the document
  pipeTok = new GroupBy(pipeTok, new Fields("document"),
    new Fields("sentnum"));
  // Apply TokenBuffer
  pipeTok = new Every(pipeTok, new TokenBuffer(), new Fields(
    "documentname","sentnumber", "wordnum", "word"));

  // The resultant tail pipes: the sentence pipe and the token
  // pipe
  setTails(pipeSent,pipeTok);

}
```

You noticed that setTails() returned two pipe assemblies. It can return any number of pipe assemblies, and in the next section, we will show you how to access them.

Using custom subassemblies

Subassemblies are used to create reusable modules. Using custom subassemblies is easy. Here are the steps:

1. If you are using a single-tail SubAssembly instance, create a pipe and pass it as the parameter to the SubAssembly constructor:

    ```
    // our custom SubAssembly
    Pipe inPipe = new Pipe("InPipe");
    Pipe pipeTextProcess = new SubAssemblyExample(inPipe);
    ```

2. The following code produces the same results as the code for the `TestBuffer` (tokenizer example) in *Chapter 4, Creating Custom Operations,* but we are using our `SubAssemblyExample` (with a single tail) to replace the lines of code that create the pipe with the tokenized output:

```
public class SubAssemblyTest
{
  public static void main(String[] args)
  {
    Fields fieldDeclarationInput =
      new Fields("document","text");
    Fields fieldDeclarationOutput = new Fields(
      "documentname","sentnumber","wordnum", "word");

    Scheme inputScheme = new TextDelimited(
      fieldDeclarationInput, true,"\t");
    Scheme outputScheme = new TextDelimited(
      fieldDeclarationOutput, "\t");

    Tap docTap = new FileTap (inputScheme, args[0]);
    Tap sinkTap = new FileTap(outputScheme, args[1],
      SinkMode.REPLACE );

    // Use our Pipe assembly
    Pipe inPipe = new Pipe("InPipe");
    Pipe pipeTextProcess = new SubAssemblyExample(inPipe);

    // For local mode use the flow connector below

    Flow flow = new LocalFlowConnector();
    flow.connect( "process", docTap, sinkTap,
      pipeTextProcess);

    // execute the flow, block until complete
    flow.complete();
  }
}
```

As you can see, in this single-tail example, the `SubAssembly` instance is passed directly to the `inPipe` object– a `Pipe` instance.

3. If we wanted to use our split `SubAssembly` class(`SubAssemblyExampleTails`), we would need to use the `getTails()` method to get both of the branches. The code to do it is shown as follows:

```
Pipe inPipe = new Pipe("InPipe");
// our custom SubAssembly with two tails
```

```
SubAssembly pipeSplit = new SubAssemblyExampleTails (inPipe );

// get the split branches
Pipe pipeSent = new Pipe( pipeSplit.getTails()[0]);
Pipe pipeTok = new Pipe( pipeSplit.getTails()[1]);
```

4. The re-written `SubAssemblyTest` main class to take advantage of a split `SubAssemby` is shown in the following code:

```
public static void main(String[] args) {
   Fields fieldDeclarationInput =
     new fields("document","text");
   Fields fieldDeclarationOutput = new Fields(
     "documentname","sentnumber","wordnum", "word");

   Scheme inputScheme = new TextDelimited(
     fieldDeclarationInput, true,"\t");
   Scheme outputScheme = new TextDelimited(
     fieldDeclarationOutput, "\t");

   Tap docTap = new FileTap (inputScheme, args[0]);
   Tap sinkTap = new FileTap(outputScheme, args[1],
     SinkMode.REPLACE );

   /* add fields definition, scheme, and sink tap for
      additional output. Note that you will have to pass
      another argument to the main - args[2] - a file name
      to safe Sentence file */
   Fields fieldSentenceOutput =
     new Fields("document","sentnum", "sentence");
   Scheme outputSchemeSent =
     new TextDelimited(fieldSentenceOutput, "\t");
   Tap sinkSentTap = new FileTap(outputSchemeSent, args[2],
     SinkMode.REPLACE );

   // Use our Pipe assembly
   Pipe inPipe = new Pipe("InPipe");
   // our custom SubAssembly with two tails
   SubAssembly pipeSplit = new SubAssemblyExampleTails
     (inPipe );

   // get the split branches
   Pipe pipeSent = new Pipe( pipeSplit.getTails()[0]);
   Pipe pipeTok = new Pipe( pipeSplit.getTails()[1]);

   // For local mode use the flow connector below
   FlowDef flowDef = flowDef.flowDef()
```

```
        .setName( "textflow" )
        .addSource( inPipe, docTap )
        .addTailSink( pipeSent, sinkSentTap)
        .addTailSink( pipeTok, sinkTap)

    FlowConnector flowConnector = new LocalFlowConnector();
    Flow flow = flowConnector.connect( flowDef );

    // execute the flow, block until complete
    flow.complete();
  }
```

In this code, we were able to get two branches of the split subassemby and connect them to two different sinks using the fluent interface. You will see more information about the fluent interface later in this chapter.

Using cascades

You have seen so far that in Cascading, we can create building blocks of different sizes, functionality, and granularity, and we can reuse and rearrange these blocks to build very agile, customized applications.

You have seen operations, subassemblies, and flows—each of them are a building block of sorts that we define in large grains to create our application. We can go further now and arrange flows into cascades. You may recall we defined cascades in *Chapter 2, Cascading Basics in Detail,* and have been intermittently referring to them throughout this book.

Let's revisit the definition of a cascade. A **cascade** is a collection of flows. Separate and individual flows can be placed together in a defined sequence and execution graph, and they are executed as a single process that is referred to as cascade. A cascade has an additional feature, that if one flow depends on the output of another (that is, the source of one pipe is the sink of another), the dependent flow will not be executed until all of its data dependencies are satisfied.

Building a complex workflow using cascades

Why would you want to use a cascade at all? Why not build just one big flow with subassemblies? Having cascades addresses several problems:

- Breaking down a workflow into smaller logical units for better component reuse and debugging

- Using pre-existing flows that we may want to incorporate into the new workflow

- Using a MapReduce job as a part of the workflow
- Using other external components as a part of a workflow

You will soon see a section entitled *Using existing MapReduce jobs*, which will give you an example of how to wrap a flow around a MapReduce job and connect it with other flows into a cascade. In order to do this, a cascade is needed. Here is a code example of a very simple cascade:

```
CascadeConnector connector = new CascadeConnector();
Cascade cascade = connector.connect( flow1, flow3, flow2, flow4 );
```

The order of the flows passed to the connector is not important. Since Cascading uses a CascadeConnector class to identify dependencies among flows. This class automatically connects them in the right order based on their taps. If flows do not have tap (that is file) dependencies, they are executed in parallel.

CascadeConnector builds an internal directional execution graph where each flow is a node, and each file is a directional link between these flows. An output from one flow becomes the input to another. Following these links (input and output files) to the flows will access each flow in the correct order. When a flow has all its files available, it is scheduled on the cluster.

The following diagram illustrates a cascade with four flows. It shows how the dependencies are resolved, and how the flows are executed.

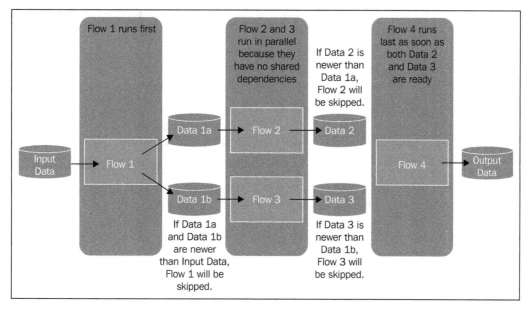

Figure 4.1 – Example of a cascade

Skipping a flow in a cascade

A flow can be skipped within a cascade. You would want to do this if the work done by the flow was already completed and there was no need to rerun it. You can set the flow skip strategy based on the existence and the age of the sink (that is, the output file). The sink is considered to be *stale* if the sink does not exist or if the sink is older than any feeding source.

> A sink's **feeding sources** are all the source taps that are required to produce the output of the sink. These are found by tracing backwards through the execution graph to locate every required input.

In a cascade, the `Flow.isSkipFlow()` method is called before `Flow.start()`. The `isSkipFlow()` method returns true if any of the sinks are stale. You can change the flow skip strategy by using `Flow.setFlowSkipStrategy(FlowSkipStrategy fss)` and `Cascade.setFlowSkipStrategy(FlowSkipStrategy fss)`. One of these methods can be called before or after a flow is created.

There are two flow skip strategies. These are actual classes that must be instantiated and passed to `Flow.setFlowSkipStrategy()` and `Cascade.setFlowSkipStrategy()`:

- `FlowSkipIfSinkNotStale` - `cascading.flow.FlowSkipIfSinkNotStale` - is the default strategy for skipping a flow. A sink tap is considered stale if the sink's resources are older than their feeding sources, or if the sink does not exist. If the `SinkMode` value for the sink tap is `REPLACE`, then the sink tap is treated as stale.

- `FlowSkipIfSinkExists` - the `flow.FlowSkipIfSinkExists` strategy skips the flow if the sink tap exists, regardless of age. If the `SinkMode` value for the sink tap is `REPLACE`, then the sink tap is treated as stale.

  For example: `cascade.setFlowSkipStrategy(new FlowSkipIfSinkExists());` will set up the flow skip strategy for the cascade to skip a flow if the sink tap it creates already exists.

Additionally, you can implement custom skip strategies by using the interface `cascading.flow.FlowSkipStrategy` and implementing one method: `boolean skipFlow(Flow flow)`. This method can examine all aspects of the flow that it is given and can return `true` if the flow should be skipped. The following is a step-by-step example of the code to run a simple cascade with two flows. We are using our sentence splitter and word `tokenizer` from the previous examples, but this time the sentence splitter will run as a separate flow and will output an interim text file with the split sentences. This text file will become an input for the second flow. If, however, this file already exists, the first flow will be skipped as per our skip strategy.

1. Here are the necessary classes to import for the code example:

```
import cascading.cascade.Cascade;
import cascading.cascade.CascadeConnector;
import cascading.flow.Flow;
import cascading.flow.FlowSkipIfSinkExists;
import cascading.flow.FlowSkipStrategy;
import cascading.flow.local.LocalFlowConnector;
import cascading.operation.Debug;
import cascading.pipe.Each;
import cascading.pipe.Every;
import cascading.pipe.GroupBy;
import cascading.pipe.Pipe;
import cascading.scheme.Scheme;
import cascading.scheme.local.TextDelimited;
import cascading.tap.SinkMode;
import cascading.tap.Tap;
import cascading.tap.local.FileTap;
import cascading.tuple.Fields;
```

2. In our `main` class, the inputs are as follows:

   `args[0]` – input file with text (see example in *Chapter 4, Creating Custom Operations*), `args[1]` – name of the interim sentence output (this file may or may not exist before running this program), `args[2]` – token output (this file may or may not exist before running this program). We are setting up three taps: `docTap` is our input document, `sink1Tap` is our interim output from the sentence splitter, which becomes an input to the tokenizer, and `sink2Tap` is our final output. Please see the input and output examples in the section *Writing a buffer* in *Chapter 4, Creating Custom Operations*. Here is the code to do so.

```
public class TestCascade {

  public static void main(String[] args) {

    Fields fieldDeclarationInput = new
      Fields("document","text");
    Fields fieldDeclarationInterim = new Fields(
      "document","sentnum", "sentence");
    Fields fieldDeclarationOutput = new Fields(
      "documentname","sentnumber","wordnum", "word");

    Scheme inputScheme = new
      TextDelimited(fieldDeclarationInput, true,"\t");
    Scheme interimScheme = new TextDelimited(
      fieldDeclarationInterim, "\t");
```

```
    Scheme outputScheme = new TextDelimited(
      fieldDeclarationOutput, "\t");

    Tap docTap = new FileTap (inputScheme, args[0]);
    Tap sink1Tap = new FileTap(interimScheme, args[1]);
    Tap sink2Tap = new FileTap(outputScheme, args[2],
      SinkMode.REPLACE );
    ...
```

3. Now let's create two flows, one for sentence splitter and one for `tokenizer`. Each flow must start with a "head" pipe:

```
Pipe inPipe = new Pipe("InPipe");
inPipe= new Each(inPipe, new SentFunc());
// Debug is optional here
// inPipe = new Each(inPipe, new Debug());

Flow flow1 = new LocalFlowConnector().connect( "Flow1",
  docTap, sink1Tap, inPipe );

Pipe inPipe2=new Pipe("InPipe2");
inPipe2 = new GroupBy(inPipe2, new Fields("document"),
  new Fields("sentnum"));

inPipe2 = new Every(inPipe2, new TokenBuffer(),
  fieldDeclarationOutput);
// Debug is optional here
// inPipe2 = new Each(inPipe2, new Debug());

Flow flow2 = new LocalFlowConnector().connect( "Flow2",
  sink1Tap, sink2Tap, inPipe2);
    ...
```

4. Finally let's create a cascade connector. We do not need to worry about the order of the flows. We are also setting a flow skip strategy to skip the flow if its sink tap (or output) already exists. Finally we complete the cascade to make it execute:

```
CascadeConnector connector = new CascadeConnector();

Cascade cascade = connector.connect( flow2, flow1 );
cascade.setFlowSkipStrategy(new FlowSkipIfSinkExists());
cascade.complete();
  }
}
```

5. When we run this code the first time, none of the output files will exist yet, so Cascading will produce the following output, showing us the flow execution detail:

```
[main] INFO cascading.property.AppProps - using app.id:
F042F058731343CEAD7FBF66F0561FD4

[cascade Flow2+Flow1] INFO cascading.util.Version - Concurrent,
Inc - Cascading 2.6.1

[cascade Flow2+Flow1] INFO cascading.cascade.Cascade -
[Flow2+Flow1] starting

[cascade Flow2+Flow1] INFO cascading.cascade.Cascade -
[Flow2+Flow1]  parallel execution is enabled: true

[cascade Flow2+Flow1] INFO cascading.cascade.Cascade -
[Flow2+Flow1]  starting flows: 2

[cascade Flow2+Flow1] INFO cascading.cascade.Cascade -
[Flow2+Flow1]  allocating threads: 2

[pool-1-thread-1] INFO cascading.cascade.Cascade - [Flow2+Flow1]
starting flow: Flow1

[pool-1-thread-1] INFO cascading.flow.Flow - [Flow1] at least one
sink does not exist

[flow Flow1] INFO cascading.flow.Flow - [Flow1] starting

[flow Flow1] INFO cascading.flow.Flow - [Flow1]  source: FileTap[
"TextDelimited[['document', 'text']]"]["C:\AnalyticsInside\files\
sent.txt"]

[flow Flow1] INFO cascading.flow.Flow - [Flow1]  sink: FileTa
p["TextDelimited[['document', 'sentnum', 'sentence']]"]["C:\
AnalyticsInside\files\sent1.txt"]

[flow Flow1] INFO cascading.flow.Flow - [Flow1]  parallel
execution is enabled: true

[flow Flow1] INFO cascading.flow.Flow - [Flow1]  starting jobs: 1

[flow Flow1] INFO cascading.flow.Flow - [Flow1]  allocating
threads: 1

[pool-2-thread-1] INFO cascading.flow.FlowStep - [Flow1] starting
step: local

[pool-1-thread-1] INFO cascading.cascade.Cascade - [Flow2+Flow1]
completed flow: Flow1

[pool-1-thread-2] INFO cascading.cascade.Cascade - [Flow2+Flow1]
starting flow: Flow2

[pool-1-thread-2] INFO cascading.flow.Flow - [Flow2] at least one
sink is marked for delete

[pool-1-thread-2] INFO cascading.flow.Flow - [Flow2] sink oldest
modified date: Wed Dec 31 18:59:59 EST 1969

[flow Flow2] INFO cascading.flow.Flow - [Flow2] starting
```

```
[flow Flow2] INFO cascading.flow.Flow - [Flow2]  source: FileT
ap["TextDelimited[['document', 'sentnum', 'sentence']]"]["C:\
AnalyticsInside\files\sent1.txt"]
```

```
[flow Flow2] INFO cascading.flow.Flow - [Flow2]  sink: FileTap["T
extDelimited[['documentname', 'sentnumber', 'wordnum', 'word']]"]
["C:\AnalyticsInside\files\tok1.txt"]
```

```
[flow Flow2] INFO cascading.flow.Flow - [Flow2]  parallel
execution is enabled: true
```

```
[flow Flow2] INFO cascading.flow.Flow - [Flow2]  starting jobs: 1
```

```
[flow Flow2] INFO cascading.flow.Flow - [Flow2]  allocating
threads: 1
```

```
[pool-5-thread-1] INFO cascading.flow.FlowStep - [Flow2] starting
step: local
```

```
[pool-1-thread-2] INFO cascading.cascade.Cascade - [Flow2+Flow1]
completed flow: Flow2
```

6. Notice what happens when we run the same program for the second time.
   The first flow — `flow1` is skipped because the interim file with the split
   sentences already exists from the first run of this program. Here is the output:

```
[main] INFO cascading.property.AppProps - using app.id:
1361B0454E2C45E7A35EB1D1142D8789
```

```
[cascade Flow2+Flow1] INFO cascading.util.Version - Concurrent,
Inc - Cascading 2.6.1
```

```
[cascade Flow2+Flow1] INFO cascading.cascade.Cascade -
[Flow2+Flow1] starting
```

```
[cascade Flow2+Flow1] INFO cascading.cascade.Cascade -
[Flow2+Flow1]  parallel execution is enabled: true
```

```
[cascade Flow2+Flow1] INFO cascading.cascade.Cascade -
[Flow2+Flow1]  starting flows: 2
```

```
[cascade Flow2+Flow1] INFO cascading.cascade.Cascade -
[Flow2+Flow1]  allocating threads: 2
```

```
[pool-1-thread-1] INFO cascading.cascade.Cascade - [Flow2+Flow1]
starting flow: Flow1
```

```
[pool-1-thread-1] INFO cascading.flow.Flow - [Flow1] sink oldest
modified date: Wed Feb 18 17:00:36 EST 2015
```

```
[pool-1-thread-1] INFO cascading.cascade.Cascade - [Flow2+Flow1]
skipping flow: Flow1
```

```
[pool-1-thread-2] INFO cascading.cascade.Cascade - [Flow2+Flow1]
starting flow: Flow2
```

```
[pool-1-thread-2] INFO cascading.flow.Flow - [Flow2] at least one
sink is marked for delete
```

```
[pool-1-thread-2] INFO cascading.flow.Flow - [Flow2] sink oldest
modified date: Wed Dec 31 18:59:59 EST 1969
```

```
[flow Flow2] INFO cascading.flow.Flow - [Flow2] starting
```

```
[flow Flow2] INFO cascading.flow.Flow - [Flow2]   source: FileT
ap["TextDelimited[['document', 'sentnum', 'sentence']]"]["C:\
AnalyticsInside\files\sent1.txt"]

[flow Flow2] INFO cascading.flow.Flow - [Flow2]   sink: FileTap["T
extDelimited[['documentname', 'sentnumber', 'wordnum', 'word']]"]
["C:\AnalyticsInside\files\tok1.txt"]

[flow Flow2] INFO cascading.flow.Flow - [Flow2]   parallel
execution is enabled: true

[flow Flow2] INFO cascading.flow.Flow - [Flow2]   starting jobs: 1

[flow Flow2] INFO cascading.flow.Flow - [Flow2]   allocating
threads: 1

[pool-2-thread-1] INFO cascading.flow.FlowStep - [Flow2] starting
step: local[pool-1-thread-2] INFO cascading.cascade.Cascade -
[Flow2+Flow1] completed flow: Flow2
```

Intermediate file management

An intermediate file is defined to be a file that is intended to exist temporarily. These files exist as a single tap that serves as a sink for one pipe and a source for another that immediately follows it.

 Please note that Cascading does not clean up intermediate files by default unless Hadoop is the underlying platform. In the case of Hadoop, separate jobs can be connected through (usually) HDFS resident data directories, and so the intermediate files (and the containing directory) are deleted by Hadoop when the second job completes normally.

Dynamically controlling flows

One interesting aspect of Cascading is that flows can be dynamically controlled. Other similar languages and paradigms such as Pig and Hive allow a high degree of programmability, but their defined work runs from beginning to end, with no ability to control the execution flow through examination of data or conditions. With Cascading, program control can be used to alter the processing of a flow, to run it multiple times, to prevent it from running, or to programmatically control the very sequence and choice of flows that run. This is an important feature of Cascading and differentiates it from many other higher level frameworks. So the dynamic control of a flow is a "programmable" ability to run one or more flows iteratively, or alternately to control the sequence of execution. For instance:

1. In a loop, run a flow.
2. Check the status when the flow ends.

3. Decide whether to run the flow again. Alternately, based on the outcome, determine which flow to run next.

4. End when some iteration count is met or when some final state or condition has occurred.

This feature can be used to do sophisticated recursive-style processing. Some examples of how dynamic control can be used are:

- Graph algorithms
    - Paths, cycles, partitioning, and so on

- General recursion
    - Monte Carlo methods
    - Markov iteration

- Natural language processing refinements
- Machine learning
    - Stochastic methods
    - Hill climbing or other gradient descent methods

So we can see that many tasks do require this type of iterative control. Let's take a look at what is required to achieve this in Cascading.

In order to do much of this, it is necessary to provide instrumentation, or internal counters and state information that can be interrogated to provide information to make a decision about what to do next. Let's see how to do that.

Instrumentation and counters

Flows allow the creation of internal counters, often referred to as **instrumentation**. Counters track interesting things that happen within your job.

A counter is incremented from an operation. An operation is always passed a `FlowProcess` object and this is where the counter is kept. There is no need to define a counter. It is identified by group name and counter name. A counter is always initialized to zero. Nothing special needs to be done to create a counter. When it is first encountered, it is created for you and set to zero. Here is code to do this:

```
String counter_group = "group_name";
String counter_name = "counter";
flowProcess.increment(counter_group, counter_name, 1);
```

It is also possible to define counters using enums:

```
public enum COUNTERS
{
   COUNTER1,
   COUNTER2
}
flowProcess.increment(COUNTER1, 1);
```

The counter's value can be retrieved by the flow executor:

```
int counter = flow.getFlowStats().getCounterValue(counter_group,
   counter_name);
```

Using counters to control flow

We can dynamically control iterations of a Cascading flow. The execution sequence looks like this:

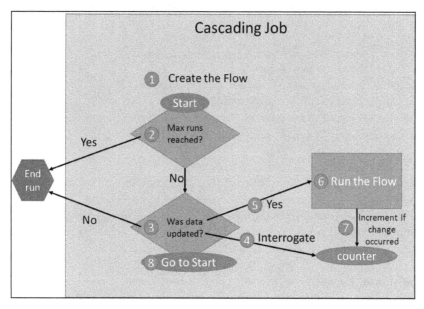

Figure 5.2 – Dynamic flow control using counters

We can use the following code:

```
// Set a max iteration count so that we won't run forever
int maxIterations = 100;
// updatedCount will be a counter managed by one of our flow pipes
int updatedCount;
```

```
boolean done = false;
//// Build our Flow called flowDef
...
while (!done)
{
  flowConnector.connect(flowDef).complete();
  // A counter is always initialized to zero
  updatedCount =
    flow.getFlowStats().getCounterValue(counter_group,
    counter_name);
  maxIterations--;
  done = (maxIterations == 0 || updatedCount == 0);
}
```

Using existing MapReduce jobs

In many cases, you may already have existing MapReduce jobs that you have written, and you may want to execute them as part of a Cascading flow. This can be accomplished with several classes that integrate MapReduce with Cascading. Here is code to do this:

```
JobConf mrconf = new JobConf();
mrconf.setJobName("mapreduce");
mrconf.setOutputKeyClass(LongWritable.class);
mrconf.setOutputValueClass(Text.class);
mrconf.setMapperClass(IdentityMapper.class);
mrconf.setReducerClass(IdentityReducer.class);

// Set other JobConf items as necessary
// Now connect it to some predefined source and sink taps.
// Note that we use the actual (HDFS) path names.
FileInputFormat.setInputPaths(mrconf, flow1SinkTap.getPath());
FileOutputFormat.setOutputPath(mrconf, flow2SourceTap.getPath());
Flow mrFlow = new MapReduceFlow("mrflow", mrconf);

// Now use a cascade
Cascade cascade = CascadeConnector.connect(flow1, mrFlow,
  flow2);cascade.complete();
```

Using fluent programming techniques

The fluent style of programming has become quite popular. This is mentioned briefly in *Chapter 1*, *The Big Data Core Technology Stack*. The name "fluent" was coined by Eric Evans and Martin Fowler in about 2005. It is often also referred to as **method cascading** since it allows a chain or sequence of method calls to be specified as a single statement.

A fluent style of programing is implemented by having each method call return the object that it is operating on. This then allows one to write code that looks like this:

```
object.methodA().methodB().methodC();
```

It aids in code readability and maintainability due to its concise representation of a programming process. The method calls `methodA()`, `methodB()`, and `methodC()` use a concept known as a **monad**, which is a single step of a mathematical operation. Monads are then organized into pipelines of processing as is evident in the chain of preceding functions.

The FlowDef fluent interface

In Cascading, one primary place where you will use fluent programming is with the `FlowDef` class. `FlowDef` allows one to create the execution flow for the job. `FlowDef` is a very rich interface and it can be used to connect taps (sources, sinks, and tails) to pipes or pipe segments, to add traps (see *Chapter 6, Testing a Cascading Application, Managing exceptions with traps,* section), to add checkpoints to the flow (see *Chapter 6, Testing a Cascading Application*), and even to add JAR files to the `CLASSPATH` variable. Several useful method signatures are shown as follows. Each is self-explanatory, adding sources and sinks, adding traps, defining checkpoints, supplying JAR files to `CLASSPATH`, and so on.

```
FlowDef addCheckpoint(String name, Tap checkpointTap)
FlowDef addSource(Pipe pipe, Tap sourceTap)
FlowDef addSink(Pipe pipe, Tap sinkTap)
FlowDef addTailSink(Pipe pipe, Tap tailSinkTap)
FlowDef addToClassPath(String jarPath)
FlowDef addTrap(Pipe pipe, Tap trapTap)
```

1. Note how each method call returns its `FlowDef` definition, which again enables method chaining. We can then construct our flow like this:

```
// Connect the taps and pipes into a flow and execute it
FlowDef flowDef = FlowDef.flowDef()
                        .addSource( pipe, inputTap )
                        .addTailSink(pipe, outputTap );
Flow flow = flowConnector.connect( flowDef );
flow.complete();
```

2. There is another way to add taps, and that uses a map that associates taps with pipes. Using this method, here is how multiple taps are connected to the pipes that use them:

```
List<Pipe> pipes = new ArrayList<Pipe>(2);
pipes.add(authorPipe);  // Pipe is named "authors"
pipes.add(keywordPipe); // Pipe is named "keywords"
Map<String, Tap> taps = new HashMap<String, Tap>();
taps.put("authors",  authorSourceTap);
```

```
taps.put("keywords", keywordSourceTap);
FlowConnector flowConnector = new LocalFlowConnector();
Flow flow = flowConnector.connect(source,taps,pipes);
flow.complete();
```

3. The same actions as above should now be performed using the `FlowDef` fluent style as follows:

```
FlowDef flowDef = FlowDef.flowDef()
.addSource(authorPipe, authorSourceTap)
.addSource(keywordPipe, keywordSourceTap)
.addTailSink(tailPipe, outputTap );
Flow flow = flowConnector.connect(flowDef);
flow.complete();
```

Note how the `addSource()` method is called twice, once for each pipe that we are connecting a source tap to. One other method is also available, and it defines the `AssemblyPlanner` that will be used when the execution graph is created, `FlowDef addAssemblyPlanner(AssemblyPlanner assemblyPlanner)`. `AssemblyPlanner` is responsible for actually building the Cascading code that will be run by `FlowConnector`. Typically, you will only use `AssemblyPlanner` instances and not write them. `AssemblyPlanner` instances provide the way in which Cascading can use different underlying frameworks such as Hadoop MapReduce, Hadoop YARN, Tez, Spark, and others.

Integrating external components

In these sections, we will discuss how to make Cascading interoperate with external systems. Interoperation is an important aspect of "shoe-horning" a new technology into an existing infrastructure. Additionally, new technologies are emerging almost daily now, so using these capabilities in Cascading is important when migrating or evolving systems.

Flow and cascade events

Each flow and cascade has the ability to execute callbacks via an event listener. This ability is useful when an external application needs to be notified that either a flow or cascade has started, halted, completed, or thrown an exception. Flows and cascades generate events that can be handled by your client-side code.

 For instance, at the completion of a flow that runs on an Amazon EC2 Hadoop cluster, an Amazon SQS message can be sent to notify another application to fetch the job results from S3 or begin the shutdown of the cluster that you are paying for.

1. These events are managed by a `FlowListener` object, which is an interface with the following signature:

```
FlowListener listener = new FlowListener()
{
    public void onStarting(Flow flow) { /* Do something */ }
    public void onStopping(Flow flow) { /* Do something */ }
    public void onCompleted(Flow flow) { /* Do something */ }
    public boolean onThrowable(Flow flow, Throwable throwable)
    {
        return false;
    }
};
/* Now use it */
flow.addListener(listener);
assertFalse( "no listener found", flow.hasListeners());
flow.removeListener(listener);
assertTrue("listener found", flow.hasListeners());
```

2. Here is a short method that allows a Cascading job to issue messages to a UNIX-style syslog server using syslog4j configured to run as a UDP server (see `http://syslog4j.org/`). It could be called from the `main()` method of any job that ran a Cascading flow:

```
import org.productivity.java.syslog4j.Syslog;

public void setSyslogger(Flow flow) {
    FlowListener listener = new FlowListener() {
        public void onStarting(Flow flow) {
            Syslog.getInstance("udp").info(flow.getName() + "
                started at " + new Date().toString());
        }
        public void onStopping(Flow flow) {
            Syslog.getInstance("udp").info(flow.getName() + "
                stopped at " + new Date().toString());
        }
        public void onCompleted(Flow flow) {
            Syslog.getInstance("udp").info(flow.getName() + "
                completed at " + new Date().toString() + " with
                status " +
                flow.getFlowStats().getStatus().toString());
        }
        public boolean onThrowable(Flow flow, Throwable
            throwable) {
            return false;
        }
    };
    /* Add it to the flow */
    flow.addListener(listener);
}
```

Using external JAR files

So much code already exists, written by other people, that we often need to make use of it. In Java, it almost always comes packaged as a set of **Java Archive (JAR)** files that are external to our code. In many cases, the source code that was used to produce these libraries is also unavailable to us. But, these external JAR files are easy to use in Cascading, but the trick is getting them to the cluster. To use an external JAR, it simply has to be placed on the Java `CLASSPATH` variable, the proper import statement must be defined, and then the JAR members can be used as normal.

In Cascading local mode, this can all be accomplished through the Java command line by specifying the `-cp` option: `java -cp myjob.jar:external.jar:cascading-lib/* com.ai.jobs.MainJob`.

In Cascading Hadoop mode, things get a bit more complicated. So another way to package our code is to produce a fat JAR. A **fat JAR** is a single consolidated JAR file that contains everything necessary to run the job, including Cascading:

1. Generate a fat JAR—for instance, using the `Export` option from Eclipse.

2. Run the following command line:

```
hadoop jar myjob.jar com.ai.jobs.MainJob data/input data/output
```

> Note that the Hortonworks distribution now contains all of Cascading, so bundling it with the job, whether using a fat JAR or on the command line, is not necessary. Note that "executable JAR" cannot be used.
>
> Also, fat JARs can become quite large and unwieldy. However, when they are generated, one can select the contents, so it is important not to include the Hadoop JARs or anything else that will be supplied by your runtime.

Hadoop provides a way to get all of the JAR files needed to the mappers and reducers with the following command. You can also pass JARs as command line parameters with the following command:

```
hadoop jar myjob.jar com.ai.jobs.MainJob -libjar external.jar data/input
data/output
```

> If the configuration scripts in $HADOOP_CONF_DIR are configured to use a cluster, the JAR is pushed into the cluster for execution. Cascading does not rely on any environment variables like $HADOOP_HOME or $HADOOP_CONF_DIR, only Hadoop does.

Using Cascading as insulation from big data migrations and upgrades

Cascading affords a major benefit that is often overlooked. Cascading produces an execution graph based on the code that you define, and this graph is not dependent on the execution framework that will run it. This is the job of the various assembly planners and connectors that one chooses. This then allows Cascading to be used to move between these different frameworks with very little effort. Essentially one can write code once and run it on many frameworks. This gives us a high degree of code reuse and enables this integration with other frameworks to be as painless as the architectural differences allow.

This aspect is not seamless. Some newer frameworks are very different than Hadoop MapReduce and will require new job properties and setup functions, and sometimes additional run methods must be called. However, subsequent versions of Cascading will hide this complexity to the best degree possible. This is important because we are seeing great volatility in various big data platforms, and we are also seeing the rapid introduction and evolution of alternative frameworks. Hadoop itself has moved through three major revisions, with the most current being YARN. We see the introduction of alternative frameworks such as Tez and Spark, and there are others coming.

We can therefore view Cascading as *insulation* that protects our investment in writing code, and allows it to more nimbly move forward to the constant advance of technology.

- **Preparing for Tez**: Tez is a new big data architecture that is similar to MapReduce, but it eliminates the concept of mappers and reducers and allows generic processors to be created. Tez is designed to reduce or eliminate a lot of the data transfers (and disk reads/writes) that must occur between a mapper and reducer only architecture.

  The easiest way for Cascading to take advantage of Tez would have been to just create the MapReduce mappers and reducers and make them processors within Tez. This is not what Cascading does though. It does so much more. In fact, the execution graph is analyzed for patterns and more localized and specific processors are created and handed over to the Tez framework for execution. This achieves significant optimization. Tez was implemented in Cascading version 3.0 by creating Tez specific planners, connectors, flows, taps, and statistics classes. Converting a Cascading job to use Tez involves a little more than switching to use the new connector though. Cascading is implementing a "platform" object that will attempt to make moving to different platforms easier.

- **Moving from MapReduce version 1 to MapReduce version 2 using YARN**: Little is actually necessary to move a Cascading job from MapReduce version 1 to version 2. The systems administrators that manage the Hadoop cluster perform the upgrade and our Cascading MapReduce version 1 jobs go on working, but they are running under version 2. However, they do continue running in simple MapReduce mode. Only the underlying platform has changed, and instead of using Hadoop's `JobTracker` and `TaskTracker`, we are now using the YARN resource managers and node managers. Our jobs are none the wiser.

  At some time in the future, we may want to take advantage not just of the YARN infrastructure, but also of its new programming facilities. Cascading has the capability to allow this.

- **Real-time Cascading using Spark**: Much of what was said earlier about moving Cascading jobs to Tez also applies to Spark. Spark uses processors that are known as Executors. Spark too attempts to provide efficiencies by reducing disk I/O. One of its main methods of doing so is by using in-memory data sets. These are generally referred to as **Resilient Distributed Datasets**. As of the time of writing this, the Spark connectors are not yet available. We believe that they will follow the same design pattern as with Tez.

 Concurrent, Hortonworks, and Databricks are all collaborating on this effort. Concurrent is the primary software developer of Cascading. Hortonworks is an Apache Hadoop open source platform vendor. Databricks is the primary software development company behind Spark.

Summary

In this chapter, we discussed how Cascading fits into the overall processing infrastructure. You learned how to build subassemblies to gain better code reuse, how to use cascades to create more complex workflows, and also how to control intermediate files. We also addressed more advanced topics of how to integrate Cascading with external systems. You also learned how to use existing JAR files as well as how to use existing MapReduce jobs for better integration with existing system components. Finally, you learned how use Cascading instrumentation and counters and how these counters can be used to dynamically control the execution of your flows.

In the next chapter, we will discuss how to test and debug Cascading applications. We will review common debugging techniques that can be used when coding a Cascading application and we will also look at "lifecycle" testing when we begin to integrate our code, and then later begin to determine how scalable the application will be.

6
Testing a Cascading Application

Debugging, testing, and **Quality Assurance (QA)** processes are essential but often overlooked skills for the development of a robust system. As with many distributed software systems, Cascading can be difficult to debug, but using the techniques in this chapter, the mysteries of a Cascading application can be unlocked and understood. While there is little documentation on this topic, this chapter will provide in-depth information on how to efficiently test a Cascading application using many techniques.

Debugging a Cascading application

We will now discuss several different techniques and capabilities that will help you debug a Cascading application that you have built. These techniques will help you pinpoint bugs and errors in your code, aid in developing tests that can help to maintain correctness through a full development and maintenance life cycle, show you how to handle run-time errors, and also ensure that your application runs as fast as possible.

Getting your environment ready for debugging

Setting up your development environment is relatively straightforward, but there are a lot of details needed. Here we are going to discuss setting up Eclipse in order to be able to develop and test Cascading applications. We will look at doing this in Cascading local mode, and then will also discuss how to modify the environment to be able to produce JAR files that can be run against a Hadoop cluster. Lastly, we will discuss some of the techniques that are used to create a Hadoop environment that can be tested against. Specifically, we will discuss many of the virtual machine environments that you can obtain and test against without requiring a full Hadoop cluster.

Using Cascading local mode debugging

The local mode is important because it gives the developer an easy to use, familiar method to debug their Cascading application as if it were a simple, standalone Java program. At its most basic, developing local mode applications allows you to debug in a single JVM using an **integrated development environment** (**IDE**) such as Eclipse, NetBeans, or IntelliJ, and many others. We have seen that in the local mode, a Cascading job runs as a single application. It relies upon the required JAR files that are made available to it either through the Java CLASSPATH variable, or that have been placed into a single JAR file as a Fat JAR.

So, it makes sense that we can use an IDE and trace our code execution, supply breakpoints in our code, and generally observe the internal variables and objects that perform the job that we are running.

Setting up Eclipse

We will now look at the most basic steps that are required to set up Eclipse to allow you to develop a Cascading local mode application. We will assume that you have downloaded and installed Eclipse from `https://eclipse.org/`:

1. Start Eclipse.

2. Create a project called `LearningCascading` by navigating to **File | New | JavaProject**.

3. Select the **LearningCascading** project, right-click and select **New** and then **Folder**. Create a folder named `lib`. You may also want to create a folder named `data`. You will put your data files here later.

4. Now we have to add the required Cascading JAR files. At this point, you will need to locate the JAR files that are shown in the following list. See *Chapter 9, Planning for Future Growth*, for information about where these JAR files can be downloaded. Copy them into the `lib` directory that you just created. You may want to right-click on this directory and select **Refresh**. It looks like a lot, but it is a one-time setup. One other thing to notice here is that the embedded version numbers will change over time for just about everything. The following list is for Cascading 2.6.1, and these numbers can be changed if you need to use other older or newer versions.

   ○ `cascading-core-2.6.1.jar`: This is the Cascading core library

   ○ `cascading-local-2.6.1.jar`: This is the Cascading core library for the local mode

   ○ `cascading-xml-2.6.1.jar`: The is the Cascading core library for XML processing

- ° `cascading-hadoop-2.6.1.jar`: This is the Cascading core library for YARN
- ° `cascading-hadoop2-mr1-2.6.1.jar`: This is the Cascading core library for YARN running MapReduce v1
- ° `janino-2.6.1.jar`: This is the Janino library
- ° `jgrapht-jdk1.6-0.8.1.jar`: This is the Cascading library used to build and manage execution graphs
- ° `log4j-1.2.15.jar`: This is a Java logging library
- ° `riffle-0.1-dev.jar`: This is a Java library used to manage the execution of Java processes and tasks
- ° `tagsoup-1.2.jar`: This is the Tagsoup HTML-to-XHTML converter
- ° `slf4j-api-1.7.10.jar`: This is the simple logging facility for Java framework
- ° `slf4j-simple-1.7.10.jar`: This is the simple logging facility for the Java framework

5. Right-click on the `LearningCascading` project and select **Properties**. This will open a dialog box where you will make the JAR files that you just copied to the `lib` directory available to your application. Select the **Libraries** tab, click on **Add JARs...**, navigate to the `lib` directory in your `LearningCascading` project and select all of the JAR files that you just copied and press **OK**. This activity looks like this:

Setting up Cascading JAR files in Eclipse

6. Now that the JAR files have been added to the project, you can begin to develop your Cascading application. You can get some sample code to use here, which is included in the code library supplied with this book. At this point, your Eclipse environment should look like this:

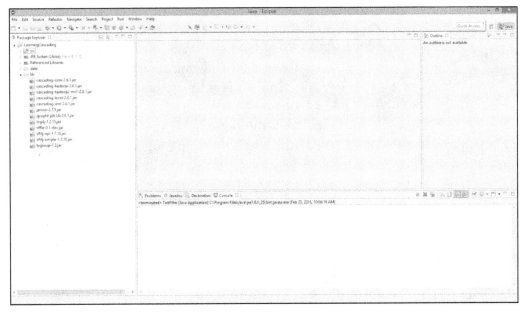

The Eclipse workspace

7. Now set up a **Run** configuration. Select the job file to run, right-click and choose **RunAs** from **RunConfigurations…**. In this dialog, you specify the command-line parameters for the class that contains your job. Here's a screenshot showing some code that has been set up from the code companion to this book:

Setting up Cascading data files

8. After that, you can select a Cascading job and either run the application or start the application in debug mode. By placing a breakpoint near the beginning of the application, we can single-step trace its flow.

9. Lastly, here is an example of the output that you will see when you run one of these test programs:

Running a Cascading job in Eclipse

When we step into our application, normally we will not be able to trace into Cascading code since we will be using JAR files only. However, we can get the full source code for Cascading and we can then trace into this code as well. This code is on GitHub, and any released version is available, as well as new releases that are marked as WIP or WorkInProgress. While it can be beneficial to have the Cascading source code and to occasionally step into it for learning purposes, it is not generally required. In most cases, setting breakpoints in your custom operations will be sufficient. In this manner, you will be able to see how your `prepare()` and `cleanup()` methods work, and you will also be able to see your context, tuple, and `TupleEntry` objects as they pass through the various operation methods.

Remote debugging

Remote debugging is also possible. Remote debugging allows a local machine (probably a desktop or laptop) to debug a Cascading application on a remote system. This can be useful if you have another system or server that has a different system configuration (operating system version, installed libraries, and so on) that you need to test. Here is the procedure to do this using Eclipse:

1. Start the Java program on the remote system by using remote debugging command-line parameters. Note that you will have to be able to log in to this server to do this.

   ```
   java -Xdebug -agentlib:jdwp=transport=dt_socket,address=9999,serve
   r=y,suspend=y -jar myCascadingJob.jar
   ```

2. Configure Eclipse to connect to the remote application.

The steps to configure Eclipse are as follows:

1. Right-click on the project and navigate to **Debug As | Debug Configurations…**.

2. In the dialog box that appears, select **Remote Java Application** and then:
   1. Create a new configuration if one does not exist.
   2. Specify the host (server) and port number (address) that you used when running the command.
   3. Select **Allow Termination of the VM**. This will allow the program that you are debugging to terminate and that will stop the remote debugging process.
   4. Press **Debug**.

3. If you have specified **suspend=y**, you should now enter the debugger and have normal Eclipse control over the running (debug mode) application.

After this, you will be able to do every debugging task that you would normally do on your local version of Eclipse (such as setting breakpoints, stepping, analyzing data, and so on), but the actual application that you will be debugging will be running on another system.

Using assertions

The next technique that we will discuss is the usage of the assertions that we discussed in *Chapter 3, Understanding Custom Operations*. Assertions can be liberally inserted into your pipes to test for the existence of desired or required conditions. Since custom assertions can also be created, they can be highly customized to invoke very complex conditions within your code. For instance, they may be based on some customer information, or a product number may require some very specific type of validation, and in this case we would create a custom ValueAssertion. Also, maybe a set of orders for a given customer needs to be validated, ensuring that no more than two discount codes were used. In this case, we would create a custom GroupAssertion. Then, if asserted conditions are not met, an exception will be thrown, and these can be caught with exception blocks and logged.

The Debug() filter

Inserting a Debug() filter into a pipe involves only creating the pipe and attaching a Debug() filter to it, and inserting the pipe into the flow. Output from this filter can be routed to STDOUT or STDERR, and it goes to STDERR by default. Here are some code examples to use the Debug() filter.

```
// Write all Tuples to STDOUT
inPipe = new Each(inPipe, new Debug());
// Write all Tuples to STDERR
inPipe = new Each(inPipe, new Debug(Debug.Output.STDERR));
// Write all Tuples with a lot of detail
inPipe = new Each(inPipe, DebugLevel.VERBOSE, new Debug());
```

As we saw in *Chapter 3, Understanding Custom Operations*, Debug() filters are set on individual pipes. However, they can be turned off globally if so desired using this code:

```
// tell the planner to remove all Debug operations
flowDef.setDebugLevel(DebugLevel.NONE);
```

When a `Debug()` filter is used, it will output all tuples that pass through the pipe to `STDERR` by default. You may use a construct that looks like this to view tuples before and after some other pipe operation:

```
Pipe inPipe = new Pipe("InPipe");
inPipe = new Each(inPipe, new Debug());
inPipe = new Each(inPipe, new SampleFilter("test"));
inPipe = new Each(inPipe, new Debug());
```

Here, we are trying to see the input and output tuples of the `SampleFilter()` operation. In our case, `SampleFilter()` removes any tuples that contain the word `test` in the `data` column. Let's run this code segment against the following data:

```
count,data
1,good data 1
2,test data 1
3,test data 2
4,good data 2
5,good data 3
6,test data 3
7,good data 4
8,good data 5
```

However, when we run this, we will see an output that looks like this:

```
[main] INFO cascading.property.AppProps - using app.id:
623AFA266EB34C789FFA3F207B549940
[flow InPipe] INFO cascading.util.Version - Concurrent, Inc -
Cascading 2.6.1
[flow InPipe] INFO cascading.flow.Flow - [InPipe] starting
[flow InPipe] INFO cascading.flow.Flow - [InPipe]  source:
FileTap["TextDelimited[['line_num', 'line']]"]["data\input.txt"]
[flow InPipe] INFO cascading.flow.Flow - [InPipe]  sink:
FileTap["TextDelimited[['line_num', 'line']]"]["data\output.txt"]
[flow InPipe] INFO cascading.flow.Flow - [InPipe]  parallel execution
is enabled: true
[flow InPipe] INFO cascading.flow.Flow - [InPipe]  starting jobs: 1
[flow InPipe] INFO cascading.flow.Flow - [InPipe]  allocating threads:
1
[pool-1-thread-1] INFO cascading.flow.FlowStep - [InPipe] starting
step: local
['1', 'good data 1']
['1', 'good data 1']
['2', 'test data 1']
['3', 'test data 2']
['4', 'good data 2']
['4', 'good data 2']
```

```
['5', 'good data 3']
['5', 'good data 3']
['6', 'test data 3']
['7', 'good data 4']
['7', 'good data 4']
['8', 'good data 5']
['8', 'good data 5']
tuples count: 8
tuples count: 5
```

See how the output of the two `Debug()` filters has been interleaved? Data is flowing freely through the pipes and we are seeing a very typical Java indeterminate thread sequencing as a result. We can aid this a little by using this code:

```
Pipe inPipe = new Pipe("InPipe");
// Supply a prefix string to the Debug Filters
inPipe = new Each(inPipe, new Debug("Before"));
inPipe = new Each(inPipe, new SampleFilter("test"));
inPipe = new Each(inPipe, new Debug("After"));
```

This will then produce an output like this, where each tuple printed by the two `Debug()` filters has an identifier prepended:

```
[main] INFO cascading.property.AppProps - using app.id:
6D9D087D6D5149D2B199A4CDD418312B
[flow InPipe] INFO cascading.util.Version - Concurrent, Inc -
Cascading 2.6.1
[flow InPipe] INFO cascading.flow.Flow - [InPipe] starting
[flow InPipe] INFO cascading.flow.Flow - [InPipe]  source:
FileTap["TextDelimited[['line_num', 'line']]"]["data\input.txt"]
[flow InPipe] INFO cascading.flow.Flow - [InPipe]  sink:
FileTap["TextDelimited[['line_num', 'line']]"]["data\output.txt"]
[flow InPipe] INFO cascading.flow.Flow - [InPipe]  parallel execution
is enabled: true
[flow InPipe] INFO cascading.flow.Flow - [InPipe]  starting jobs: 1
[flow InPipe] INFO cascading.flow.Flow - [InPipe]  allocating threads:
1
[pool-1-thread-1] INFO cascading.flow.FlowStep - [InPipe] starting
step: local
Before: ['1', 'good data 1']
After: ['1', 'good data 1']
Before: ['2', 'test data 1']
Before: ['3', 'test data 2']
Before: ['4', 'good data 2']
After: ['4', 'good data 2']
Before: ['5', 'good data 3']
After: ['5', 'good data 3']
Before: ['6', 'test data 3']
```

```
Before: ['7', 'good data 4']
After: ['7', 'good data 4']
Before: ['8', 'good data 5']
After: ['8', 'good data 5']
Before: tuples count: 8
After: tuples count: 5Writing Log Messages
```

Taps exist for STDOUT and STDERR: StdOutTap and StdErrTap. These taps can be used like any other tap. But remember that they will just contain dumps of tuples! You can just create them and connect them to pipes using FlowDef. The only real reason that you might want to do this would be to save your output. Otherwise you can use a Debug() filter just as easily. Remember that in Hadoop mode, these files will be distributed across HDFS. In Hadoop, they will be spread across the many log files created by the mappers and reducers! Lastly, you can always just use a good old System.out.println() call to write things out, but this is best done in the mainline job, not in Cascading-specific classes (remember that writing billions of log records may not be advisable and your cluster administrator will likely remind you of this!). But, when debugging in the local mode, they work quite well and can be very valuable when used to print information in a custom operation.

Managing exceptions with traps

A trap is very useful special purpose sink tap that can be attached to one or more pipes. The difference here between a sink tap and a trap is that a trap can be bound to an intermediate pipe, not just to the end point of a flow. A trap is used to catch errors, but it is relatively expensive to use, so other methods (filters and functions) are generally preferred. In order to trigger the usage of a trap, an operation just needs to throw an exception. Here is an example of how to use a trap:

```
Tap trapTap = new Hfs(new TextDelimited( true, "\t" ), trapPath);
Pipe sumPipe = new Pipe("summarize");

// set the trap on the "summarize" branch
flowDef.addTrap("summarize", tapTrap);
```

The following diagram shows how traps are configured relative to a flow. The diagram shows how versatile traps are, with one handing errors detected by an assertion, and a single one handling errors detected by both a function and an operation. Looking at the previous code snippet, to accomplish this, trapTap simply needs to be added to each pipe that requires it. In the following diagram that is the each_func pipe and the every_agg pipe like this:

```
flowDef.addTrap("each_func", trap2);
flowDef.addTrap("every_agg", trap2);
```

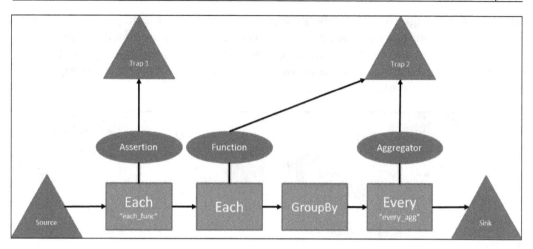

Using traps

Checkpoints

The Cascading checkpointing facility is a Hadoop-only function. It allows the state to be saved in the form of an intermediate file. Then, if a failure should occur in a subsequent Hadoop job, the flow can be restarted at this intermediate point without requiring all of the prior steps to be executed. Checkpoints are useful when some prior resource-intensive work (CoGroup, HashJoin, or some complex function) has completed and we want to prevent this work from reoccurring if a subsequent error occurs.

After a subsequent step has been completed successfully, the checkpoint file is automatically cleaned up by Cascading for you. When a checkpoint is inserted into a flow, it will automatically cause another Hadoop job to be generated beyond those that have already executed before the checkpoint.

The following diagram shows how a checkpoint is used. In this diagram, we run two parallel pipes and then do a join (CoGroup). When we have completed this join, we take a checkpoint, and then perform an aggregation. Should the aggregation fail, the job can be restarted and when this occurs, only the aggregation will run using the checkpoint file as input.

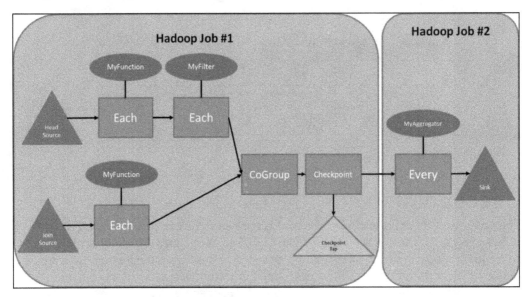

Using checkpoints

Here is an example of how we create the checkpoint in the preceding diagram. Since a checkpoint is actually just a specialized pipe that has a sink tap attached to it, the checkpoint is just inserted as part of the flow as follows:

```
// The head pipe
Pipe headPipe = new Pipe("head");
headPipe= new Each(headPipe, new MyFunction() );
headPipe= new Each(headPipe, new MyFilter() );
// A Join head with an identical transformation function run against
it
Pipe joinPipe = new Pipe( "join" );
joinPipe = new Each(joinPipe, new MyFunction());
// Join the head and joinpipes
Pipe join = new CoGroup(headPipe, joinPipe);
// Take a Checkpoint here by inserting it into the flow
Checkpoint checkpoint = new Checkpoint("checkpoint", join );
// Group by some field and apply an aggregator
Pipe groupPipe = new GroupBy(checkpoint, new Fields("group_field");
groupPipe= new Every(groupPipe, new MyAggregator());
```

```
Tap headSource = new Hfs(new TextLine(), "main_data" );
Tap joinSource = new Hfs(new TextLine(), "join_data" );
Tap outSink = new Hfs(new TextLine(), "output_data" );
Flow flow = new HadoopFlowConnector().connect(flowDef);
```

To use this checkpoint, all we need to do is to rerun the job. If the anonymous checkpoint exists, the job will be restarted from that point. Now, should we need to restart this job from its defined (that is, non-anonymous) checkpoint. Here is how we do that:

```
// Set up all Taps as before
Tap checkpointTap = new Hfs(new TextDelimited( true, "\t" ),
"checkpoint");
FlowDef flowDef = new FlowDef()
.setName("restarted_checkpointed_join")
  .addSource(headPipe, headSource)
  .addSource(joinPipe, joinSource)
  .addTailSink(groupPipe, outSink)
.addCheckpoint( checkpoint, checkpointTap )
.setRunID("some-unique-value");
Flow flow = new HadoopFlowConnector().connect(flowDef);
```

We can optionally write the checkpoint as a tab delimited file with headers. This step is not required, and if it is not specified, the output file will be anonymous and will be automatically deleted if the following step completes successfully. Note that if this non-anonymous method is used, this file will now exist persistently and may need to be manually cleaned up if this job is run multiple times. Here is the code to do this:

```
Tap checkpointTap = new Hfs(new TextDelimited( true,
"\t" ), "checkpoint");
// And now put it all together and run it
FlowDef flowDef = new FlowDef()
        .setName("checkpointed_join")
        .addSource(headPipe, headSource)
        .addSource(joinPipe, joinSource)
        .addTailSink(groupPipe, outSink)
        .addCheckpoint(checkpoint, checkpointTap)
```

Managing bad data

Bad data appearing in an input stream is inevitable. We have all seen it and experienced it. It is important to understand your options to handle it.

One very easy way to manage bad data is to throw an exception and let the framework handle it. We can write custom assertions to do this. If you do this, you'll want to set up a trap to handle the exception that will be thrown by the assertion. If you do not do so, it will terminate your application. You can try to catch the error and log it, but there is sometimes limited control over where this can be done. For instance, coercion can be an uncontrollable area.

Another easy way of handling bad data is to simply create a filter for it and check the condition, removing the bad data tuple if required. While this is simple to do, it is often very insufficient. We probably want to know that the bad data is there and track it, so we could always create a counter, or more likely a set of counters, and be able to print a count of all of our bad data by type. We may want to log it or otherwise print it, but if there is a lot of it, this can produce very long log files. We probably also want to know if a tuple has bad data in it, which specific entry was bad. All of these factors make simple filters a bad idea.

A better idea is to build a subassembly that validates the data and flags each tuple that contains an error with an indicator of what the specific error was. Then, later we can use a filter to divert data flagged as bad into a sink tap that we can later examine and correct. Here is some code that shows you how to do this:

```
public class ValidatorAssembly extends SubAssembly{
    public ValidatorAssembly (Pipe inPipe)
    {
            // Insert error and message fields
            Fields fields = new Fields( "error", "errormsg" );
            Insert function = new Insert( fields, "0", "" );
    inPipe= new Each(inPipe, function, Fields.ALL );
            // Run validators
    inPipe= new Each(inPipe, new ValidatorFunction1() );
    inPipe= new Each(inPipe, new ValidatorFunction2() );
    Pipe tailPipe= new Each(inPipe, new ValidatorFunction3() );
            setTails(tailPipe);
    }
}
```

This subassembly can now be attached as a validation pipe to any data flow and it will apply the set of validations to all data that flows through it. It can accumulate errors in the added fields. Users of this subassembly can then split its tail and route good and bad data into different sink taps.

When using this method, it is a good idea to define some sort of naming convention for your `TupleEntry` fields. For instance, you might want all fields added by a special subassembly to be prefixed with one or more underscores, and maybe also to be prefixed with some indicator that specified the subassembly that added them. By taking these steps, you can prevent name field collisions and can also allow errors to accumulate over more than one validator, if so required.

Viewing flow sequencing using DOT files

DOT is a text graph description language that is used to save the representation of the execution graph of a flow in a file. A DOT file can be very valuable to help you understand how flows and assemblies actually work and are good to produce and examine when you are testing. A DOT file can be created easily using the `Flow` object:

```
FlowConnector flowConnector = new LocalFlowConnector();
Flow flow =flowConnector.connect(source,taps,pipes);
flow.writeDOT("/tmp/mcovert/myjob.dot");
```

Let's look at a relatively complicated flow and see how visualizing its DOT file can help us. Here is the flow part of a Cascading job:

```
// define source and sink Taps.
Scheme sourceScheme = new TextDelimited( new Fields( "author",
"organization", "document", "keyword" ), true, "," );
Tap source = new FileTap( sourceScheme, args[0] );
Scheme sinkScheme = new TextLine( new Fields( "line") );
Tap sink_authors = new FileTap( sinkScheme, args[1] + "/authors.txt" ,
SinkMode.REPLACE );
Tap sink_keywords = new FileTap( sinkScheme, args[1] + "/keywords.txt"
, SinkMode.REPLACE );
Tap sink_orgs = new FileTap( sinkScheme, args[1] + "/orgs.txt" ,
SinkMode.REPLACE );
Tap sink_orgkws = new FileTap( sinkScheme, args[1] + "/org_kws.txt" ,
SinkMode.REPLACE );
// the 'head' of the pipe assembly
Pipe assembly = new Pipe( "summarizer" );
assembly = new Each(assembly, new Fields( "author", "organization",
"document", "keyword" ), new Identity());
// For each input Tuple
Pipe p_author = new Pipe("authors", assembly);
p_author        = new GroupBy(p_author, new Fields("author"));
p_author        = new Every(p_author, new Fields("author"), new
Count(), new Fields("author", "count"));
Pipe p_keyword = new Pipe("keywords", assembly);
```

```
p_keyword      = new GroupBy(p_keyword, new Fields("keyword"));
p_keyword      = new Every(p_keyword, new Fields("keyword"), new
Count(), new Fields("keyword", "count"));
Pipe p_org     = new Pipe("orgs", assembly);
p_org          = new GroupBy(p_org, new Fields("organization"));
p_org          = new Every(p_org, new Fields("organization"), new
Count(), new Fields("organization", "count"));

Pipe p_orgkw   = new Pipe("orgkws", assembly);
p_orgkw        = new GroupBy(p_orgkw, new Fields("organization",
"keyword"));
p_orgkw        = new Every(p_orgkw, new Fields("organization",
"keyword"), new Count(), new Fields("organization", "keyword",
"count"));
// initialize app properties, tell Hadoop which jar file to use
Properties properties = new Properties();
AppProps.setApplicationJarClass( properties, Exercise1.class );
// Connect all of the Taps to their respective Pipes
final List<Pipe> pipes = new ArrayList<Pipe>(4);
pipes.add(p_author);
pipes.add(p_keyword);
pipes.add(p_org);
pipes.add(p_orgkw);
final Map<String, Tap> taps = new HashMap<String, Tap>();
taps.put("authors",  sink_authors);
taps.put("keywords", sink_keywords);
taps.put("orgs",     sink_orgs);
taps.put("orgkws",   sink_orgkws);
// And run the flow
FlowConnector flowConnector = new LocalFlowConnector();
Flow flow = flowConnector.connect(source,taps,pipes);
flow.complete();
// Produce a DOT file to visualize
flow.writeDOT("flow.dot");
System.out.println("Done....");
```

The DOT file shown in the following code snippet is a textual representation of the execution graph. It is ugly and pretty much incomprehensible, although you can see how the graph is represented, first with numbered vertices, and later with edges that connect pairs of vertices. Remember that a vertex is a pipe segment (sometimes with an attached operation), and an edge is a flow of tuples between pipe segments.

```
digraph G {
  1 [label = "Every('authors')[Count[decl:[{1}:'count' | Long]]]"];
```

```
    2 [label = "FileTap['TextLine[['line']->[ALL]]']['c:\temp/authors.
txt']"];
    3 [label = "GroupBy('authors')[by:['author']]"];
    4 [label = "Each('summarizer')[Identity[decl:[{4}:'author',
'organization', 'document', 'keyword']]]"];
    5 [label = "FileTap['TextDelimited[['author', 'organization',
'document', 'keyword']]']['c:\temp\small1.csv']"];
    6 [label = "Every('keywords')[Count[decl:[{1}:'count' | Long]]]"];
    7 [label = "FileTap['TextLine[['line']->[ALL]]']['c:\temp/keywords.
txt']"];
    8 [label = "GroupBy('keywords')[by:['keyword']]"];
    9 [label = "Every('orgs')[Count[decl:[{1}:'count' | Long]]]"];
   10 [label = "FileTap['TextLine[['line']->[ALL]]']['c:\temp/orgs.
txt']"];
   11 [label = "GroupBy('orgs')[by:['organization']]"];
   12 [label = "Every('orgkws')[Count[decl:[{1}:'count' | Long]]]"];
   13 [label = "FileTap['TextLine[['line']->[ALL]]']['c:\temp/org_kws.
txt']"];
   14 [label = "GroupBy('orgkws')[by:['organization', 'keyword']]"];
   15 [label = "[head]\n2.2.1\nlocal:2.2.1:Concurrent, Inc."];
   16 [label = "[tail]"];
    1 -> 2 [label = "[{2}:'author', 'count']\n[{4}:'author',
'organization', 'document', 'keyword']"];
    3 -> 1 [label = "authors[{1}:'author']\n[{4}:'author',
'organization', 'document', 'keyword']"];
    6 -> 7 [label = "[{2}:'keyword', 'count']\n[{4}:'author',
'organization', 'document', 'keyword']"];
    8 -> 6 [label = "keywords[{1}:'keyword']\n[{4}:'author',
'organization', 'document', 'keyword']"];
    9 -> 10 [label = "[{2}:'organization', 'count']\n[{4}:'author',
'organization', 'document', 'keyword']"];
   11 -> 9 [label = "orgs[{1}:'organization']\n[{4}:'author',
'organization', 'document', 'keyword']"];
   12 -> 13 [label = "[{3}:'organization', 'keyword', 'count']\
n[{4}:'author', 'organization', 'document', 'keyword']"];
   14 -> 12 [label = "orgkws[{2}:'organization', 'keyword']\
n[{4}:'author', 'organization', 'document', 'keyword']"];
   15 -> 5 [label = ""];
   10 -> 16 [label = "[{2}:'organization', 'count']\
n[{2}:'organization', 'count']"];
    2 -> 16 [label = "[{2}:'author', 'count']\n[{2}:'author',
'count']"];
    7 -> 16 [label = "[{2}:'keyword', 'count']\n[{2}:'keyword',
'count']"];
   13 -> 16 [label = "[{3}:'organization', 'keyword', 'count']\
n[{3}:'organization', 'keyword', 'count']"];
```

```
    5 -> 4 [label = "[{4}:'author', 'organization', 'document',
'keyword']\n[{4}:'author', 'organization', 'document', 'keyword']"];
    4 -> 14 [label = "[{4}:'author', 'organization', 'document',
'keyword']\n[{4}:'author', 'organization', 'document', 'keyword']"];
    4 -> 11 [label = "[{4}:'author', 'organization', 'document',
'keyword']\n[{4}:'author', 'organization', 'document', 'keyword']"];
    4 -> 8 [label = "[{4}:'author', 'organization', 'document',
'keyword']\n[{4}:'author', 'organization', 'document', 'keyword']"];
    4 -> 3 [label = "[{4}:'author', 'organization', 'document',
'keyword']\n[{4}:'author', 'organization', 'document', 'keyword']"];
}
```

Now let's visualize this execution graph using Graphviz (http://www.graphviz.org/). To visualize this graph, we use the following command. The -T option tells Graphviz to output a .png file. The -O option tells it to create a file that will be named flow.dot.png:

```
dot -Tpng -O flow.dot
```

The following diagram shows the flow.dot.png file. We can see each pipe split, how it connects to a prior pipe, the input tap, the output taps, and each pipe segment, its operation, and even the tuple structure that connects the pipe segments:

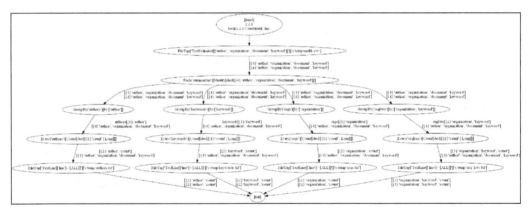

DOT file visualized with Graphviz

Flow DOT files can also be produced relative to how they will execute on the underlying platform, specifically Hadoop. When a flow is created by a `HadoopFlowConnector`, and this flow produces its DOT file by calling `writeDot()`, this execution graph will show how intermediate taps will be used to connect multiple Hadoop jobs (that is, MapReduce jobs) that the larger Cascading job may require. You can also use the `writeStepsDOT()` method to produce details about the Hadoop jobs. The code mentioned earlier produces the following diagram when the `writeStepsDOT()` method is used. From the following diagram, we can see that the Cascading job will produce four Hadoop jobs and that they will run in parallel. This makes sense since each Hadoop job is a `GroupBy` and `Every` (and therefore will consist of Mappers and Reducers):

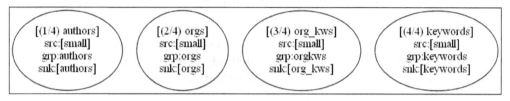

A Hadoop job DOT file visualized with Graphviz

Testing strategies

In this section, we will discuss three test strategies. We will start with unit testing, then discuss integration testing, and finally load testing.

Unit testing involves creating very specific test cases that ensure that individual components are working as expected. In many cases, this will be at the custom operation level. Typically unit tests are coded by the developer who created the to-be-tested code. Unit tests are also important to check when code can be broken by maintenance or fixes. In many cases, the local mode is used for unit testing.

Integration testing is used when the individual components are assembled into a more complex function or full application. Integration testing is often also called **end-to-end testing**. It involves not only ensuring that all processing is correct, but it typically involves negative testing where erroneous conditions such as bad data must be handled.

Load testing is performed to test the overall scalability of the application. This is done by generating a large amount of data and running it through a Cascading job, or maybe even a set of jobs run simultaneously, to determine how the system (typically a Hadoop cluster) will perform. In these tests, we monitor performance, and it is quite typical to tune the application based on results.

Unit testing and JUnit

Several methods exist to create unit test cases. The most standard way of doing this is by using the JUnit framework. JUnit is a Java framework to create and run repeatable tests. It is a set of JAR files that must be downloaded and incorporated into your project. After this is done, it is very easy to create a unit test.

JUnit creation, running, and debugging is highly integrated into Eclipse, which handles all the includes, annotations, and so on, and automatically creates the source Java files for you.

To begin building our unit testing apparatus, we create a class to contain our test methods. Nothing special needs to be done with this class except that the proper includes must be supplied.

Write method calls where each method implements a particular test. Annotate the method with the @Test decorator. In each method, many other utility functions exist to help you perform the tests. Here is a typical JUnit test class:

```
package com.ai.test;
import org.junit.Test;
import org.junit.runner.RunWith;
import org.junit.runners.JUnit4;
/**
 * Tests module.
 */
public class MyTest {
    @Test
    public void myTest1() { … }
    @Ignore
    public void myTest2() { … }
}

Run the tests from the command line and check the results.

java -cp .:/usr/share/java/junit.jar org.junit.runner.JUnitCore MyTest
```

Cascading uses JUnit Version 3. This version is subtly different from the preceding code example. It uses a base class from JUnit called `TestCase`, and your test cases should derive from this class. When using this technique, all methods defined in this class will be automatically called by the JUnit framework. It is still considered a best practice to place the @Test decoration on each defined test method to ensure future compatibility when tests are converted to version 4. This class definition would then be coded as follows:

```
public class MyTest extends TestCase
```

Cascading provides customized classes that make this even easier. Cascading has the CascadingTestCase and PlatformTestCase classes. The CascadingTestCase class is perfect for unit tests. It derives from JUnit's TestCase (that is, version 3) and it has a lot of special methods that make testing Cascading conditions very easy. These methods allow you to test the length of a flow of pipes, the size of an output tuple, and the contents of a tuple's fields. Here is an example of a test case for Cascading that simply verifies that the head pipe is constructed correctly:

```
package com.ai.test;
import cascading.CascadingTestCase;
import org.junit.Test;
public class PipeTest extends CascadingTestCase {
  @Test
  public void testFirstPipe()
  {
    Pipe headPipe = new Pipe("head");
Pipe pipe = new Pipe(headPipe);
    pipe = new Pipe(pipe);
    assertEquals(headPipe, pipe.getHeads()[0]);
  }
}
```

Now let's look at a simple test case for an operation. There is a lot of code here for such a simple test, but after you get the hang of it, writing these test cases will become second nature. Also, take a look at the Cascading source code and in many test cases that they provide, you will find many utility routines that you can use to simplify the task of writing test cases:

```
package com.ai.test;
import cascading.CascadingTestCase;
import cascading.tuple.Fields;
import cascading.tuple.Tuple;
import cascading.tuple.TupleEntry;
import cascading.tuple.TupleListCollector;
import org.junit.Test;

/**
 * Test an Expression Function
 */
public class ExpressionTest extends CascadingTestCase {
  public ExpressionTest() { }
  @Test
  public void testExpressionFunction() {
    Fields fields = new Fields("a", "b");
    Tuple values = new Tuple(1, 2);
```

```
    TupleEntry tupleEntry = new TupleEntry(fields, values);
    TupleListCollector tuples = invokeFunction(new ExpressionFunction(
new Fields( "c" ), "a + b", int.class ), tupleEntry);
    assertEquals( 3, tuples.entryIterator().next().getObject( 0 ));
  }
}
```

Note the usage of the `invokeFunction()` call in the preceding code snippet. This allows a test case to call this operation directly. Unfortunately, much of the verbosity of the code comes as a result of having to implement the internal data structures used by Cascading (`Fields`, `Tuples`, `TupleEntries`, and `TupleListCollector`). As we discussed earlier in this chapter, Cascading can also be tested very simply by using a `LocalFlowConnector`. In fact, when coupled with simple `System.out.println()` messages, this is a very easy way to test and can be a great first step to testing out a concept or some form of basic algorithm test.

As we have seen before, this involves just changing the types of taps and connectors to use the local mode rather than a platform specific mode (that is, Hadoop). It is a little more work to convert, but it is generally worth it during the early stages of development. A better solution involves using the Cascading `PlatformTestCase` class, which is itself a subclass of the `CascadingTestCase` class. The `PlatformTestCase` class allows you to write test cases that are platform-independent. This class is a little bit complex to use though. You must define the platform itself through a properties file. In the cascading-platform source project that is found on GitHub (see *Chapter 9, Planning for Future Growth*, for details) there is a lot of information about how to do this, along with several examples that can be used to test the local mode, Hadoop mode, and Hadoop YARN mode.

Mocking

Mocking is a technique that allows a more controllable interface to be used during testing. For instance, if we are testing a production database, it may be desirable to test it using a mocked interface that supplies tuples to the application without actually accessing the database at all. Such a routine is often referred to as a stub. A stub is called by a program in the same manner that the actual database would be accessed, and it returns controlled data to the application without the application being aware that it is actually using a stub. Mocking also allows rapid switching between interfaces. Because of these two attributes, mocking can be invaluable when testing Cascading or any big data applications.

Mocking is useful when testing these sort of things:

- Stubbing out external system calls
- Stubbing out database calls

- Testing states that are difficult to create naturally (various errors, interrupts, and so on)

- Testing things that do not yet exist

- Testing things that tend to be indeterminate or non-static (time of day, sensor data, and so on)

In the preceding example, we see how a sort of mocked call is used in the invokeFunction() call. This call performs the required wiring and the mocked data is passed in the TupleEntry class that we create. In general, our mocks will be much more sophisticated. Often when pulling data from a database, we see mocks used to stub out JDBC calls. We also see many mocks that implement fixed versions of some Java interface.

Mocking is best used during unit testing, but is also often used in integration testing. It is generally much less useful during load testing though. There are many mock libraries to use. Some of the more popular ones are shown in *Chapter 9, Planning for Future Growth*.

Integration testing

Integration testing is arguably the most detailed type of testing. An integration test is often conducted by a team of QA specialists, but it is also usually conducted by a development team when the software that they are developing has reached the point of stability. The purpose of integration testing is to ensure that all components work together as expected. Whereas unit testing is concentrated on the part itself, integration testing is focused on the entire system.

There are many methodologies for integration testing, but an integration test strategy usually follows this process:

1. Build the master JAR files with all the code, as follows:

    1. Create some sort of naming convention for this build that references the version, build number, date/time, and so on.

    2. Examine the build script and ensure that there are no errors in the build.

        There are many systems that can be used to do these builds, such as Make, Ant, Maven, Gradle, and others. There are also many automated build systems, such as Jenkins, Cruise Control, and others.

2. Define a standard set of inputs for each tap that is required. This will consist of a fixed set of data from which we can expect a given output.

3. Make sure you have a clean environment. Delete any old files left over from prior tests.

4. Run the job, or jobs if the integration test involves more than one Cascading job. It may be advisable to put this set of commands into a script file. In a complex system, there will generally be many tests that will need to be run.

5. Examine the results as follows:

    1. Examine the log files for any errors.

    2. Examine any traps that may have been set and ensure that they contain the expected tuples.

    3. Examine the output taps and ensure that they contain correct results.

Following a successful integration test, the build is usually placed in a controlled location and the source code is marked with a designated label. In fact, these are often the designators that one sees in various compressed downloads that one finds on the Web. You often see downloads that look like this: `application_name-major_version-minor_version-build-SNAPSHOT`.

Load and performance testing

Data volume is always an issue, and while this is fundamentally what big data solutions are designed to handle, you can often be surprised at the results that you obtain. Much can go wrong, ranging from physical hardware issues (slow disks, too few systems, asymmetric configurations, memory shortages, and so on). Therefore, it is important to obtain or generate a large dataset and test. During initial tests, using a `Sample()` filter can be used to limit the length of the testing runs by setting a low sample size (maybe 10 percent).

The Load tool (described in more detail in *Chapter 9, Planning for Future Growth*) is useful, but it generates mainly random data, and it may be necessary to generate more meaningful sets of data by writing your own data generator, using some open source tools, or even using a commercial generator. It has a command-line interface that allows relatively sophisticated load testing against a cluster. It can be customized, but not easily, and is probably best for initial or baseline testing with various configuration changes. You should also consider using MultiTool (described in more detail in *Chapter 9, Planning for Future Growth*) for quick and dirty processes.

Also, when testing how your program will function, generate bad data to ensure that it can handle it! These are called **negative tests** and they exercise the error handling functionality of your application. Build these tests into all of your tests (unit, integration, and load) to determine how this impacts performance. This will allow you to test out your skill using the techniques that we discussed in the *Managing bad data* section.

Here, we must also reference the Concurrent Driven monitor. This tool is available as commercial product, but there is a free online version for developers. See *Chapter 9, Planning for Future Growth,* for details of where to locate this tool. Driven is invaluable in tuning and optimizing Cascading applications. It gives detailed statistics about the activities of your Cascading jobs, not only at the Cascading function level, but also relative to how your application is mapped onto the underlying framework. Here is an example of the type of information that Driven can provide from the Cascading job viewpoint:

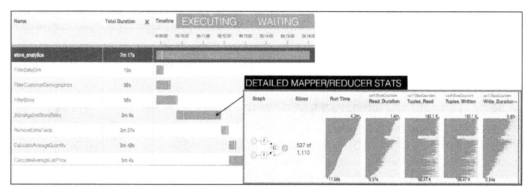

Driven performance monitor Cascading job view

This information can be further viewed in terms of pure MapReduce components as well. The following diagram shows how Cascading maps onto Hadoop MapReduce:

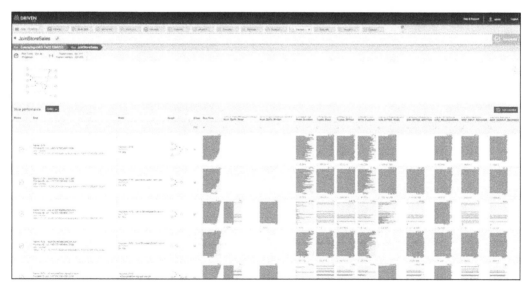

Driven performance monitor Cascading Hadoop job view

For more information on Driven, see *Chapter 9, Planning for Future Growth*. In *Chapter 7, Optimizing the Performance of a Cascading Application*, we will discuss more detailed information about Hadoop performance.

Summary

In this chapter, we completed an in-depth review of many techniques used to debug and test a Cascading application. You learned how to set up Cascading developer configurations for rapid and thorough testing. We looked at several facilities and techniques for debugging, including the use of specialized filters such as Debug(), how to write log messages, and how to review the overall structure of your Cascading application visually. We also reviewed various testing strategies for unit, integration, and load/performance testing.

In the next chapter, we will take a look at some specific techniques that you can use to optimize the performance of your Cascading applications, and also how the performance and tuning of the underlying platform (that is, Hadoop) can be optimized to further assess and improve performance.

7
Optimizing the Performance of a Cascading Application

Optimizing performance by tuning a Cascading application is essential in order to ensure speedy and reliable execution. This chapter will provide in-depth information on how to efficiently optimize a Cascading application and configure the underlying framework (Hadoop) for maximum performance.

You will learn what to look for when determining performance characteristics. We will be:

- Examining practices for improving the performance of a Cascading application
- Discussing how to make performance changes to the underlying Hadoop system when Cascading is running on a specific platform
- Showing how to effectively use checkpoints to help with processing time when failures occur
- Overviewing several open source and commercial tools that can help us to diagnose performance of a Cascading application

Optimizing performance

Performance optimization can be divided into a set of disciplines, each one focused on some sphere of control. The following diagram shows these disciplines:

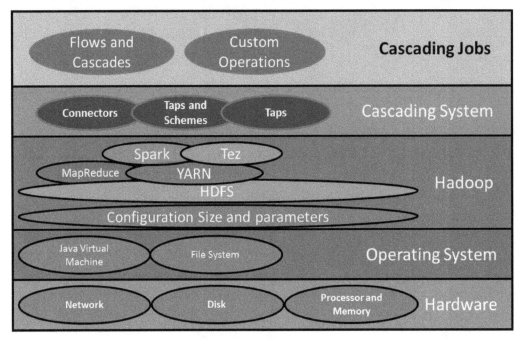

Performance and tuning layers

At the highest level, we will concern ourselves with the Cascading code that we write. This level of performance is concerned with the pipes, operations, and data flows that we assemble.

The level below this is concerned with the fabric that our job will run on, in this case, Cascading and Hadoop (by version), Tez, Spark, and whatever else may come along. Here, we will be concerned with how we partition our data, the number of reducers that we use, buffer sizes, and other parameters that we can supply to Hadoop.

Finally, at the lowest level, we will be concerned with the operating system and hardware configuration on which our cluster actually runs.

We will focus almost exclusively on our applications, Cascading, and the underlying fabric—in our case, Hadoop.

Optimizing Cascading

When we begin to design a Cascading application, we start with some understanding of the functionality that we wish to perform, whether this be various forms of summarization and reporting, or this application is more sophisticated and involves machine learning, discovery, and iterative algorithms. Next, we must understand the data that we will use, how it is structured, and how it must be assembled. Here we will pay close attention to joins that may be required. Data analysis will also consider how we need to emit data, what format we will use, and look at the known consumers of this data—web servers, relational databases, NoSQL databases, or just flat files that will be fed to other systems. In *Chapter 8, Creating a Real-world Application in Cascading*, we will discuss a methodology to handle all of this, but for now we are only listing those areas of concern and we will look closely at these, since they will define our performance characteristics.

In Cascading, and in most applications, there are some general rules that we will try to adhere to. In many of the following items, we will be discussing performance optimization with a specific look towards Hadoop, and then later we will take a very brief look at some Hadoop-specific performance tips. Let's look at some of these concepts and guidelines:

- First, we should run parallel processes when possible. This involves splitting pipes. These processes will then run simultaneously. While input data may be read twice, in many cases this is preferable to running the processes sequentially.

- Always try to reduce the amount of data that you must process whenever possible. This involves reducing unnecessary disk I/O and network I/O. Disk I/O comes from persisting data to taps (including checkpoints) and from running reducers, which also causes network I/O.

    ° Data volumes are key. Understand the volume of data that you will process. Start with the set of input taps. Get some idea of the origin of this data, its format, and the number of records that it will contain during a typical processing run.

    ° Perform as much filtering as possible early on. We always seek to reduce the amount of data that will flow through our system. Typically we will filter based on dates, locations, or other domain-specific selectors. This is the functional equivalent of a SQL SELECT WHERE clause. This is usually handled by a filter, and it can be one of our generic filters that use field level compares, or maybe regex matching. Where possible, be specific. Regex matches are expensive!

- ○ Eliminate unnecessary fields early. Use input and output selectors to get rid of data that you just do not need. You can also use the `Retain` subassembly:

```
Pipe main = new Pipe("main");
main = new each(main, …);
pipe = new Retain(pipe, new Fields("name", "address", "phone"));
```

- ○ Eliminate duplicate records if you can. If you have a stream of tuples that have a unique primary key, use the Unique subassembly early to eliminate these duplicates:

```
Pipe pipe=new Pipe("main");
pipe=new Each(pipe, … ,new MyFunction(), new Fields("key",
"value"));
pipe=new Unique(pipe, new Fields("key"));
```

- Another technique is to use map side partial aggregators (`AggregateBy` and derived classes). See *Chapter 6, Testing a Cascading Application*, for examples of how to do this. This is a sort of Cascading combiner technique and will minimize the amount of data that needs to be passed from Mapper to Reducer. These Map side functions may even help limit the number of Reduce steps that are required. Remember that every `GroupBy` and `CoGroup` pipes will cause a MapReduce pair to be created.

> Take a look at the `cascading_ext` project on GitHib (`https://github.com/LiveRamp/cascading_ext`) and the `MultiCombiner` class. The code provides highly efficient multidimensional summaries. See *Chapter 9, Planning for Future Growth*, for more details.

- Always use Java's capabilities to your advantage. Java has many different classes that can be used, and many have differing performance characteristics. Understanding how you intend to use them in your custom operations will aid in overall performance.

  - ○ Reuse objects wherever possible and reduce the impact of garbage collection. Hadoop encourages the creation of reusable objects once, clearing them, and reusing them in Mappers and Reducers. In Cascading, this can be accomplished in the operation's `prepare()` method, and the reusable object can be saved in the `Context`. One such technique is to create a tuple once to generate output, and then use its `clear()` method before it is reused.

- The Java `Collections` classes are especially important. Use maps and lists efficiently. Use the correct types of these classes by understanding how inserts will be used. Consider `LinkedList` implementations, sorted implementations (`TreeSet`), priority queues, and so on.

- Manage the JVM through command-line parameters. Give it sufficient virtual memory and sensible expansion values.

- In Cascading, understanding the flow plan is essential. Generate and review the DOT files. Generate them in all modes—specifically Hadoop cluster-side. Visualize these DOT files. See *Chapter 6, Testing a Cascading Application*, for information about how to do this. Within the flow diagram, we will be able to see the segments that we will attempt to measure and optimize. We will look for parallel processes, and if they do not exist, we will consider creating them.

- Be aware of data-skewed joins. A data-skewed join is one where one of the datasets to be joined has many more of some keys than of others. Since joins are usually done in Reducers, the result will be that one or more Reducers will be much more heavily used than the others. In Hadoop, the longest running process determines that overall run time. If we know this skew exists in advance, we can take measures to minimize its impact. One way to do this would be to split the skewed file on the skewed keys using a Cascading filter and then to run the joins in parallel on the subsets.

- When joining, use memory optimization with a `HashJoin` if it is feasible. This is very important. It will be influenced by virtual machine memory settings, but if you can reasonably expect to load all of the data for one side of the join into memory, you can do a Map side join using this Cascading pipe type.

- Review every `CoGroup` and `GroupBy` since these pipes will lead to a Reducer being run, and the presence of a Reducer means that with its Mapper, this will form a full Hadoop job. So, every sequence of sequential (not parallel) pipe splits will run back to back Hadoop jobs, and they will be connected to each other through a file that will be persisted to disk! This read/write cycle takes time, and even starting a Hadoop job does too, so minimizing this will reduce your overall run time.

- Effective data partitioning can also be a useful technique. Hadoop will read all data that is in its input directory. Sometimes it is useful to partition this data by date range, or by some other business element (company, department, customer segment, geography, and so on). Then various Hadoop read schemes can be used to only process the data that you need to process. This can significantly reduce the amount of I/O required. Cascading has several tap types that can be used for this. One such is GlobHfs, which is a MultiSourceTap. It allows Hadoop HDFS resident files to be read using a Unix style "glob", or wildcard matching expression. This can be very useful if HDFS files are arranged in some sort of directory structure, maybe something such as year/month/date/*. To use this tap, just selective date ranges can be read. Here is an example of how to do this:

```
String inPath = "/invoices/2015/1q/*";
GlobHfssourceGlob = new GlobHfs(sourceTextLineScheme, inPath);
// Createa tap to read a resource from the HDFS glob
Tap sourceTap = new MultiSourceTap(sourceGlob);
```

> A Cascading MultiSourceTap is a tap that can be used to effectively treat multiple taps as a single tap. In other words, it is a sort of composite tap. All such taps must share a common scheme.

Optimizing Hadoop

Like Cascading, Hadoop performance and tuning too has some best practices. Here we are only going to discuss some of the things that you should consider. Hadoop contains hundreds of tuning parameters, so tuning is a very large topic.

Optimizing Hadoop comes in one of two ways. One is to modify the Hadoop system itself. This is done by making changes to the Hadoop conf files (see *Chapter 1, The Big Data Core Technology Stack*). This requires you to be a system administrator, or to know how to get one to do your bidding.

Another more commonly used technique is to modify settings just for your job or for a portion of your job. Let's look at this latter method in more detail. We must then first discuss how we get parameters to Hadoop from Cascading. Here is some code that shows how this is accomplished in our job that defines our Cascading workflow. We are using a Cascading class named cascading.flow.hadoop.util.HadoopUtil. This class contains many helpful method calls to manipulate the underlying Hadoop configuration from within a Cascading application:

```
// Create a Hadoop JobConf object
JobConf jobConf = new JobConf();
```

```
// Set some values on it
jobConf.setJobName("Jobtest");
// Allow speculative execution. Allows Hadoop to start new identical
tasks if
// started ones are running slowly!
jobConf.setSpeculativeExecution(true);
// Do some other setup
...
// Use HadoopUtil to create a properties map for us
Map<Object, Object> properties = HadoopUtil.createProperties(jobConf);
// Pass it to the Hadoop flow connector
FlowConnectorflowConnector = new HadoopFlowConnector(properties);
```

It is also possible to set specific properties just for a small section of the Hadoop job. Later we will take a look at many of the property names and values that you are likely to use. To do that, we set the property on just the affected pipe. Of course, you will need to understand what the pipe segment does in order to understand what you should and should not set. So, here is how to set a property in this manner:

```
pipe.getStepConfigDef().setProperty(property_name, property_value);
```

There are several reasons why we might want to modify the default behavior of Hadoop in this manner. We may want to change the number of Reducers that will be run as the result of a GroupBy or CoGroup. We may want to increase memory to our Mappers or Reducers. We may want to allow some more complex Hadoop features to become active, such as speculative execution. We may just want to change some log file settings too.

Now that we understand the mechanisms for doing so, let's discuss some basic rules that we should follow to optimize the performance of Hadoop:

- Manage your memory, both real and virtual. Try to use it efficiently for lookups, sorts, and so on. Increasing the amount of virtual memory to your task managing Java virtual machines provides additional storage for in-memory joins, larger buffer sizes (for instance with AggregateBy), and so on. Here are some options that can be used. These must be placed into your Hadoop configuration files (see *Chapter 1, The Big Data Core Technology Stack,* for more information):

```
<property>
<name>mapred.child.java.opts</name>
<value>-Xms1024M -Xmx2048M</value>
</property>
```

- Monitor and minimize data spills. A data spill occurs when a memory buffer becomes full and must be emptied to disk to allow space for more incoming data. Spills in Hadoop occur in two places: on the Mapper side when data is being accumulated to be sent to a Reducer, and on the Reducer side when the data arrives and must be sorted before it is given in aggregated form to the Reducer. Let's take a look at an abbreviated MapReduce log file so that we can see how to identify spills:

```
12/29/14 16:44:01 INFO input.FileInputFormat: Total input paths to
process : 2
12/29/14 16:44:01 INFO mapred.JobClient: Running job:
job_201412332103_0001
12/29/14 16:44:08 INFO mapred.JobClient:  map 0% reduce 0%
12/29/14 16:44:18 INFO mapred.JobClient:  map 40% reduce 10%
12/29/14 16:44:27 INFO mapred.JobClient:  map 60% reduce 20%
12/29/14 16:44:34 INFO mapred.JobClient:  map 80% reduce 30%
12/29/14 16:44:40 INFO mapred.JobClient:  map 100% reduce 70%
12/29/14 16:44:44 INFO mapred.JobClient:  map 100% reduce 100%
12/29/14 16:44:46 INFO mapred.JobClient: Job complete:
job_201412332103_0001
12/29/14 16:44:46 INFO mapred.JobClient: Counters: 17
12/29/14 16:44:46 INFO mapred.JobClient:   Job Counters
12/29/14 16:44:46 INFO mapred.JobClient:     Launched reduce
tasks=4
12/29/14 16:44:46 INFO mapred.JobClient:     Launched map tasks=4
12/29/14 16:44:46 INFO mapred.JobClient:     Data-local map
tasks=4
...
12/29/14 16:44:47 INFO mapred.JobClient:   FileSystemCounters
12/29/14 16:44:47 INFO mapred.JobClient:     FILE_BYTES_
READ=894120000
12/29/14 16:44:47 INFO mapred.JobClient:     HDFS_BYTES_
READ=372060000
12/29/14 16:44:47 INFO mapred.JobClient:     FILE_BYTES_
WRITTEN=373900000
12/29/14 16:44:47 INFO mapred.JobClient:     HDFS_BYTES_
WRITTEN=1647560000
12/29/14 16:44:47 INFO mapred.JobClient:   Map-Reduce Framework
...
12/29/14 16:44:47 INFO mapred.JobClient:     Map input
records=150124
...
12/29/14 16:44:47 INFO mapred.JobClient:     Reduce output
records=91235
12/29/14 16:44:47 INFO mapred.JobClient:     Spilled Records=1803
...
```

From this log, we can see the progress of our Mappers and Reducers. We see HDFS I/O information, and in bold, we see that 1,803 records were spilled to disk during the sort just before the Reducers were run.

The steps that need to be taken to reduce spills are relatively complex, but there are two properties that you need to understand:

- ○ `io.sort.mb`: This is the total buffer size allocated to sorting (the default is 100 MB)
- ○ `io.sort.spill.percent`: This is the portion of the buffer that, when it becomes full, means a spill will occur (the default is 75%)

Working in conjunction with the JVM memory parameters described earlier, increasing these values can reduce or eliminate many spills, thereby improving the performance of your jobs.

In Hadoop 2.0, these properties have been renamed as `mapreduce.task.io.sort.mb` and `mapreduce.map.sort.spill.percent` respectively.

- Reuse your JVMs. Every time a new Mapper or Reducer is started by Hadoop, a new JVM is launched. A JVM can take several seconds to initialize. There is a property named `mapred.job.reuse.jvm.num.tasks` that can be set to a number greater than 1 to cause the JVM to be "reset but not terminated and restarted," thereby reducing the initialization time. If this property is set to -1, the JVM will be reused as many times as possible. The example of setting this property to -1 is shown as follows:

```
<property>
<name>mapred.job.reuse.jvm.num.tasks</name>
<value>-1</value>
</property>
```

In Hadoop 2.0, this property has been renamed `mapreduce.job.jvm.numtasks`.

- Manage the number of Mappers relative to your input data by using the Hadoop `dfs.block.size` parameter. Remember that the number of Mappers run will be the total file size divided by this number. Block sizes can be increased globally, but can also be increased per file using the following command:

```
hadoop fs -D fs.local.block.size=<size> -put <local_file><hdfs_
file>
```

You can also set this programmatically within Cascading by using the technique described earlier. This will cause all output files to use this setting:

```
// Set the HDFS block size to 256 MB
properties.set("dfs.block.size", 256*1024*1024);
```

As of Hadoop 2.0, this property is now called `dfs.blocksize`.

It is actually preferable to increase the block size on a per pipe basis in Cascading. The block size change will then apply to the sink taps that are connected to the pipe. To do this, use code like the following:

```
// Set the HDFS block size to 256 MB
pipe.getStepConfigDef().setProperty("dfs.block.size",
256*1024*1024);
```

While it is difficult to figure out how long to set this, a good rule of thumb is to try get your Mappers to run for at least 3 minutes. This is a good amount of time that will make JVM startup time a small percentage of the overall execution time. Also, check out JVM reuse in the following points.

- Reducers can become a bottleneck when there are too few of them. We can increase parallelism by increasing the number of Reducers that will run out of a `GroupBy` or `CoGroup`. We would typically do this at the pipe level (that is, for a particular Map and Reduce pair) using a statement like this:

```
// Set the number of Reducers to 13
pipe.getStepConfigDef().setProperty("mapred.reduce.tasks", 13);
```

 We might be tempted to try and define a custom partitioner as well. This is currently no easy or intuitive way to do this. Cascading uses a hashed partitioner that uses the `hashCode` of the tuple as its standard partitioner for a group. You can modify the number of Reducers as shown earlier, and you could also generate a custom partitioning key to be used. We do not recommend doing this!

- Also in HDFS, if you find that you have files that are very heavily used, you can increase their replication factor. By default, each block of data written to HDFS is replicated three times. This number can be increased. To do this on a per file basis, use this command:

```
hadoopdfs -setrep -w replication_factorfile_path
```

This can also be changed globally (across all files or all files below a given directory), but be careful using this since it may dramatically increase the amount of disk space that you require. The `-R` parameter specifies that the command is to be applied recursively, and / indicates that it should start at the HDFS root directory:

```
hadoopdfs -setrep -R -w replication_factor /
```

A more typical command might be to simply change the replication factor for some data directory that you own. Say, for instance, that we had a 20-data-node cluster. Then, the following command would place all files in the HDFS `/user/mcovert/masterdata` directory on every node:

```
hadoopdfs -setrep -R -w 20 /user/mcovert/masterdata
```

- Where possible, compress your data. Data compression is specified using one of several codecs (coder-decoder) that perform various types of compression. Compressing data will reduce the amount of disk I/O that is required to read and write the data. However, like with all optimizations, this comes at an expense. If your cluster is heavily CPU bound (meaning that your slave nodes are running close to 100 percent CPU utilization), data compression will have less of an impact, and in some cases can actually make your jobs run slower. Remember that Hadoop will split your files into blocks and hand these blocks to your Mappers. Some compression schemes are non-splittable. What this means is that when certain compression algorithms are used, the only way to uncompress the file is to read it from beginning to end. In this case, Hadoop will hand the entire file to one Mapper or Reducer. If the file is large, this is probably not what you want to happen. In this case, either do not compress the file or switch to a compression algorithm that is splittable. Another option is to create many smaller compressed files rather than a single larger one. Hadoop will start a Mapper on each file, so the problem of single-threading through only one Mapper because a large file is non-splittably compressed is eliminated. Here is a short table describing some compression schemes and how they will work, relative to block splits:

Compression format	File extention	Is It Splittable?
gzip	gz	No
bzip2	bz2	Yes
LZO	lzo	Yes (if indexed using Hadoop LZO indexing tool)
Snappy	snappy	No

Compression formats and splittability

Here is an example command for how to use gzip compression:

```
hadoop jar myjar.jar                      \
  -Dmapred.output.compress=true \
  -Dmapred.compress.map.output=true \
  -Dmapred.output.compression.codec=org.apache.hadoop.io.compress.
GzipCodec \
  …
```

In Hadoop 2.6.0, the `mapred.output.compress` property is now called `mapreduce.output.fileoutputformat.compress`. The `mapred.compress.map.output` property is called `mapreduce.map.output.compress`.

- Consider more elaborate data storage formats. In many cases, you will just store your file as text, either tab or comma delimited. In some cases, when heavy parsing of this data is required, other formats will allow this parsing to occur much more efficiently. Consider using Avro, Thrift, Protobuf, SequenceFiles, ORCFiles, SerDe, or Parquet formats. These are binary formats and they can be de-serialized very efficiently. JSON is another encoding option. Avoid it unless the stored information is final and will be fed to a Web server. JSON encoding and decoding is very inefficient otherwise.

- Beware of custom Writables. It is best to stay away from them if you can. Remember that a Writable is a Hadoop custom class that can be very efficiently serialized and thereby transmitted between Mappers and Reducers. They generate data payload overhead since custom Writable information is kept in the record. If you must use them, use Hadoop tokens. Hadoop tokens allow efficient encoding of custom Writables by substituting a smaller amount of metadata in the payload (a key), which is then mapped back to the actual Writable information (type, length, and so on) that is stored in the `conf/core-site.xml` file. These keys are numeric values, and the values chosen must be greater than 128. Another thing to note here is that with Cascading, many times custom Writables just aren't needed. Tuples are quite flexible and a tuple field can contain another tuple, so it is pretty easy to create composite objects that will satisfy your data needs without having to resort to custom Writables at all!

- We again mention the Concurrent Driven product. It is multipurpose and can help diagnose and tune both Cascading and Hadoop. There is a developer-only free version of this product, and there is also a larger commercial version that must be purchased. See *Chapter 6, Testing a Cascading Application*, and *Chapter 9, Planning for Future Growth*, for more information.

- Another open source product that we will mention here is called **Vaiyda**. It is an Apache open source post-processing system that can be used to identify common performance problems that occur within MapReduce jobs. It processes the output of MapReduce log files and applies a set of rules to produce various recommendations for tuning options. It is relatively easy to set up and use, and it can also be extended with custom rules. It can be found at `http://hadoop.apache.org/docs/r1.2.1/vaidya.html`.

A note about the effective use of checkpoints

Checkpoints can be used very effectively to prevent long-running workflows that encounter errors from having to restart and reprocess all data from the beginning. Typically, checkpoints are placed after complicated steps (joins, complex calculations, or even in some cases transformations that may involve database I/O). But with checkpoints, there are some things that you need to know that may help you make them work correctly.

Restarting a checkpoint requires that the first downstream pipe be aware of the format of the checkpoint file, which will serve as its source tap. So, while you should actually do this anyway, if you do insert a checkpoint, supply the full list of field names to the user of the checkpoint.

Another thing to note is that since the checkpoint will be serialized to disk, it is a good idea to make it fast, and since it is really a temporary file anyway (but see *Chapter 6, Testing a Cascading Application*, for more information!), a `SequenceFile` is a good choice to use. Let's look at how to do this:

```
importcascading.scheme.hadoop.SequenceFile;
…

// Define the Fields that the Checkpoint will persist and build the
Tap
Fields checkpointFields = new Fields( … );
Scheme seqScheme = new SequenceFile(checkpointFields);
Tap    checkpointTap = new Hfs(seqScheme, path);
…

// Begin processing
Pipe pipe = new Pipe("main");
…

Checkpoint checkpoint = new Checkpoint("checkpoint1", pipe);
…

// Resume processing after the checkpoint, but supply the fields
Pipe nextPipe = new Each(checkpoint, checkpointFields, …);
FlowDefflowDef = new FlowDef()
            …
                .addCheckpoint(checkpoint, checkpointTap);
```

Summary

In this chapter, you learned some useful techniques to tune a Cascading workflow. We discussed what to look at when determining performance characteristics. We looked at many best practices that can be considered when improving the performance of a Cascading application. You also learned how to make performance changes to the underlying Hadoop system when Cascading is running on this platform. We discussed how to effectively use checkpoints to help with processing time when failures occur. And finally, we looked at several tools that can help us to diagnose the performance issues of a Cascading application.

In the next chapter, we will finally put everything that you have learned so far together and create a real-world Cascading application. This application will be fully-featured. We will build a **natural language processing (NLP)** application that will process free form text files, and extract various forms of information from them using OpenNLP software. In this application, we will utilize some sophisticated machine learning algorithms. In doing so, we will also outline a comprehensive methodology that can be used to design, develop, test, and extend a Cascading application.

8
Creating a Real-world Application in Cascading

Now it is time to take everything we learned and create a real-world application in Cascading. We will use a practical case study, which could be easily adapted to a functional component of a larger system within the reader's organization. This case study uses techniques of **text analytics** (**TA**) and **natural language processing** (**NLP**). We will start with a brief introduction to the basic concepts and show you how to design and develop a domain-specific Cascading project. The reader will utilize all the knowledge acquired in the previous chapters and learn how to apply it to a specific situation.

Project description – Business Intelligence case study on monitoring the competition

It is imperative for any organization to monitor their competition in order to stay on top of its game. Thankfully, there is a plethora of open source information, both structured and unstructured, that can be easily obtained from the Web and other publically available sources. When the sources are narrowed down by the topic of interest, finding specific organizations, people, and products mentioned in these sources will enhance Business Intelligence results.

Let's say that we are an organization specializing in chemical products. Having a collection of trade literature, we would like to know what our competition is doing. This involves following competing organizations, their products, and people who are "influencers" in an industry. The goals of this project are as follows:

- Finding mentions of all organizations in the collection of trade literature
- We also want to identify the "movers and the shakers" in the industry, that is, people who are mentioned in this document collection
- We want to identify all the chemical products mentioned in this trade literature collection
- The frequency of the mentions of these entities throughout the document collection signifies their importance, so we want to count how many times specific people, organizations, and chemical products are mentioned throughout our trade literature collection
- Finally, we would like to discern the relationships among people, organizations, and chemical products
- This will be a Hadoop project, so our inputs and outputs will reside in HDFS, and we will running this project on a Hadoop cluster

In this project, we will deal with the text documents already collected and preformatted for the consumption of this project. We will have these two files:

- A very large file that contains document names and texts (similar to the example of the *Writing a buffer* section of *Chapter 4*, *Creating Custom Operations*)
- A list or a dictionary of chemical products of interest

You may be wondering how we are going to glean people's names and organization names without a list? The answer to this is: we will utilize the OpenNLP functionality to extract named entities (people's names and organization names, in our case) without a list, and we will learn how to integrate this functionality with Cascading in the Hadoop mode.

 OpenNLP is an Apache open source project that performs a variety of natural language processing tasks, such as sentence parsing, word tokenization, and part-of-speech tagging.

The other question you may ask is "How do we determine relationships among entities?" We will use a simple method: if two or more entities occur within a sentence, we will assume that they are related.

In the next section, we will decompose the project and guide you step by step through the Cascading architecture and implementation of this project.

 Please note that the Eclipse workspace with fully functional project code for this application for both local and Hadoop modes, as well as the sample data files and necessary instructions, can be downloaded from this book's website.

Project scope – understanding requirements

Just like most real-life situations, this project consists of both structured and unstructured data. Unstructured and semi-structured data are media articles, press releases, trade literature, blog posts, tweets, and so on. Unstructured files can arrive to a researcher in the form of text, PDF, Word, HTML, and many other formats. Structured data is usually delimiter-separated (most often comma-separated, such as CSV, or tab-separated, such as TSV) text files with or without a header. These structured files can be used by Cascading as they are, but unstructured data needs preprocessing.

The steps that we used to pre-pre-process our unstructured data are:

1. First convert unstructured files of different formats into text. You can write your own utility to do this, or you can download it from the Web. In this book, we will not provide a conversion utility, since it is outside our scope.

2. Then normalize the unstructured data. For this project, after we've converted our data files into text, we created a large structured file that contains the document name and the document text, as follows:

```
Name   Text
Doc1   Text inside of doc1.It can have many sentences.
Doc2   Text inside of doc2.It can be very long.
...    ...
DocXX  It can have many documents
```

Hadoop renders itself for processing very large files like this one.

 Sometimes, it would be more practical to use indexing, such as Lucene indexing, and work against an index file. While this is outside the scope of this book, many of the techniques that we will demonstrate can be adapted to create such search indexes.

Understanding the project domain – text analytics and natural language processing (NLP)

Since we are using unstructured text, we are going to touch on text analytics and natural language processing – just enough to accomplish our task. In a nutshell, text analytics is the art and the science of making sense of text by extracting some qualitative data (such as the concepts that are mentioned), and quantitative measures, such as how often and when something was mentioned. Natural language processing is "how" we do it. On the simplest level, we break text into sentences and words, and we use dictionaries and machine learning to discern specific entities, such as organizations, proper names, locations, dates, and so on.

We've already discussed sentence extraction and tokenization in *Chapter 4, Creating Custom Operations*. We've also learned how to use a dictionary to find abbreviations. A similar method will be applied to the list of chemicals.

What happens, however, if we do not know the names of the people that may appear in our document collection in advance? We could try to utilize a very large list of possible first names, and an even larger list of possible last names, but this would be incredibly inefficient and inaccurate. It is close to impossible to get a name combination correctly (last-first-middle, first only, last only), especially if they are foreign or unusual. This is where specialized natural language libraries, which utilize machine learning to find proper names (and other named entities, such as the names of organizations), come into play. We have not yet discussed how to extract these entities without using dictionaries. In the next section, we will talk about a simple named entity extraction using another Apache open source project – OpenNLP. Later in the chapter, we will show you how to integrate OpenNLP into a Cascading application.

Conducting a simple named entity extraction

A **Named entity** is a word a phrase that identifies something or someone by a specific name. For example, the name of an organization, such as ACME, Inc., is a named entity. The name of a person, such as John Smith, is a named entity as well, as is the name of a chemical compound, such as carbon dioxide.

From the previous chapters, we know how to break text into sentences, "correct" sentences with ambiguous punctuation, and break a sentence into tokens (or words). Having tokens allows us to use dictionary extraction, that is, compare tokens to dictionary entries, to glean specific words out of the text stream. The following diagram outlines this process through the lens of Cascading processing. Here, you see the processing steps, inputs and outputs, interim steps, and necessary operations.

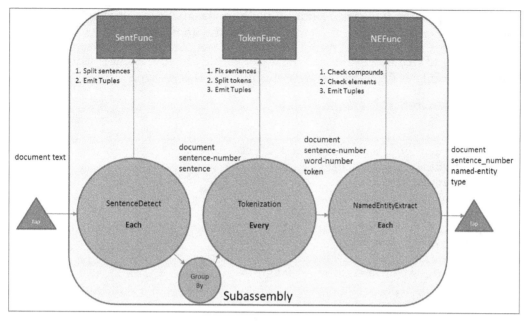

Figure 8.1 – A parsing subassembly

Everything in this diagram has been covered in the previous chapters, except how to integrate the OpenNLP components into a Cascading project.

OpenNLP supplies trained machine learning models that are used to find a named entity—in our case, this includes a person and an organization's name in a stream of tokens.

> Machine learning is the outgrowth of artificial intelligence. It is a set of algorithms that are capable of learning from the data that they are given. This learning comes in the form of a "model", which is then applied to new data to predict some aspect of it (in this case, whether it is a name, address, and so on.)

The following code shows how to load such a model from a local filesystem. A model is a binary file:

```
//Person
InputStreammodelInPerson = new
  FileInputStream("models/en-ner-person.bin");
TokenNameFinderModelmodelPerson = new
  TokenNameFinderModel(modelInPerson);
//modelInPerson.close();
```

In the Hadoop mode, however, loading a file from the HDFS is a little bit more complicated. For one, the file name will be prefixed with hdfs:.

We are going to create a customized file loading utility to address the loading of files from either local or HDFS. The code for this utility is shown here:

```
public class Utilities
{
  /**
    * Return an InputStream from a file name
    * @paramfileName - name of file
    * @return InputStream
    * @throws IOException
    */
  public static InputStreamgetInputStream(String fileName)
    throws IOException
  {
    if (fileName.startsWith("hdfs:"))
    {
      Path pt=new Path(fileName);
      FileSystem fs = FileSystem.get(new Configuration());
      return fs.open(pt);
    }
    return new FileInputStream(fileName);
  }
  ...
}
```

So, loading a model from an HDFS will use the following code:

```
// get proper HDFS   path
String pathPrefix = "hdfs:/user/" +
  System.getProperty("user.name") + "/";

// load the mode, assuming the model is in the HDFS directory
  "models"
InputStreammodelInPerson = Utilities.getInputStream(pathPrefix +
  "models/en-ner-person.bin");
```

After loading the OpenNLP model, extracting named entities is simple, as shown in the following code. All we need is an array of tokens (words) to pick the named entities (such as a person's names) out of String[] tokens and our trained person detection modelPerson model:

```
TokenNameFindernameFinder = new NameFinderME(modelPerson);

Span nameSpans[] = nameFinder.find(tokens);
```

```
for (Span span: nameSpans) {
  String name = "";
  for (inti=span.getStart(); i<span.getEnd(); ++i)
    name +=" "+ tokens[i];
  // Get and print people's names
  System.out.println ("Name="+name.trim());
  // Do something else with these names
  ...

}
```

In order for this code to work, the following classes must be included:

```
import opennlp.tools.namefind.*;
import opennlp.tools.tokenize.*;
import opennlp.tools.util.*;
```

Defining the project – the Cascading development methodology

Now, let's dive into the full development methodology. We will talk about composing your team, analyzing your data and problem set, and also how to decompose the problem set in a way that will make developing a solution in Cascading straightforward and understandable.

Project roles and responsibilities

Here are the roles of projects and their key responsibilities:

- The process owner is a person who is sees the "big picture". This person understands the ultimate purpose of the application, the inputs required, and the outputs that need to be produced. He or she is the **subject matter expert (SME)** in the underlying domain of the application. In effect, this person is more of an analyst than a technician, although some knowledge of the underlying operating system and HDFS is important. He or she runs an application on a given cluster either on a command line, using a prepackaged Java JAR file compiled against the Apache Hadoop and Cascading libraries, or through a customized user interface.

- The process architect is a person who assembles Cascading data, processing workflows into Cascades and consequently into applications. This person is a Cascading developer, but also has strong system administrative skills, and is well versed in the Hadoop framework. He or she communicates with the process owner in order to understand the requirements of the system and the application goals. The process architect describes to the workflow developer the "building blocks" of the application: the subassemblies and workflows that need to be implemented.

- The workflow developer is a person who creates individual operations, reusable subassemblies, as well as workflows that act on a specific set of data. This person is usually a string Cascading and Java developer who is capable of not only developing in Cascading, but also integrating external components into a lower-level Cascading "building block".

- Finally, there is often a need for one or more external "utility" Java developers who can create Java (non-Cascading) domain-specific (such as NLP) classes that are used in Cascading operations.

In this chapter, we will assume all of these roles.

Conducting data analysis

This step in the beginning of the project is the job of the **process owner**. The process owner knows what inputs and outputs are expected. He or she examines the incoming data, looking for what can be extracted from it, and what possible errors or pitfalls this data can hold. He or she, knowing what the requirements of the project are, proposes the output content and format for the project.

Performing functional decomposition

The process of the architect is to be a "middleman" between the project requirements and the ultimate final product. It is their job to break down the project into functional components.

The following diagram shows a possible functional decomposition of our project.

1. We start with sentence extraction (through the `Each` pipe).
2. Then we break every sentence into tokens (through the `Each` pipe).
3. Next, we group results by document and sentence number (through the `GroupBy` pipe) so that we can extract named entities.

4. Now we are ready to extract people's names, organizations, and chemical compounds (through the `Every` pipe).

> Since we are performing several similar but independent tasks based on the same input, could we run these tasks in parallel?

5. The output from a named entity extraction process (such as the `Each` pipe) becomes an input for a relationship finder task and named entity counts (such as the `GroupBy` and `Every` pipe). These tasks are independent of each other, so they can be run in parallel.

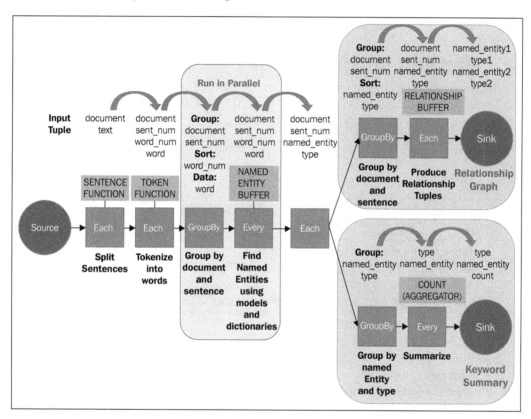

Figure 8.2 – A possible functional decomposition of a project

Please keep in mind that it may take several iterations to come up with an optimal Cascading project design. The preceding diagram shows us the initial step—the straightforward design project to get from point A to point B. Having done this, we want to optimize our process. Remember, we are dealing with big data, and we want to make our application fast and efficient.

Designing the process and components

Now, after we've designed the high-level process, we need to assess which lower-level components will do the job. In this section, we are going to put on the "Workflow developer" hat.

We need to consider which operations—such as functions, buffers, filters, aggregators, or assertions—will be most appropriate for each stage of the process. We also need to consider which pipe assemblies can be reused in multiple areas of the project so that we can create subassemblies. In order to make the application robust, we need to discern which tasks do not depend on each other and, thus, can run in parallel. Ultimately, we need to design flows and integrate them into a cascade for utmost efficiency, while taking advantage of the underlying big data framework.

Creating and integrating the operations

Having an understanding of the project domain as well as the overall picture of the application functionality, we are now ready to look at the necessary Cascading operations.

These are the steps to create operations in our project:

1. You may remember from *Chapter 4, Creating Custom Operations* that we created a function to break text into sentences. We also created a buffer to break sentences into tokens and to fix sentences with incorrect punctuation.

2. Having sentences and tokens ready for "consumption", we are going to extract named entities. Named entities are explained in the preceding section, and the code shows how to use OpenNLP to do it. Hypothetically, an external utility Java developer will create a non-Cascading class for us to extract named entities from a single array of tokens as shown previously.

3. Code reuse is important for a modular, well-functioning product, so we are going to create an operation that could be used to extract any named entity (it could be in the form of people, organizations, chemicals, or anything else, depending on a dictionary or an OpenNLP model). Along with the named entities, we need to keep track of the document it came from, and the sentence number within this document where the named entity occurred. The best fit for this operation is a buffer, because it can process multiple tuples at a time and return any number of resultant tuples.

4. The code for the `NameBuffer` is as follows. Here are all the imports necessary for this buffer:

```
import java.io.IOException;
import java.util.ArrayList;
```

```
import java.util.HashSet;
import java.util.Iterator;
import java.util.List;
import opennlp.tools.namefind.TokenNameFinderModel;
import cascading.flow.FlowProcess;
import cascading.operation.BaseOperation;
import cascading.operation.Buffer;
import cascading.operation.BufferCall;
import cascading.operation.OperationCall;
import cascading.tuple.Fields;
import cascading.tuple.Tuple;
import cascading.tuple.TupleEntry;
```

5. The following code shows the properties of the `NameBuffer` class. We declared input and output tuple fields. Since we are using both dictionaries and trained NLP models, we are going to have a `isDict` Boolean property to tell us if we are using a dictionary to extract named entities or an OpenNLP model. We also have the name of the `String modelName` OpenNLP model, and the type of entity we are extracting is the `String` type. If we are using a dictionary, then `isDict` is true, and `modelName` becomes the dictionary name. You may have noticed that we have allocated similar properties in `Context`:

```java
public class NameBuffer<Context> extends
  BaseOperation<NameBuffer.Context> implements
  Buffer<NameBuffer.Context>
{
  static Fields fieldInput = new Fields(
    "documentname","sentnumber", "wordnum", "word");
  static Fields fieldOutput = new Fields(
    "documentname","sentnumber", "word","type");
  String modelName="";
  Boolean isDict=false;
  String type="";

  public class Context
  {
    TokenNameFinderModel model=null;
    HashSet<String> dictionary=null;
    String modelName ="";
    Boolean isDict=false;
    String type="";
  }
```

6. Now we are able to pass these parameters via the class constructor and store them in the Context object in the prepare method. We load dictionaries and/or OpenNLP models (depending on the setting of the isDict property) and store them in the Context object as well. Finally, we write the cleanup method to empty the Context object at the end of the process:

```
public NameBuffer(String model, Boolean dict) {
   super(4, fieldOutput);
   modelName=model;
   isDict=dict;
   type="unknown";
}


public NameBuffer(String model, Boolean dict, String
   entityType) {
   super(4, fieldOutput);
   modelName=model;
   isDict=dict;
   type= entityType;
}


@Override
public void prepare (FlowProcess flowProcess,
   OperationCall<NameBuffer.Context>bufferCall)
{

   bufferCall.setContext(newNameBuffer.Context());
   Context context = bufferCall.getContext();
   context.modelName=modelName;
   context.type=type;
   context.isDict=isDict;
   if (context.isDict==false)
   {
      try {
         context.model =
            Utilities.getNamedEntityModel(context.modelName);
         System.out.println("Model loaded");
      } catch (IOException e) {
         // TODO Auto-generated catch block
         e.printStackTrace();
      }
   }
   else
   {
```

```
      try {
        context.dictionary =
          Utilities.getDictionary(context.modelName);
        System.out.println("Dictionary loaded");
      } catch (Exception  e) {
        // TODO Auto-generated catch block
        e.printStackTrace();
      }
    }
  }
  public void cleanup(FlowProcessflowProcess,
    BufferCall<NameBuffer.Context>bufferCall)
  {
    bufferCall.setContext(null);
  }
```

7. Finally, the following code shows the `operate()` method. We will use our low-lever utility to extract named entities based on an OpenNLP model or a dictionary. The resultant tuples will include a document name, sentence number, named entity, and the type of named entity (that is, a person, organization, chemical, and so on):

```
public void operate( FlowProcessflowProcess,
  BufferCall<NameBuffer.Context>bufferCall )
{
  TupleEntry group = bufferCall.getGroup();
  List<NamedEntity> NamedEntityArr= new
    ArrayList<NamedEntity>() ;
  //get all the current argument values for this grouping
  Iterator<TupleEntry> arguments =
    bufferCall.getArgumentsIterator();

  // create a Tuple to hold our result values
  Tuple result = Tuple.size(4);
  Context context = bufferCall.getContext();
  List<String>tokenList= newArrayList<String>() ;

  while( arguments.hasNext() )
  {
    Tuple tuple = arguments.next().getTuple();
    tokenList.add( tuple.getString(3));
  }
  String[] tokens = new String[tokenList.size()];
  tokens = tokenList.toArray(tokens);
```

```
if (context.isDict==false)
{
  try {
    NamedEntityArr =
      Utilities.detectNamedEntity(context.model,
      tokens,group.getString("documentname"),
      context.type);
  } catch (IOException e) {
    e.printStackTrace();
  }
}
else
{
  try {
    NamedEntityArr =
      Utilities.detectDictionary(context.dictionary,
      tokens,group.getString("documentname"),
      context.type);
  } catch (IOException e) {
    e.printStackTrace();
  }
}
for (inti = 0; i<NamedEntityArr.size(); i++)
{
  result.set(0, group.getString("documentname"));
  result.set(1, group.getString("sentnumber"));
  result.set(2, NamedEntityArr.get(i).getName());
  result.set(3, NamedEntityArr.get(i).getType());
  // Return the result Tuple
  bufferCall.getOutputCollector().add( result );
}
  }
}
```

8. Another task for our project is to find relationships among the named entities in our dataset. As you may recall, if two or more named entities occur in the same sentence, they are assumed to be related. Our input tuples will consist of a document name, sentence number, named entity, and the type of named entity (that is, a person, organization, chemical, and so on):

Here is the output produced by the named entity extraction. For the output tuples, we have a document name, sentence number, and a pair of related named entities with their types. We will output a tuple with this format for each named entity within a sentence. For example, if in Doc1, we had Bob works at Concurrent, and so does Chris., the output tuples will look similar to this:

```
Doc1, 1, Bob, person, Concurrent, organization
Doc1, 1, Bob, person, Chris, person
Doc1, 1, Concurrent, organization, Chris, person
```

In other words, all possible relationships will be taken into account.

For this, we need another buffer, since we are processing groups of tuples (grouped by a document name and sentence number) in time.

9. The following code for RelationshipBuffer is shown in its entirety. Since we are only passing tuples and not any external parameters, this is a much simpler buffer that does not need a Context object or a prepare method:

```java
public class relationship Buffer<Context> extends
  BaseOperation<Context> implements Buffer<Context>
  {
    static Fields fieldOutput = new
      Fields("documentname","sentnumber",
      "word1","type1","word2","type2");
    static Fields fieldDeclaration = new Fields(
      "documentname","sentnumber", "word", "type");

    public RelationshipBuffer() {
      super(4, fieldOutput);
    }

    public void operate( FlowProcessflowProcess,
      BufferCallbufferCall )
    {
      TupleEntry group = bufferCall.getGroup();
      //get all the current argument values for this
        grouping
      Iterator<TupleEntry> arguments =
        bufferCall.getArgumentsIterator();
      //create a Tuple to hold our result values and set
        its document name field
      Tuple result = Tuple.size(6);
      ArrayList<NamedEntity> entities = new ArrayList<>();
      intname_count = 0;
      while( arguments.hasNext() )
```

```
      {
        Tuple tuple = arguments.next().getTuple();
        NamedEntitytempEntity = new NamedEntity();
        tempEntity.setName(tuple.getString(2));
        tempEntity.setType(tuple.getString(3));
        tempEntity.setDoc(tuple.getString(0));
        entities.add(tempEntity);
        name_count++;
      }
      for (int i=0;i<name_count;i++)
        for (int j=i+1; j<name_count; j++)
        {
          // document name
          result.set(0, group.getString(0));
          // sentence number
          result.set(1, group.getString(1));
          // head of relationship entity
          result.set(2, entities.get(i).getName());
          // type
          result.set(3, entities.get(i).getType());
          // other relationship entity
          result.set(4, entities.get(j).getName());
          // other type
          result.set(5, entities.get(j).getType());
          // Add result
          bufferCall.getOutputCollector().add( result );
        }
      }
    }
  }
}
}
```

Creating and using subassemblies

As we mentioned earlier, code reuse and abstraction are very important for a
Cascading project. Subassemblies are great building blocks on a Cascading project.
They are used in several cases:

- When a functional block requires several operations

- When a functional block can be reused within different flows or cascades

- To abstract a functional block — that is, if the same functional block can be
  rewritten without affecting the rest of the flow

For our project, we will build subassemblies for all these reasons.

The first subassembly we will build is BasicNLPSubassembly. It will include our sentence function and token buffer. Breaking documents into sentences and tokens is the first step of any project that deals with the processing of unstructured text. So, the subassembly we are building could be reused in different projects. Also, our BasicNLPSubassembly is using our simple sentence and token operations based on our simple utility classes. It is possible to create more sophisticated sentence and token operations using OpenNLP classes, as well as further refine them with the usage of stop lists.

A **stop list** is the list of words that are filtered out before or after the processing of natural language text. Usually, these words are just common words, such as "a", "an", "the", and so on, which are not needed for the NLP project. Sometimes, these are domain-specific words, such as certain names, which are not of importance to the project.

Thus, as long as this subassembly takes the same inputs and produces the same outputs, it could be rewritten at some point without affecting the rest of the processes that include it.

Here is the BasicNLPSubassembly code in its entirety:

```
Public class BasicNLPSubAssembly extends SubAssembly {
  Public Basic NLP SubAssembly (Pipe headPipe)
  {
    headPipe = new Each(headPipe, new SentFunc());
    headPipe = new GroupBy(headPipe, new Fields("document"), new
      Fields("sentnum"));
    headPipe = new Every(headPipe, new TokenBuffer(),
      Fields.RESULTS);
    setTails(headPipe);
  }
}
```

All we did is create an Each pipe that has sentence extraction applied to it, grouped it by the document and sentence number, and passed it to the Every pipe, which has a tokenizer applied to it.

Our next subassembly will deal with named entity extraction. We already have
`NameBuffer`, which we would like to use to extract people, organizations, and
chemicals. The logical way would be to run these tasks in parallel, as shown on the
following diagram—that is, group the incoming stream by the document and sentence,
sort it by the word number, and then split it into the `Every` pipe for each named entity.
Ultimately, we would like to merge the resultant pipes into a single stream.

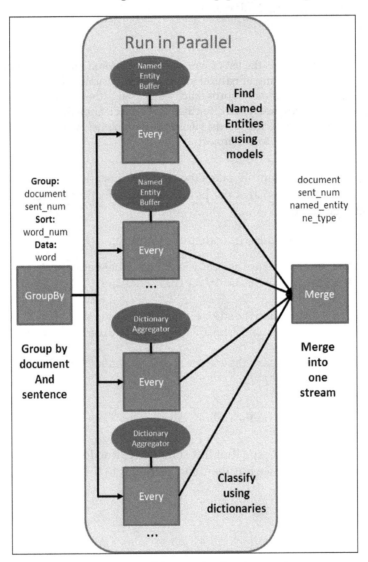

Figure 8.3 – Parallel processing done incorrectly

Unfortunately, this will not work! You will get an "Every instances may not split
after a `GroupBy` or `CoGroup` pipe." error message

Chaining buffers is not technically possible. If we look closer under the hood into the MapReduce layer, we will see why. The primary reason for this is that, in MapReduce, the `GroupBy` sort and the `Every` reducer are inextricably intertwined. They both run within a single JVM instance on the same `TaskTracker` node. So, splitting `GroupBy` cannot be done unless the sort itself could be made into a separate unit of work. Additionally, a buffer does some internal assembly, essentially creating the iterator that is used through `BufferCall`, and this also makes chaining them difficult.

A better way to do it is to create three identical `GroupBy` pipes for people, organizations, and chemicals, and then apply `NameBuffer` with different extraction types to the three `Every` pipes. Unfortunately, this is a bit inefficient, but that is something that we will just have to live with, and the fact that we are running everything in parallel makes it a little more palatable.

Here is the corrected diagram of this subassembly:

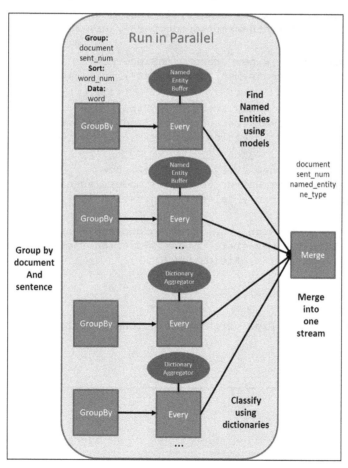

Figure 8.4 - Parallel processing done correctly

The code to demonstrate the NamedEntityExtractor subassembly (in local mode) is shown here:

```
public class NamedEntityExtractor extends SubAssembly
{
  public NamedEntityExtractor (Pipe inPipe)
  {
    Fields fieldDeclarationOutputInterim = new Fields(
      "documentname","sentnumber","wordnum", "word");

    Fields fieldDeclarationOutput = new Fields(
      "documentname","sentnumber","word","type");

    Pipe groupPipe1 = new GroupBy(inPipe, new
      Fields("documentname","sentnumber"), new Fields("wordnum"));

    Pipe groupPipe2 = new GroupBy(inPipe, new
      Fields("documentname","sentnumber"), new Fields("wordnum"));

    Pipe groupPipe3 = new GroupBy(inPipe, new
      Fields("documentname","sentnumber"), new Fields("wordnum"));

    Pipe peoplePipe = new Every(groupPipe1, new
      NameBuffer<NameBuffer.Context>("models/en-ner-person.bin",
      false,"person"), Fields.RESULTS);

    Pipe orgPipe = new Every(groupPipe2, new
      NameBuffer<NameBuffer.Context>("models/en-ner-
      organization.bin", false,"organization"), Fields.RESULTS);

    Pipe dictionaryPipe = new Every(groupPipe3, new
      NameBuffer<NameBuffer.Context>("dictionaries/chemicals.csv",
      true,"chemical"), Fields.RESULTS);

    setPrevious(inPipe);

    setTails(peoplePipe, orgPipe, dictionaryPipe);
  }
}
```

Note that this is a split subassemby, and we are producing three resultant pipes. Also, note the setPrevious() call. If you do not use it, you will get a warning message that says "setTails, previous pipes not set via setPrevious() or constructor". The setPrevious(pipe) method allows the current subassembly to become the parent of any pipe instances between the previous pipe and the tails. If setPrevious() is set incorrectly, anything that would act on the pipe assembly represented by this subassembly will be incorrect.

Once again, this subassembly can be reused for different processes or modified without affecting the existing process.

Our final custom subassembly is the one used to extract relationships from the stream of named entities, grouped by document name and sentence number. We have already created RelationshipBuffer, so all we need to do is to group the incoming stream by document name and sentence number, and apply RelationshipBuffer to the Every grouping. The code to do it is shown as follows:

```
public class RelationshipExtractor extends SubAssembly {
  public RelationshipExtractor (Pipe relPipe){
    relPipe = new GroupBy(relPipe, new Fields("documentname",
      "sentnumber"));
    relPipe = new Every(relPipe, new RelationshipBuffer(),
      Fields.RESULTS);
    setTails(relPipe);
  }
}
```

One of the tasks of our project is to count named entities. For this, we will use Cascading's built-in assembly, CountBy. We will be counting named entities that come in a tuple stream, consisting of a document name, sentence number, named entity (word), and named entity type (type). This is the code to do it:

```
Pipe countPipe = new Pipe("CountPipe");
countPipe = new CountBy(countPipe, new Fields("word", "type"),
  new Fields("count"));
```

Now we have completed designing processes and components for our project, and it is time to build the workflow.

Building the workflow

We are finished with the components of our workflow, and are assuming the role of the process architect. Keeping in mind the high-level task given to us by our process owner, and also our functional decomposition diagram, we are going to assemble the workflow for this project using flows then and assemble them into a cascade.

There is more, however, to building the workflow. We also need to come up with an efficient test plan for the project and, since we are developing in a local mode, we need to port it to a Hadoop cluster. Here is an in-depth decomposition of our project:

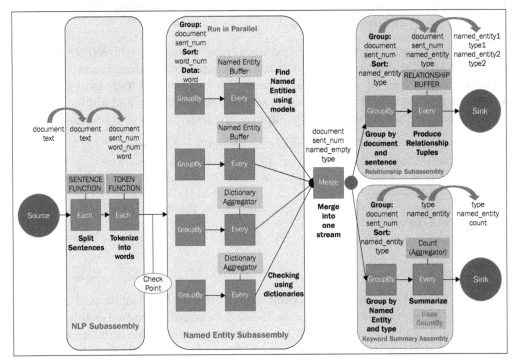

Figure 8.5 - Final project decomposition

Building flows

The following steps describe the process of creating flows for both sequential and parallel processing of the tasks within our project.

1. There is no need for us to save tokenized text as an individual output, but we do want to save extracted named entities with a corresponding document name and sentence number. So, our first flow will include two subassemblies: the basic NLP subassembly (`BasicNLPSubAssembly`), which will feed the named entity subassembly (`NamedEntityExtractor`).

You may recall that the `NamedEntityExtractor` subassembly returns three "tails", that is, three pipes structured identically but with different data: one contains people, the other contains organizations, and the last contains chemicals. We need to merge these pipes into a single pipe for the output file and for use by other processes. Here is a simple diagram of the named entities flow:

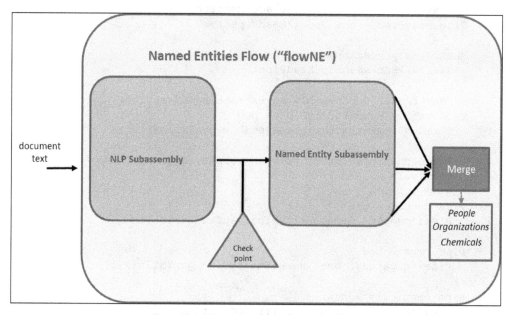

Figure 8.6 – Extraction flow of named entities

 You may have noticed a **Checkpoint** on our diagram. The checkpoint is inserted here for debugging and refining purposes, and we will discuss it shortly.

2. This code shows how the flow is created. Please note that `<inputFileName>` and `<namedEntityFile>` are the file names provided by the user:

```
Fields fieldDeclarationInput = new
  Fields("document", "text");

Scheme inputScheme = new
  TextDelimited(fieldDeclarationInput, true,"\t");

Fields fieldDeclarationOutput = new
  Fields("documentname","sentnumber", "word","type");
```

```
Scheme outputScheme = new
  TextDelimited(fieldDeclarationOutput, true,"\t");
Tap docTap = new FileTap(inputScheme, <inputFileName>);

Tap finalOutTap = new FileTap(outputScheme,
  <namedEntityFile>, SinkMode.REPLACE);

// Basic subassembly to extract sentences and tokenize text
Pipe headPipe = new Pipe("HeadPipe");

SubAssembly headAssembly = new
  BasicNLPSubAssembly(headPipe);

// our custom SubAssembly to extract named entities
SubAssembly namedEntityPipe = new
  NamedEntityExtractor(headAssembly.getTails()[0]);

// grab the split branches with People, Organizations and
  Chemicals

Pipe people = new
  Pipe("people",namedEntityPipe.getTails()[0]);

Pipe orgs = new
  Pipe("organizations",namedEntityPipe.getTails()[1]);

Pipe chemicals = new
  Pipe("chemicals",namedEntityPipe.getTails()[2]);

// Merge into a single pipe
Pipe inPipe = new Pipe("NamePipe");
inPipe = new Merge(people, orgs, chemicals);

// Create the named entities flow in local mode for now

Flow flowNamedEntities = new
  LocalFlowConnector().connect("flowNE",docTap,finalOutTap,
  inPipe);
```

3. The relationship flow feeds on the output from the named entity extraction flow. It uses our custom relationship subassembly (RelationshipExtractor). The code for this pipe is shown here. Please note that the user provides outputRelationshipFile:

```
/* Flow to extract relationships
 * Relationship pipe feeds on the output by document name
 * and sentence number*/
```

```
Fields fieldDeclarationRelationships = new
  Fields("documentname",   "sentnumber", "word1",
  "type1","word2", "type2");

Scheme relScheme = new
  TextDelimited(fieldDeclarationRelationships, true, "\t");

Tap relOutTap = new
  FileTap(relScheme,<outputRelationshipFile>,
  SinkMode.REPLACE);

Pipe relPipe = new Pipe("RelationshipPipe");

SubAssembly relAssembly =
  newRelationshipExtractor(relPipe);

FlowDef flowREL = new FlowDef().setName("flowREL")
  .addSource(relPipe, finalOutTap)
  .addTailSink(relAssembly.getTails()[0],relOutTap);

Flow flowRelationships = new
  LocalFlowConnector().connect(flowREL);
```

It is possible to examine the execution of the flow by adding this line of code to create a DOT file, and then using a visualizer such as graphviz to see the phases of mapper and reducer:

```
flowRelationships.writeDOT( "data/rel.dot" );
```

4. The named entity count flow also feeds on the output from the named entity extraction flow. Here, we just going to use CountBy as described in the preceding section about components. The code for the flow will look similar to this:

```
Fields fieldDeclarationCountOutput = new Fields("word",
  "type", "count");

Scheme countScheme = new
  TextDelimited(fieldDeclarationCountOutput, true, "\t");

Tap countOutTap = newFileTap(countScheme,
  <outputtCountFile>, SinkMode.REPLACE);

// CountBy code here
. . .
FlowDefflowCNT = new FlowDef().setName("flowCount")
.addSource(countPipe, finalOutTap)
```

```
        .addTailSink(countPipe, countOutTap);

    Flow flowCounts = new
        LocalFlowConnector().connect(flowCNT);
```

Before we embark on connecting these flows into a cascade, a few words have to be said about managing a context within flows and cascades.

Managing the context

The `Context` object is just a class that is instantiated by an operation that is attached to a pipe. It is then passed to each operation call where it can store state information. In most cases, this `Context` object will simply hold a tuple where we store temporary results before emitting them. However, in our `NameBuffer`, there is one nuance that we must discuss.

The context for this buffer looks similar to this:

```
    public class Context
    {
        TokenNameFinderModel model=null;
        HashSet<String> dictionary=null;
        String modelName ="";
        Boolean isDict=false;
        String type="";
    }
```

This `Context` object holds a lot of information. The `NameBuffer` buffer is used for multiple purposes, since it extracts multiple different types of named entities. Therefore, it will require either a named `TokenNameFinderModel` entity or a "dictionary." In the first case, the model is a binary file that will be loaded from HDFS and will contain the information that will be used to find named entities. In the second case, `HashSet<String>` will be loaded with a text file, which is also stored in HDFS, and it will contain words that we wish to check for. For instance, our dictionary text file might contain chemical elements, anger words, profanity, and so on that, when found, would indicate some special type of word that we wish to know about.

We saw before that we usually declare our context as static. In this case, since the same class, `NameBuffer`, will be used many times with the `Each` pipe being passed a different file name and type, we cannot declare it as static. Doing so would cause the buffer instances to interfere with each other, since only one such context would be created across all classes.

So, to accomplish all of this, we omit the static keyword on the Context class definition, pass NameBuffer a parameter on its constructor, telling it whether it is to use a model or a dictionary, and then we use the prepare() method to load the specified file and store it in the context.

Building the cascade

Finally, our flows are built, and we can put them together into a robust cascade. Both the process owner and the process architect will come together for this task. You may recall from the previous chapters that the Cascading planner will execute some flows sequentially and in parallel, according to whether these flows depend on each other or not. In our project, the **Named Entities** flow will be executed first, because other flows depend on its output. The **Relationship Flow** and **Named Entity Count** flows will be executed in parallel, because they do not depend on each other. This diagram shows the cascade for our project in its entirety:

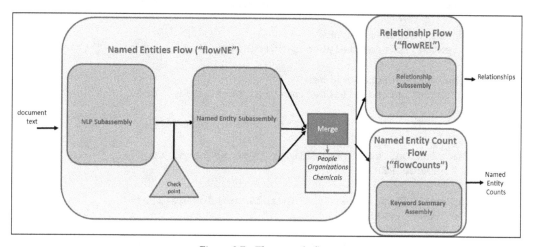

Figure 8.7 – The cascade flow

The following code shows the main method for the job that runs the entire project, including linking all of the flows into a cascade. We are going to set FlowSkipStrategy to skip a flow if the sink tap created by this flow already exists. This code is shown in the local mode:

```
public class Chapter8JobLocal {
    // args[0] - initial data file, args[1] - named entity output,
    // args[2] - relationship output, args[3] -count output

    public static void main(String[] args) {
        // TODO Auto-generated method stub
        Fields fieldDeclarationInput = new Fields("document", "text");
```

```
      Fields fieldDeclarationOutputInterim = new
        Fields("documentname", "sentnumber", "wordnum", "word");

      Fields fieldDeclarationOutput = new Fields("documentname",
        "sentnumber", "word", "type");

      Fields fieldDeclarationRelationships = new
        Fields("documentname",  "sentnumber", "word1", "type1",
        "word2", "type2");

      Fields fieldDeclarationCountOutput = new Fields("word",
        "type", "count");

      Scheme inputScheme = new TextDelimited(fieldDeclarationInput,
        true,"\t");

      Scheme outputScheme = new
        TextDelimited(fieldDeclarationOutput, true,"\t");

      Scheme relScheme = new
        TextDelimited(fieldDeclarationRelationships, true, "\t");

      Scheme countScheme = new
        TextDelimited(fieldDeclarationCountOutput, true, "\t");

      Tap docTap = new FileTap(inputScheme, args[0]);

      Tap finalOutTap = new FileTap(outputScheme, args[1],
        SinkMode.REPLACE);

      Tap relOutTap = new FileTap(relScheme, args[2],
        SinkMode.REPLACE);

      Tap countOutTap = new FileTap(countScheme, args[3],
        SinkMode.REPLACE);

      // Basic sub assembly to extract sentences and tokenize text
      Pipe headPipe = new Pipe("HeadPipe");

      SubAssembly headAssembly = new BasicNLPSubAssembly(headPipe);

      // Checkpoint code, described later, would go here

      // our custom Named Entity  Extraction SubAssembly
      SubAssembly namedEntityPipe = new
        NamedEntityExtractor(headAssembly.getTails()[0]);
```

```
// grab the split branches - People, Organizations and
   Chemicals
Pipe people = new Pipe("people",
   namedEntityPipe.getTails()[0]);

Pipe orgs = new Pipe("organizations",
   namedEntityPipe.getTails()[1]);

Pipe chemicals = new
   Pipe("chemicals",namedEntityPipe.getTails()[2]);

// Merge pipes
Pipe inPipe = new Pipe("NamePipe");
inPipe = new Merge(people, orgs, chemicals);

// Flow to extract named entities
Flow flowNamedEntities = new
   LocalFlowConnector().connect("flowNE", docTap,finalOutTap,
   inPipe);

/* Flow to extract relationships
 * Relationship pipe feeds on the output by
 *   document name and sentence number
 */
Pipe relPipe = new Pipe("RelationshipPipe");
SubAssembly relAssembly = new RelationshipExtractor(relPipe);

FlowDef flowREL = new FlowDef().setName("flowREL")
.addSource(relPipe, finalOutTap)
.addTailSink(relAssembly.getTails()[0], relOutTap);

Flow flowRelationships = new
   LocalFlowConnector().connect(flowREL);

// Create dot file
Flow Relationships.writeDOT( "data/rel.dot" );

// Flow to count named entities
Pipe countPipe = new Pipe("CountPipe");
countPipe = new Each(countPipe, new Debug());
countPipe = new CountBy(countPipe, new Fields("word",
   "type"),new Fields("count"));

FlowDef flowCNT = newFlowDef().setName("flowCount")
.addSource(countPipe, finalOutTap)
.addTailSink(countPipe, countOutTap);
```

```
Flow flowCounts = new LocalFlowConnector().connect(flowCNT);

CascadeConnector connector = new CascadeConnector();
Cascade cascade = connector.connect( flowNamedEntities,
  flowRelationships, flowCounts );

cascade.setFlowSkipStrategy(new FlowSkipIfSinkExists());
cascade.complete();
    }
  }
```

Now that the cascade is designed and coded, let's take a quick look at the DOT file that it produces. Note that a cascade itself also implements with the `writeDOT()` method.

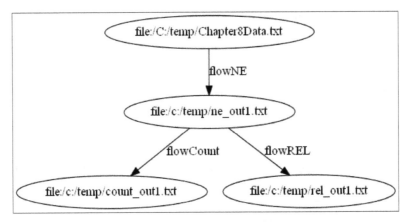

Figure 8.8 – A cascade DOT file

Designing the test plan

Efficient testing is an often overlooked, but an enormously important, part of any application development, especially in Cascading development. Therefore, we are going to define a very simple test plan for our application. It will consist of a set of one or more unit tests and an integration test. The unit test will perform a calculation using each of our custom operations. Our integration test will perform an end-to-end test on our subassemblies.

> See the description of the Plunger project in the next chapter. This is a testing framework from Hotels.com that is getting a lot of attention right now.

Performing a unit test

Let's start with a unit test. Creating unit tests is part of the job of any developer, workflow, or utility. For conciseness, we will just test our `SentFunc()`. To perform this test, we create our `CascadingTestCase`, and define a method that is annotated with the JUnit `@Test` decorator. In this method, we will construct some data as `Tuple` and `TupleEntry` and then we will use the `invokeFunction()` call to perform it. Lastly, we will use an assertion to make sure that it performed as we expected. Here is the code to do all of this:

```
package com.ai.learning.test;
import static org.junit.Assert.*;
import org.junit.Test;
import com.ai.learning.SentFunc;
import cascading.CascadingTestCase;
import cascading.tuple.Fields;
import cascading.tuple.Tuple;
import cascading.tuple.TupleEntry;
import cascading.tuple.TupleListCollector;

/**
 * Define a JUnit function test case
 */
public class UnitFuncTest extends CascadingTestCase {

  @Test
  public void testSentenceFunction()
  {
    // SentFunc expects two fields
    Fields fields = new Fields("document", "text");

    // Define the data
    Tuple values = new Tuple("doc", "This is a test.
      There are two sentences.");

    // Create the TupleEntry
    TupleEntrytupleEntry = new TupleEntry(fields, values);

    // Invoke the function
    TupleListCollector tuples = invokeFunction(new SentFunc(),
      tupleEntry, new Fields( "document","sentnum", "sentence"));

    // Make sure that it returns two Tuples
    assertEquals( 2, tuples.size());
  }
}
```

If this function performs as we expect, and is run within Eclipse, we will see this output:

Figure 8.9 – A successful unit test

Note from the upper left-hand corner, where the list of tests that were run by JUnit appears, that this test is marked as successful.

> It is a common practice to group all our unit tests into a single class in this manner, each annotated with `@Test`. In this case, Eclipse can run all these tests in a single invocation. To do this, right-click on the class name and select **Run As -> JUnit Test**.

Performing an integration test

Now let's define an integration test. Integration tests are generally constructed by process architects. To do this, we will use the same basic technique, but we will start with our base job, which runs the entire workflow. We will start by creating a file of known test data. It will look similar to this:

```
document,text
doc1,There is one sentences with the name Winston Churchill.
```

We will then use our basic code, but will add some code at the end of the merge pipe to perform this assertion test:

```
inPipe = new Merge(people, orgs, chemicals);

inPipe = new Each(inPipe, AssertionLevel.STRICT, new
  AssertSizeEquals(4));

inPipe = new Each(inPipe, AssertionLevel.STRICT, new
  AssertEquals("doc1", 1L, "Winston Churchill", "person"));
```

We will also check out count pipe output as well. Here is the code to be added after the CountBy statement:

```
countPipe = new Each(countPipe, AssertionLevel.STRICT, new
AssertSizeEquals(3));

countPipe = new Each(countPipe, AssertionLevel.STRICT, new
  AssertEquals("Winston Churchill", "person", 1L));
```

We can follow a similar pattern and test the output of each subassembly, or even of each pipe, if we so desire. After determining all the places that we wish to test, we can run our entire flow and then check the contents of our output after making certain that the noAssertion we coded failed and, therefore, did not pass its validity check.

These assertions could also then be turned on and off using the assertion control that we discussed in *Chapter 6, Testing a Cascading Application*.

The next set of tests is usually performed by a specialized testing group. These tests look at the performance of the application and the system as a whole.

Performing a cluster test

Lastly, we mention that we then wish to do a cluster (MapReduce) test as well. In order to do this, we must move from the local mode to the Hadoop mode. We saw how to do this in *Chapter 5, Code Reuse and Integration*. We replace the FileTap instances with Hfs instances. We replace our LocalFlowConnector with a HadoopFlowConnector. Remember that import statements will need to be edited as well! Then, we submit the job to the cluster and use the same assertions and other techniques to test the result.

Performing a full load test

The last test in our plan will be a full load test to determine performance. In order to do this, we need a large amount of data. Many open source datasets do exist, but one may also want to use some sort of data generator. Many data generators also exist, but generating valid sentences is relatively difficult. One may want to find a set of proper names and generate very simple sentences in large volumes. The software download has a small file that you can use for this purpose. See the *Appendix, Downloadable Software* to this book for more information.

Refining and adjusting

When the cascade is created and the application produces the desired results, it is time to refine and adjust the process. For instance, the process owner, or whoever did the data analysis, should look for ways to streamline and tighten up the output. Here are some ways that we can do that:

- Is there meaningless data in the output? If so, maybe a Cascading filter operation should be used for any stage of the process, where some unnecessary data can be eliminated. For example, a custom filter operation described in *Chapter 4, Creating Custom Operations* could be modified to filter out words based on a stop list.

- Are there more assertions that could be added to detect changes that may occur in the future?

- Is there further parallelization that could occur? Always look for ways to take full advantage of your cluster!

- Should a checkpoint be added? Look for places where failures may occur. Protect your job by making it restartable if failure is likely. In our project, we insert a checkpoint between the NLP subassembly and the named entity subassembly. These two processes interact without an intermediate persistent tap; so, if the named entity subassembly fails and we want to rerun the job, we will have to restart the job, rerunning the named entity subassembly. If we have a checkpoint there, however, we will not need to rerun the named entity subassembly, because its results will be stored in a temporary location created by the checkpoint. In our example, the code will go after creating `BasicNLPSubAssembly` and look like this:

```
// Checkpoint code
Checkpoint checkpoint = new Checkpoint("checkpoint", headAssembly.
getTails()[0]);
```

The checkpoint will only work in Hadoop mode. We attach this checkpoint pipe to the first tail pipe produced by the subassembly. Should flow step skipping be enabled? If there are files that are reused, this may be advisable since it may be possible to eliminate entire process steps. In our example, we are skipping flows that create intermediate files, if these files exist.

Software packaging and delivery to the cluster

As you have seen, we created and tested our project code in the local mode for expedited development, testing, and debugging. The full power of Cascading, however, is only utilized when our program is running in the Hadoop mode. So, after we are done testing and debugging in the local mode, we are going to move our project to the Hadoop cluster. Several things are required to make all of this work:

1. We need to remember to move our data files and any other support files into the HDFS. So, our NLP model files and dictionaries must be placed into HDFS. Alternately, a distributed cache could be used but, since it is likely that these files will be reused, we recommend placing them at a known HDFS file location.

   Many people create a well defined directory structure by application, but also using a common location to hold shared files. It is likely that, in the application we have developed, the model and dictionary files will be used by many jobs, so this is a good idea here.

2. As we discussed in *Chapter 4, Creating Custom Operations*, we need to initialize application properties, and let Hadoop know which JAR file to use:

   ```
   Properties properties = new Properties();
   AppProps.setApplicationJarClass( properties, OurProject.class );
   ```

3. Also, as we discussed in *Putting it all together* section of *Chapter 2, Cascading Basics in Detail* before, we need to conduct the following replacements (and use the correct syntax to include application properties):

   1. Replace all local flow connectors with Hadoop connectors and make sure to use `import cascading.flow.hadoop.HadoopFlowConnector`.

   2. Replace local taps with `Hfs` taps, and make sure to import the correct class, such as `import cascading.tap.hadoop.Hfs`.

   3. Replace local imports for your schemes with Hadoop imports, such as `import cascading.scheme.hadoop.TextDelimited`.

4. A fat JAR must be generated with all of the required libraries. See *Chapter 5, Code Reuse and Integration,* for details on how to generate a fat JAR file. The libraries that we used to make this application run are shown in this screenshot:

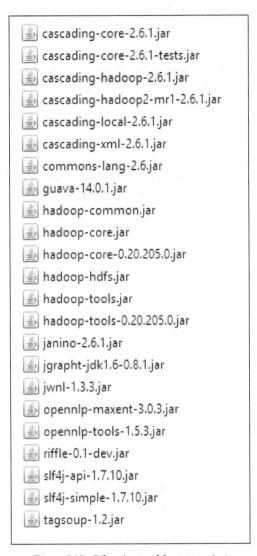

Figure 8.10 – Libraries used for our project

Note that the Hortonworks distribution contains Cascading so, in this environment, inclusion of these JAR files is not required.

5. The job must be parameterized to pass the required information, which mainly consist of file locations, to the operations. In our case, these parameters are our text input file and three text output files. To make the application more flexible, you can also modify the `NamedEntityExtractor` subassembly and pass the NLP model file names as parameters.

6. After this, the job can be run using the Hadoop command. It will look similar to this:

```
hadoop jar chapter8.jar com.ai.LearningCascading.jobs.
Chapter8HadoopJob data/Chapter8Data.txt data/ne_out1.txt data/rel_
out1.txt  data/count_out1.txt
```

 See *Chapter 5, Code Reuse and Integration*, for more details

The complete source code for this application in both Local and Hadoop modes is available for download.

Next steps

We just completed a relatively simple NLP application using Cascading. As we saw through the example code in this chapter, Cascading is the perfect fit for "pipeline processing" (pun intended) of large volumes of unstructured text. Considering that Cascading is optimized for big data and parallel processing, we are in the unique position of being able to improve the area of text analytics by several orders of magnitude. Using Cascading on top of Hadoop, we are addressing the issues of volume, speed, veracity, and complexity of text analytics.

Take a look at the following diagram, which covers most of the domain of text analytics. With Cascading, we implemented the subassemblies with * in their names with elegance and ease. However, we are only scratching the surface. The other components of the art and science of NLP and text analytics are shown in the diagram. Using the methodology we described in this chapter, all we really need is NLP/TA domain expertise to implement the rest of the text analytics suite. Now, quick and accurate knowledge discovery over large volumes of data is within our reach.

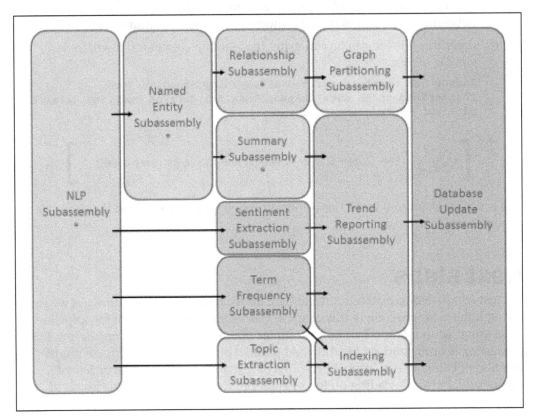

Figure 3.11 – A project follow up

Summary

In this chapter, we learned how to conduct project functional decomposition, data analysis, and design process, specifically targeting big data/Cascading implementation, as well as how to design and develop components in the Cascading API. Having acquired knowledge of every aspect of Cascading design and development, we were able to develop a fully functional and reusable application to satisfy the requirements of a specific use case based on text analytics and NLP.

While developing this application, we learned how to integrate external Java libraries and frameworks into a fully functional Cascading application. We also learned various options for file storage, specifically HDFS versus local files, for data needed by the integrated software. We also addressed the roles and responsibilities of the project team.

Remember our brewery at the beginning of this book? Now we understand the works of the intricate pipe networks and what makes a "delicious beverage" out of a "gray liquid". In fact, we just built a Cascading "brewery" of sorts ourselves! Now, we have fulfilled our project goals. We can maybe enjoy some of our delicious beverage!

However, we are not going to stop here. In the next chapter, you will learn about the future of Cascading as well where to find many other resources that give us the power to tame big data! We will take a look at many other sites where you can get more information, places where additional software can be downloaded, and also a walk through the rich Cascading ecosystem of tools that have been created.

Planning for Future Growth

9

This chapter provides information that will allow you to continue to advance your skills. Here we will help you locate additional sources of information, explore other tools that are available, and provide forward-looking information concerning the future direction that Cascading will take.

Cascading is now in a period of expansion, and new libraries and products are emerging very quickly that facilitate integration with a variety of big data, machine learning, data management, and advanced analytics systems. It is important to get connected with this online world and to stay abreast of these new developments. The world of open source is supported by thousands of developers and testers, and becoming attuned to the places where people post their utilities and libraries can save you a lot of time by not having to "reinvent the wheel."

Finding online resources

Online resources exist, but they are sparse. There is of course a full JavaDoc online at `http://docs.concurrentinc.com/cascading/<version>/javadoc/cascading-core/`. Concurrent maintains a pretty full set of JavaDocs for each version. Currently 2.6 is the most recent, but 3.0 is coming soon!

There is also a user's guide online. This can be found at `http://docs.cascading.org/cascading/<version>/userguide/html/`. There is a six-part quick start tutorial that is located at `http://docs.cascading.org/tutorials/etl-log/`. There is a six-part tutorial that is also quite good called *Cascading for the Impatient* at `http://docs.cascading.org/impatient/` and in general, a good location for other Cascading references and documentation is `http://www.cascading.org/documentation/`.

All code is available on GitHub and can be found at `https://github.com/Cascading`. Start here. There is a lot here that will help you. In fact, in some cases it is a good idea to simply download the Cascading project (or import its POM file in Maven) and to run this code out of your favorite debugger. Actually seeing what Cascading is doing under the covers can help you become much more familiar with all that it can do for you, and also helps you better understand the myriad of constructors and method call formats that are available to you.

In a project called CascadingSDK (`https://github.com/Cascading/CascadingSDK`), there is a unit test suite that can be very valuable to examine since it contains tried and true methods for many Cascading tasks.

Conjars (`http://www.conjars.org`) is a JAR file repository hosted by Concurrent, Inc. (`http://www.concurrentinc.com/`) that is full of open source downloadable JAR files that can be very useful. The Conjars repository contains Java interfaces that allow Cascading jobs to access HBase, Pentaho, Storm, several different SQL databases, Twitter's Elephant Bird libraries, and much more. You can also join Conjars and place your own developed libraries here to share with others.

LiveRamp has another very interesting set of open source Cascading extensions available on GitHub (`https://github.com/LiveRamp/cascading_ext`). These extensions are performance-oriented and provide bloom filters and `BloomJoin` to perform high speed joins — a very useful `MultiCombiner` that allows multiple aggregations to occur with a single pass through data (that is, using a single Mapper), and also has several utility classes that aid in debugging complex workflows.

 A bloom filter is an algorithm created by Burton Bloom in 1970. It tests for the presence of an element in a hash map. It is a very efficient algorithm and can speed up hash joins by an order of magnitude in some cases. It gains efficiency by reducing the memory requirement by reducing the number of elements that must be storied in the map by only storing hashed values, not the values themselves. By doing so, it does allow false positives (indicating that an element is present in the hash map when it is not), but never indicates a false negative (indicating that the element is not present when it really is).

The Plunger project on GitHub provides a Cascading-specific testing framework developed by people from `Hotels.com`. It is gaining traction. It can be found at `https://github.com/HotelsDotCom/plunger`. And lastly, see `http://www.cascading.org/projects/cascading/` as another starting point. There are many links to other sources of information here, and it is updated frequently with new developments.

Using other Cascading tools

The Cascading ecosphere is expanding rapidly and there are many toolsets and extensions that can help you with common tasks. Let's take a look at a few of them. Many of these are available for download from the previous URLs.

Lingual

Lingual is a Cascading framework tool that allows ANSI standard SQL queries to be used to create, transform, and move data. Lingual is based on the Apache Calcite framework (formerly known as **Optiq**). Essentially, using Lingual, one can write complex workflows as SQL commands, and then they are translated into Cascading flows, taps, and so on. Since Cascading interoperates with Hadoop, this allows ingestion and storage of Hadoop resident data through this programming paradigm.

This use pattern is very similar to Hive. However, Lingual is Cascading-specific and can therefore interoperate with Cascalog, Scalding, and Java. One other advantage over Hive is that using Cascading as an insulating layer, these programs will be able to more quickly migrate to Tez, Spark, and whatever comes next.

 Cascalog and Scalding are Clojure and Scala implementations of Cascading.

Like Hive, Lingual uses a catalogue where any file can be represented as a SQL table (that is, with column names, column data types, and so on). These tables are then accessible by Cascading taps and schemes. By defining a SQL statement, a `SQLPlanner` class can be used to generate a Cascading flow that can perform the query and route it through the designated source and sink taps. In other words, a Cascading flow will be produced that will perform the requested SQL operation.

Here is an example of using Lingual to create and run a Cascading flow that is based on a SQL statement:

```
/* Create a SQL statement to join contacts with employees based on a
name */
String sql = "select *\n"
+ "from \"dbo.contacts\" as c\n"
+ "join \"dbo.employees\" as e\n"
+ "on e.\"EMPNAME\" = s.\"NAME\"";

/* Define input and output taps. All taps will be treated as tables.
*/
    Tap employeeTap = new FileTap(new SQLTypedTextDelimited( ",", "\""
),"employees.csv", SinkMode.KEEP);
```

```
    Tap contactTap = new FileTap(new SQLTypedTextDelimited( ",", "\""
),
      "contacts.csv", SinkMode.KEEP);
    Tap outputTap = new FileTap(new SQLTypedTextDelimited( ",", "\""
),"dbo.contact_employees.csv", SinkMode.REPLACE);

    /* Use the fluent interface to define the flow */
    FlowDef flowDef = FlowDef.flowDef()
      .setName("contact employee")
      .addSource("dbo.employees", employeeTap)
      .addSource("dbo.contacts", contactTap)
      .addSink("dbo.contact_employees", outputTap);

/* Use the SQLPlanner to build the plan and add it to the flow
definition */
    SQLPlanner sqlPlanner = new SQLPlanner().setSql(sql);
    flowDef.addAssemblyPlanner(sqlPlanner);

    /* Connect and run as usual */
    Flow flow = new LocalFlowConnector().connect(flowDef);
    flow.complete();
```

Pattern

Pattern is a very powerful tool that allows **Predictive Modelling Markup Language (PMML)** to be used to generate machine learning Cascading jobs. PMML is an XML dialect that allows one to specify predictive modelling processes.

Machine learning is a science that derives from data mining and artificial intelligence. Machine learning systems predict future events based on analysis of input data. For more information, refer to *Machine Learning with R* by Brett Lantz, *Scala for Machine Learning* by Patrick R. Nicolas, and *Mastering Machine Learning with scikit-learn* by Gavin Hackeling, all by Packt Publishing. There are several other books that you can refer to as well.

A predictive model consists of the following things:

- **Features**: These are data values on which the prediction will be made
- **Targets**: These are the data values that we seek to predict
- **Algorithms**: These are the machine learning functions that will be used to make the predictions

As a brief example, we may have a set data consisting of temperature, precipitation, relative humidity, longitude and latitude, and time of day. We may desire to predict the likelihood that it will rain tomorrow. In this case, the former values are features, and the probability of rain is a target. The target will have a predicted value ranging between 0.0 (no chance of rain) and 1.0 (absolutely certain that it will rain). We could use a variety of algorithms such as logistic regression, k-means clustering, and so on, to make this prediction.

Using Pattern, you can write a predictive model program in XML (not a program in the normal sense, but a set of directives that describe the model, its parameters, algorithms, and so on), supply the data, build a model, and start making predictions. The PMML program is translated into a Cascading flow for each step.

One other advantage of Pattern is that by using PMML, it is possible to obtain interoperability with other systems that also use it. One common use case is to develop the model in a language such as R, and then to export this as PMML and run it in a big data environment (that is, Cascading running on Hadoop).

PMML model definition files can be quite complex, so we will not include examples here. See the previous book references above and also the Data Mining Group website (http://www.dmg.org/) for more information. There are also several good videos and tutorials at http://www.cascading.org/projects/pattern/.

Currently, Pattern supports hierarchical clustering, k-means clustering, linear regression, logistic regression, and random forest algorithms.

Driven

Driven, developed by Concurrent, Inc., is an application performance management tool that minimizes operational risk and saves time in diagnosing complex problems. While the use of Driven to develop and deploy Cascading applications is optional, it provides significant benefits for developers and operators. We briefly mentioned Driven in *Chapter 7, Optimizing the Performance of a Cascading Application*, as one very useful solution for Cascading system tuning and optimization.

To implement business solutions, data workflows typically execute a series of processes that may or may not use the same framework. In order to track business-level SLAs, the developers and the operators need to visualize and track how the workflow executes from start to finish. Cascading uses a query planner to develop an execution plan and identify dependencies between different data flows. With the information from Cascading's query planner, Driven correlates the real-time progress and execution status from each of the tasks to provide end-to-end, application-level visibility. The following screenshot shows how Driven enables operators and system architects to get end-to-end, application-level visibility:

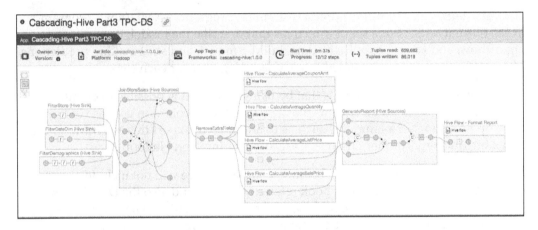

In addition, Driven collects operational metrics at the task level and rolls it up to provide instrumentation details at a flow level. This graphical representation helps the developer to identify flows that require attention for performance tuning. Driven renders these metrics in detail without acquiring extra code to print them to be placed in your Cascading application.

Finally, Driven allows the developer to drill down and see how his/her application generated native calls into the compute fabric (for example, Mapper and Reducer calls). This becomes helpful to see if particular tasks became bottlenecks in the overall application performance. The view also identifies other important issues related to poor data layout, environment issues, or bad application logic.

Driven collects metrics from the granular task level to flow to the application level. By aggregating the counters of interest and rolling them to the application level, Driven answers questions about CPU and storage consumption (also useful for capacity planning and optimizing cluster use).

IT organizations often must track applications by different segments based on the needs identified by governance policies. Segments can be based on clusters (production, development, ad hoc), organizations (marketing, fraud), use cases, or other factors. Depending on how the applications are segmented, IT organizations need to develop chargeback models, create audit artifacts for regulatory needs, or track application behavior over a period of time. Driven lets you visualize application performance based on segments defined through teams or through customizable Cascading tags.

Timely identification of application stakeholders to resolve production issues is vital for operators. Driven surfaces application errors, avoiding the need for operators to log in to the cluster and make log files available to the developers for analysis, saving valuable time and avoiding unnecessary interruptions for operations staff. Since applications execute on the Hadoop cluster as machine accounts, it is usually not possible for operations staff to tell which developers own the applications that require attention, causing a loss of valuable time when applications fail to meet their SLAs. With Driven, it is possible to create collaboration workspaces with teams, and track applications within the context of the team. As a result, when applications fail to meet SLA terms, Driven can help notify the appropriate stakeholders with the right context for the application behavior.

More information about Driven can be found at:

- **Driven documentation**: http://cascading.io/driven/documentation/
- **Screencasts**: http://cascading.io/driven/features/

Fluid

Fluid is an open source Fluent interface for Cascading. Fluid supplies an interface for almost all Cascading functions, and makes programming in Cascading more understandable and straightforward. For instance, Fluid interface allows a concise definition of various operation types, and allows them to be attached to pipes easily. Pipes can be split and joined, create assemblies, and so on.

Here is a simple example of using the Fluid interface for a simple word counter:

```
Tap source = new FileTap( new TextLine( new Fields( "offset", "line" )
), "input.txt" );
Tap sink = new FileTap( new TextLine( new Fields( "offset", "line" )
), " output.txt", SinkMode.REPLACE );

AssemblyBuilder.Start assembly = assembly();
```

```
        Pipe pipe = assembly
          .startBranch( "simple" )
            .each( fields( "line" ) )
              .function(
                function()
  .RegexParser()
  .fieldDeclaration( fields( "line" ) )
  .patternString( "[ ]+" )
  .end()
                )
            .outgoing( fields( "word" ) )
            .groupBy( fields( "word" ) )
  .every( Fields.ALL )
  .aggregator(
  aggregator().Count( fields( "count" ) )
  )
  .outgoing( fields( "word", "count" ) )
  .completeGroupBy()
  .completeBranch();

  Flow flow = new LocalFlowConnector().connect( source, sink, pipe );
```

Note how the entire sequence of actions is specified as a sort of inline program. Note also how functions and aggregators ae explicitly defined.

See `http://www.cascading.org/fluid/` and `https://github.com/Cascading/fluid` for more information.

Load

Load is an easy-to-use command-line interface that allows extensive testing and load generation processes to be run against a Cascading implementation (usually a Hadoop cluster). Using this tool, you can easily create test jobs to generate random data of any size and many formats, block sizes, files sizes, to specify the number of Mappers and Reducers, to run joins, multijoins, sorts, compares, functions, aggregations, and so on. Additionally, many Hadoop-specific parameters can be specified. Load can be very useful to create test baselines and then doing performance comparisons for modifications. It can also be useful to simply determine capacity limits that exist within clusters. See, `http://www.cascading.org/load/` for more information.

Multitool

Multitool is a general-purpose command-line interface to quickly generate Cascading jobs. It is very full-featured, but is generally only used to prototype jobs. It was designed primarily to be able to run some very common UNIX-style commands that are typically chained together to perform tasks, such as `sed`, `awk`, `grep`, `cut`, `join`, `cat`, `sort`, and a few others. For instance, to simply run a `grep` command against some Hadoop resident document files, all you need to do is run:

```
multitool source=hdfs:/data/documents select=Tuesday sink=hdfs:/
results/out.txt
```

For more information, see `http://cascadingorg.wpengine.com/multitool/` and also follow the links on this page to the GitHub site.

Support for other languages

Cascading has now been ported and can be used by many other programming languages. These other products represent language specific implementations that implement the basic Cascading paradigms of pipes, taps, schemes, operations, and so on. The following screenshot shows Cascading language support:

Programming Language	Project Name	Description of Project
Clojure	Cascalog	Clojure
Java	Cascading	Concurrent Cascading
JRuby	Cascading.JRuby	From Etsy, JRuby
PMML	Pattern	Concurrent PMML
	JPMML-Cascading	Openscoring PMML
Python	PyCascading	Twitter Python
Scala	Scalding	Twitter Scala
SQL	Lingual	Concurrent ANSI SQL shell and JDBC driver

Hortonworks

Hortonworks has now fully integrated Cascading into their **Hortonworks Data Platform (HDP)** product. This means that the Cascading libraries are now natively part of the Hadoop cluster, so much of the packaging work (Fatjar, Maven, Gradle, Ant, and so on) that we had to do is not required. Hortonworks also has a lot of information available about using Cascading. For more information, see the following links:

- `http://hortonworks.com/hadoop-tutorial/cascading-hortonworks-data-platform-2-1/`
- `http://hortonworks.com/hadoop-tutorial/cascading-pattern/`

- `http://hortonworks.com/hadoop-tutorial/cascading-log-parsing/`
- `http://hortonworks.com/blog/cascading-hadoop-big-data-whatever/`

And lastly, since Cascading 3.0 is almost here, the Apache Tez offering (originally developed by Hortonworks) will quickly become the preferred method of creating even higher performing Cascading applications. See `http://hortonworks.com/blog/cascading-on-apache-tez/` for more information.

Custom taps

Cascading can also connect to many data sources and sinks using custom developed taps. These projects allow Cascading to access a wide variety of other data source. Most significant are many of the interfaces to NoSQL databases, which can be used to access indexed data in a very scalable way. The following screenshot shows Cascading data sources:

Data Source	Project Name	Description of Project
Accumulo	Cascading.Accumulo	Accumulo data source
Cassandra	Cascading-Cassandra	Cassandra data source
Derby	Cascading-JDBC	Derby data source via JDBC
Elasticsearch	elasticsearch-hadoop	Elasticsearch data source
ElephantDB	ElephantDB	ElephantDB data source
H2	Cascading-JDBC	H2 data source via JDBC
HBase	Cascading.HBase	HBase data source
Hive	Cascading-Hive	Hive HQL
	Cascading.Hive	Hive data source
JDBC	Cascading-JDBC	Concurrent JDBC drivers
Oracle	Cascading-JDBC	Oracle database JDBC drivers
Memcached	Cascading.Memcached	Memcached data source
MongoDB	Cascading-Mongomigrate	MongoDB data source
MySQL	Cascading-JDBC	MySQL database JDBC drivers
Neo4J	Cascading.Neo4J	Neo4J data source
Parquet	Parquet-mr	Parquet data source
PostgreSQL	Cascading-JDBC	PostgreSQL database JDBC drivers
Redshift	Cascading-JDBC	Amazon Redshift database JDBC drivers
SimpleDB	Cascading.SimpleDB	Scale Unlimited SimpleDB data source
Solr	Cascading.Solr	Scale Unlimited Solr data source
Splunk	Tbana	Splunk data source
Teradata	Cascading-JDBC	Teradata database JDBC drivers

Cascading serializers

Many customer serializers have also been written for use with both local and Hadoop mode in Cascading. New serializers are also becoming quite prevalent and should be examined for applicability to your particular problem. Some offer exceptional speed, others better compression schemes, and still others offer novel forms of managing metadata. The following screenshot shows Cascading custom serializers:

Serializer	Project Name	Description of Project
Avro	Cascading.Avro	Scale Unlimited data serialization for Apache Avro
JSON	Cascading.JSON	JavaScript Object Notation (JSON) utility classes
Kryo	Cascading.Kryo	Kryo serialization
Protocol Buffers	Cascading2-protobufs	Square Protocol Buffers
Thrift	Cascading-Thrift	Thrift Serializer

Java open source mock frameworks

The following table shows a list of many Java open source mock frameworks that you can use to test your Cascading applications:

Framework	URL
Mockito	http://mockito.org/
EasyMock	http://easymock.org/
Mockachino	http://code.google.com/p/mockachino/
PowerMock	http://code.google.com/p/powermock/
jMock	http://www.jmock.org/
JMockit	http://code.google.com/p/jmockit/
Unitils	http://unitils.sourceforge.net/

Summary

In this chapter, you learned how to find other Cascading resources. This includes online help, Wikis, code sources, and various other sources of in-depth documentation. We also discussed open source and commercial software, special purpose interface software, and specialized add-on utilities that extend Cascading's capabilities and can also reduce development time.

This is the last chapter of this book. There is so much more, but we think that this book provides a solid foundation that will more than just get you started, but actually give you a great basis for further learning. So we hope that you continue to explore, learn, and most of all, write good reusable, scalable code using Cascading and the full ecosystem of tools that comes with it. We hope that you monitor the many sites that we have outlined here because Cascading and nearly all big data solutions are moving, changing, and evolving at a tremendous pace. This is a great time to be alive and to be developing code in this new world. Enjoy!

Downloadable Software

The software in this book is delivered in a downloadable ZIP file. It contains all source code, a set of Cascading libraries, and test data. It is packaged as a complete Eclipse project so that it can be easily loaded into your Eclipse development environment.

Contents

The code that is included in the ZIP file shows the following:

- Creating and testing a custom filter, function, aggregator, buffer, and assertion
- Running several types of pipe tests: GroupBy, CoGroup, Merge, and so on
- Using a subassembly
- Running a cascade, including using skipFlow
- Running the reference application that we built in *Chapter 8, Creating a Real-world Application in Cascading*
- Running unit and integration tests that we also built in *Chapter 8, Creating a Real-world Application in Cascading*

This zip file contains the following structure:

```
/Learning Cascading - Base Eclipse project folder
  /src
    /com
      /ai
        /learning
          Java classes (*.java)
          /jobs
            Java cascading jobs (*.java)
    /scripts
      Script files to make using Hadoop easier
```

```
/data
   Data files for testing
/lib
   Jar files (*.jar)
/models
   OpenNLP model files (*.bin)
/dictionaries
   Dictionary files (*.csv)
/bin
   Where Eclipse will place compiled classes
.classpath - the Eclipse classpath setting file
.project - the Eclipse project specific parameters
.gitignore - used by Git if you are using Git source code
           management
```

Installing and using

Using this code is very easy. This can be done as follows:

1. Unzip it.
2. Start Eclipse. We use Luna (Eclipse 4.4.0), but it should work with almost any version 3 or later release.
3. Import the project into your workspace as follows:

    File -> Import -> General -> Existing projects into workspace.

    We suggest checking copy projects into workspace. This will physically copy the contents of the ZIP file into the workspace that you have defined for Eclipse.

4. Build the project using **Project -> Clean**.

    Note that this project is already set up to use JUnit.

That's really all that there is to do. At this point, you are ready to begin using the code provided through the book.

Other integrated development environments can also be used. Simply maintain the preceding directory structure, but copy the /src Java files into the appropriate locations. You will then need to set up the classpath in the manner that is required using the JAR files in the /lib directory.

 For further information, go to the Analytics Inside website, at http://www.AnalyticsInside.us.

Index

classes, of operations
  aggregator 65
  assertion 65
  buffers 65
  filters 65
  functions 65
classes, simple MapReduce job
  MRComparator 19
  MRJob 19
  MRMapper 19
  MRPartitioner 19
  MRReducer 19
cluster test 221
coercion 34
CoGroup pipe 47
combiner 9
common Cascading themes
  about 27
  data flows, as processes 28-30
comparators 32
contents 241
contexts 70
counters
  about 17, 140
  used, for controlling flows 141
custom assertion, custom operations
  writing 110-112
custom operations
  aggregator, writing 101-110
  buffer, writing 112-120
  custom assertion, writing 110, 112
  filter, writing 92-96
  function, writing 96-100
  use cases, identifying 121, 122
  writing 91, 92
custom taps 238

D

data definition language (DDL) 5
Data Mining Group website
  URL 233
DataNode 14
data streams
  defining, for Cascading processing 31
  structuring, for Cascading processing 31
data typing 34

Debug() filter 155-158
declarator 34
distributed cache 16, 17
domain-specific language (DSL) 25
DOT file
  about 163
  creating 163
Driven
  about 233-235
  URL 235

E

Each operations
  about 73
  filters 73
  functions 75
Each pipe 41, 42
EasyMock
  URL 239
Eclipse
  URL 150
end-to-end testing 167
environment variables, Hadoop
  HADOOP_CONF_DIR 4
  HADOOP_HOME 4
  JAVA_HOME 4
Every operations
  about 78
  aggregator 78
Every pipe 44, 45
external components
  external JAR files, using 146
  integrating 144

F

FAT JAR 17
feeding sources 134
field algebra 33
fields
  about 32, 67
  defining 31-33
field sets
  about 33
  Fields.ALL 33
  Fields.ARGS 33
  Fields.GROUP 33

K

key field 4

L

least recently used (LRU) 127
Lingual 231
Load
  about 236
  testing 167, 172, 173
  tool 172
  URL 236
Load local mode 55

M

machine learning 232
Map process 5
MapReduce 2, 14
MapReduce execution framework
  about 14
  jobs, using 142
  JobTracker 14
  TaskTracker 15
MapReduce version 1
  to MapReduce version 2 moving to, YARN
    used 148
Merge pipe 45
method cascading 142
Mockachino
  URL 239
mocking 170
Mockito
  URL 239
monad 143
Multitool
  about 237
  URL 237

N

named field groups
  using 33
NameNode 13
natural language processing
  (NLP) 189, 192, 225
negative tests 172

nodes, Hadoop
  boundary nodes 10
  head nodes 10
  slave nodes 10

O

online resources
  searching 229, 230
OpenNLP 190
OperationCall<Context> object 71
Operation class
  about 68
  contexts 70
  FlowProcess object 71
  interface hierarchy 68
  OperationCall<Context> object 71
operations
  about 65-67
  basic operation lifecycle 69
  methods 72
  processing sequence 72
  using 66
operations, types
  about 72
  assertions 82
  buffers 81
  Each operations 73
  Every operations 78
Optiq 231
orchestration layer 25

P

partitioner 9
Pattern
  about 232
  URL, for videos and tutorials 233
  using 233
performance
  optimizing 176
performance testing 172
pipe 30
pipe assembly 30
pipe operations
  about 40
  aggregator 41
  assertion 41

test plan, designing
  cluster test 221
  full load test 222
  integration test 220, 221
  unit test 219, 220
test strategies
  about 167
  integration testing 167, 171
  load testing 167, 172, 173
  mocking 170
  unit testing 168-170
text analytics (TA) 189, 192
Tez 147
trap 158
tuple
  about 30, 31
  using 31-33
TupleEntry class 39
tuple stream 30, 40

U

Unitils
  URL 239
unit test 219, 220
unit testing
  about 168-170
  creating 168

V

ValueAssertion calling sequence 83
value field 4

W

workflow
  building 210
  cascade, building 215, 218
  context, managing 214
  delivery, to cluster 223, 225
  flows, building 210-214
  software, packaging 223, 225
  test plan, designing 218
Write phase 5

Y

YARN 17-19

Z

ZIP file
  code 241
  installing 242
  using 242

Thank you for buying
Learning Cascading

About Packt Publishing

Packt, pronounced 'packed', published its first book, *Mastering phpMyAdmin for Effective MySQL Management*, in April 2004, and subsequently continued to specialize in publishing highly focused books on specific technologies and solutions.

Our books and publications share the experiences of your fellow IT professionals in adapting and customizing today's systems, applications, and frameworks. Our solution-based books give you the knowledge and power to customize the software and technologies you're using to get the job done. Packt books are more specific and less general than the IT books you have seen in the past. Our unique business model allows us to bring you more focused information, giving you more of what you need to know, and less of what you don't.

Packt is a modern yet unique publishing company that focuses on producing quality, cutting-edge books for communities of developers, administrators, and newbies alike. For more information, please visit our website at www.packtpub.com.

About Packt Open Source

In 2010, Packt launched two new brands, Packt Open Source and Packt Enterprise, in order to continue its focus on specialization. This book is part of the Packt Open Source brand, home to books published on software built around open source licenses, and offering information to anybody from advanced developers to budding web designers. The Open Source brand also runs Packt's Open Source Royalty Scheme, by which Packt gives a royalty to each open source project about whose software a book is sold.

Writing for Packt

We welcome all inquiries from people who are interested in authoring. Book proposals should be sent to author@packtpub.com. If your book idea is still at an early stage and you would like to discuss it first before writing a formal book proposal, then please contact us; one of our commissioning editors will get in touch with you.

We're not just looking for published authors; if you have strong technical skills but no writing experience, our experienced editors can help you develop a writing career, or simply get some additional reward for your expertise.

Learning Hadoop 2

ISBN: 978-1-78328-551-8   Paperback: 382 pages

Design and implement data processing, lifecycle management, and analytic workflows with the cutting-edge toolbox of Hadoop 2

1. Construct state-of-the-art applications using higher-level interfaces and tools beyond the traditional MapReduce approach.

2. Use the unique features of Hadoop 2 to model and analyze Twitter's global stream of user generated data.

3. Develop a prototype on a local cluster and deploy to the cloud (Amazon Web Services).

Hadoop MapReduce v2 Cookbook
Second Edition

ISBN: 978-1-78328-547-1   Paperback: 322 pages

Explore the Hadoop MapReduce v2 ecosystem to gain insights from very large datasets

1. Process large and complex datasets using next generation Hadoop.

2. Install, configure, and administer MapReduce programs and learn what's new in MapReduce v2.

3. More than 90 Hadoop MapReduce recipes presented in a simple and straightforward manner, with step-by-step instructions and real-world examples.

Please check **www.PacktPub.com** for information on our titles

Mastering Hadoop

ISBN: 978-1-78398-364-3   Paperback: 374 pages

Go beyond the basics and master the next generation of Hadoop data processing platforms

1. Learn how to optimize Hadoop MapReduce, Pig and Hive.

2. Dive into YARN and learn how it can integrate Storm with Hadoop.

3. Understand how Hadoop can be deployed on the cloud and gain insights into analytics with Hadoop.

Building Hadoop Clusters [Video]

ISBN: 978-1-78328-403-0   Duration: 02:34 hours

Deploy multi-node Hadoop clusters to harness the Cloud for storage and large-scale data processing

1. Familiarize yourself with Hadoop and its services, and how to configure them.

2. Deploy compute instances and set up a three-node Hadoop cluster on Amazon.

3. Set up a Linux installation optimized for Hadoop.

Please check **www.PacktPub.com** for information on our titles

www.ingramcontent.com/pod-product-compliance
Lightning Source LLC
Chambersburg PA
CBHW060529060326
40690CB00017B/3427